D1528854

Critique and Crisis
Enlightenment and the Pathogenesis of Modern Society

Studies in Contemporary German Social Thought
Thomas McCarthy, General Editor

Critique and Crisis

Enlightenment and the Pathogenesis of
Modern Society

REINHART KOSELLECK

The MIT Press
Cambridge, Massachusetts

First MIT Press edition 1988

This English translation © 1988 Berg Publishers Ltd

Originally published as *Kritik und Krise. Eine Studie zur Pathogenese der bürgerlichen Welt* by
Verlag Karl Alber GmbH, Freiburg/Munich, West Germany
© 1959 Verlag Karl Alber GmbH

Library of Congress Cataloging-in-Publication Data

Koselleck, Reinhart.
    Critique and crisis. Enlightenment and the
    Pathogenesis of Modern Society.

    (Studies in contemporary German social thought)
    Translation of: Kritik und Krise.
    Bibliography: p.
    Includes index.
    1. Political science—History. 2. Enlightenment.
3. Divine right of kings. 4. History—Philosophy.
I. Title. II. Series.
JA83.K6613 1988   320'.09   87–15149
ISBN 0–262–11127–6

Printed in Great Britain

Contents

Foreword

Professor Koselleck's learned and influential study remains as absorbing today as it was when first published, nearly thirty years ago, under the title *Kritik und Krise*. It is good to have it available at last in English.

In Professor Koselleck's view the modern understanding of politics, and hence modern political practice, has become dangerously depoliticised. The basic differences between the political realm proper and other public but non-political realms, have become blurred. At the same time visions of eventually escaping the hard constraints of politics distort the real alternatives here and now. Professor Koselleck traces this malady — to use his own metaphor — to the changing status of political authority in the age of Absolutism and Enlightenment, the period that stretches from the Peace of Utrecht to the waning years of the *ancien régime*, from the major writings of Hobbes to those of Rousseau and Raynal. His thesis, reduced to a formula, is that during that period the widening breach, in fact and in theory, between State and society, and between politics and ethics, inevitably led to the challenge — the critique — and the eventual subversion — the crisis — of the political by the social, cultural and moral realms.

The specifically modern order which was established by the middle of the seventeenth century redistributed the public space into two sharply separate domains: that of political authority proper, the prince or State; and the strictly subordinate domain of the subjects, the domain which at about that time came to be known as society. In Professor Koselleck's view this ordering of sovereign and subject is given its clearest theoretical formulation by Hobbes.

vii

Hobbes fully recognised that such an ordering entails the strict subordination of the claims of individual morality to the require- ments of political necessity. He argues for it none the less, on the grounds that 'the state of man can never be without some incom- modity or other', and that the ordering of sovereign and subjects which he proposes makes for fewer incommodities than does any other. For it at least permits subjects to lead secure, commodious, and hence decent and just lives.

Yet when and wherever men are denied an active share in the exercise of political authority, when and wherever they are subjects without being citizens, they inevitably endow other concerns and pursuits — economic, cultural, moral — with an independent, and hence rival, authority. The absolutisms of seventeenth- and eight- eenth-century continental Europe are in large measure themselves responsible for the criticism and the challenges to which they finally succumbed. Professor Koselleck makes the point in the fascinating chapters in which he traces the gradual transformation of such free, voluntary associations as the Masonic lodges and the Republic of Letters from enclaves of internal exile into centres of moral auth- ority, and eventually into surrogates and even models for political society. In the process, existing political societies came to be judged by standards which take little or no account of the constraints which political men must inevitably take into account, standards which for all political intents and purposes are therefore Utopian.

But Utopia is not, properly speaking, a political alternative at all. In Professor Koselleck's view, political Utopianism is as much a contradiction in terms as is, for example, dogmatic scepticism. In theoretical terms, it draws from all those political constraints which, in practice, it challenges and subverts. And in so far as it either fails or refuses to take cognisance of its self-evident political role, he regards it as an outright hypocrisy as well. He does not ever consider the possibility of a politically self-conscious and respon- sible Utopia.

The study concludes with some particularly incisive analyses of how Enlightenment Utopianism becomes rationalised, radicalised and transmuted into the new philosophy of history. The philo- sopher of history or, more precisely, the philosopher of historical progress, by stationing himself in the hoped-for future, typically looks back upon the conflicts and the suffering caused by the clash between intransigently held norms and political realities as if these

conflicts had been happily resolved, and therefore had been justified. He confidently expects that, to paraphrase a remark of
Hegel's, the wounds inflicted by history invariably heal without
leaving scars. By thus justifying confrontation, conflict and crisis,
the philosophy of history abets them and so contributes further to
that depoliticisation which Professor Koselleck sees as perhaps the
most distinctive feature of the Enlightenment.

By contrast, he himself adopts the stance by which he believes
that political matters are most accurately perceived as the viewpoint
of the citizen or of the statesmen on the spot. By studying the
doctrines of the philosophers and the opinions of representative
men or groups as they appear to a political agent rather than to a
detached chronicler, he calls attention to a great deal that otherwise
goes unnoticed. This political perspective on the history of ideas
also makes for much that is fresh, original and absorbing in his
book. Admittedly a number of his judgements are impassioned;
political judgements are apt to be so. It is, indeed, altogether
striking how engaged much of the most valuable recent Enlightenment scholarship continues to be. Although Professor Koselleck
himself refrains from pointing to possible morals, he clearly recognises that his critical history of criticism and of what he regards as
its hypocrisies, from the mid-seventeenth to the late-eighteenth
century, also serves as a critique of the critical theories of the
mid-nineteenth and, especially, of the mid-twentieth century.

The reader of *Critique and Crisis* is left with the distinct impression
that it is the political teaching of Hobbes that captures what Professor Koselleck regards as the essential features of political life.
Clearly, he does not wish to restore any particular doctrine of
Hobbes's, so much as to restore the characteristically Hobbesian
awareness that there is no escaping the constraints of political life,
and that it is not possible to reduce some measure of contingency,
conflict and compulsion to the status of differences of opinion or to
resolve them by discussion and peaceful competition. He certainly
shares the conviction, so forcibly articulated by Hobbes, that the
only alternative to politics that takes these constraints into account
is the war of all against all. He is, of course, also aware of the
fact that the great and very real evils of civil strife can be exaggerated, and that such exaggerations can serve as a screen behind which
far greater evils are introduced into the civil order. It would seem
that he wants to warn against both of these extremes when he

approvingly alludes to Napoleon's remark to the ageing Goethe: 'Nowadays, fate is politics'.

Victor Gourevitch

Preface to the English Edition

This study is a product of the early postwar period. It represented an attempt to examine the historical preconditions of German National Socialism, whose loss of reality and Utopian self-exaltation had resulted in hitherto unprecedented crimes. There was also the context of the cold war. Here, too, I was trying to enquire into its Utopian roots which, it seemed, prevented the two superpowers from simply recognising each other as opponents. Instead they blocked one another and thereby destroyed the opportunity for a peace which each superpower self-confidently proclaimed to be capable of establishing single-handedly. It was in the Enlightenment, to which both liberal-democratic America and socialist Russia rightly retraced themselves, that I began to look for the common roots of their claim to exclusiveness with its moral and philosophical legitimations.

My starting-point was therefore to explain the Utopian ideas of the twentieth century by looking at their origins in the eighteenth. My original intention was to test my arguments by reference to Kant's critiques whose political function during the age of Absolutism I was planning to investigate. But, as tends to happen to German scholars, I never got beyond the preliminaries. The analysis of the concepts of 'critique' and 'crisis' became an end in itself and the basis of a new hypothesis. This hypothesis argues that the Enlightenment itself became Utopian and even hypocritical because — as far as continental Europe was concerned — it saw itself excluded from political power-sharing. The structure of Absolutism, which was rooted in the dichotomy between sovereign and subject, between public policy and private morality, prevented the Enlightenment and the emancipation movement produced by it from seeing

itself as a political phenomenon. Instead the Enlightenment developed patterns of thought and behaviour which, at the latest from
1789 onwards, foundered on the rocks of the concrete political
challenges that arose. The Enlightenment succumbed to a Utopian
image which, while deceptively propelling it, helped to produce
contradictions which could not be resolved in practice and prepared
the way for the Terror and for dictatorship. Here was an ideal-type
framework which time and again made its reappearance in the
subsequent history of the modern world.

Given that this book raised a question which was topical not only
from an historical, but also from a political point of view, its impact
went beyond the debate originally generated in Germany. Translations into Spanish, Italian and French appeared in 1965, 1972 and
1979 respectively. It appears to be more than a coincidence that all
three were continental European languages. If nothing else, their
societies had at least one thing in common with Central Europe:
they had all been ruled by Absolutist regimes, whatever the political
differences between these regimes may have been. Accordingly it
was only in these countries that there emerged a type of Enlightenment which, while trying to evade censorship and other chicaneries,
was directed against the Absolutist claims of the sovereign ruler.
Whoever refused to follow the majority, who adapted and subjected
themselves to their ruler, invented ways of camouflage and mystification as well as other indirectly operative modes of behaviour
which ultimately began to pervade the ideas of the Enlightenment
themselves. It is true that arguments about rationality and natural
justice subjected the Absolutist State to fresh pressure to legitimate
itself and to respond to change. But, none the less, such arguments
remained confined to the corridors outside the chambers of actual
political decision-making. As a result there emerged, by way of
compensation, a progressive philosophy of history which promised
victory to the intellectual elite, but one gained without struggle and
civil war.

Since 1688 at the latest Britain, by contrast, underwent a different
development. She never experienced the tension between State and
society which so shaped the nations of the European continent.
Both spheres remained sufficiently interlinked through Parliament
and the judicial constitution to appreciate that all moral questions
represented at the same time political problems. The Utopian ideas
of the continental Enlightenment therefore never gained a foothold

across the Channel. There it was the Scottish moral philosophers with their sober theories rooted in social history who set the tone and who began to respond to the economic lead gained by Britain. At first the Scots moved in the wake of Britain's progress which was soon also to affect the whole of the European continent. This was an important point to which my book gives no more than marginal attention.

Against the background of these considerations, it may be appropriate to add a few further remarks, now that this translation into English has become available. During the past two decades many and methodologically very sophisticated studies have appeared in the fields of intellectual as well as social history. It would be impossible to list them here. This research on Hobbes, Locke, Diderot, Rousseau and Raynal has become so intensified that my contribution to an interpretation of their writings may seem rather peripheral. Similarly, the social history of Freemasonry and of the Illuminati, research on the Republic of Letters and its networks of communication, on literary societies, academies and libraries, on reading habits, in short on the *mentalités* of divergent social groups in different European countries, has expanded our knowledge so much that my study will not teach the reader anything new.

However, what I hope will be of value to the interested reader of this book is its theoretical framework. This framework provides a larger, ideal-typically constructed context into which detailed events and findings can be put. Thus this book tries to interpret the origins of Absolutism as an outgrowth of religious wars. As a next step, it attempts to explain the genesis of the modern Utopia from the context of the political interaction in which the men of the Enlightenment found themselves *vis-à-vis* the system of Absolutism. It is in this way that two major themes of the early modern period have been connected, with the aim of deducing therefrom the evolution of a long-term process which went beyond what the contemporaries had intended. As a result I hope to highlight more persistent structures of the modern age which may be seen as elements of historical anthropology: the sense that we are being sucked into an open and unknown future, the pace of which has kept us in a constant state of breathlessness ever since the dissolution of the traditional *ständische* societies; and the pressure on our post-theological age to justify politics and morals without us being able to reconcile the two. These were the challenges which the

Enlightenment faced, and they produced mentalities, attitudes and behavioural patterns which have survived the special circumstances of their birth. Put in a nutshell, this book attempts to offer a genetic theory of the modern world which may help us to explain individual historical phenomena. If this assumption is correct, my central hypothesis will also serve to provoke criticism. After all, it is not merely historical problems that are being raised here, but questions which are challenging us to this day to search for an answer.

R.K.
Bielefeld, September 1987

Introduction

> In the fires of a revolution, when hatreds prevail and the
> sovereign power is split, it is difficult to write history.
> *Rivarol*

From an historical point of view the present tension between two superpowers, the USA and the USSR, is a result of European history. Europe's history has broadened; it has become world history and will run its course as that, having allowed the whole world to drift into a state of permanent crisis. As bourgeois society was the first to cover the globe, the present crisis stems from a mainly Utopian self-conception on the part of the philosophers of history — Utopian because modern man is destined to be at home everywhere and nowhere. History has overflowed the banks of tradition and inundated all boundaries. The technology of communications on the infinite surface of the globe has made all powers omnipresent, subjecting all to each and each to all. At the same time, we have seen the opening up of interplanetary space, although the result may well be to blow up mankind as well in a self-initiated process of self-destruction.

Unified, the two phenomena are historically one. They constitute the political crisis which — if it really is a crisis — presses for a decision, and they are the philosophies of history that correspond to the crisis and in whose name we seek to anticipate the decision, to influence it, steer it, or, as catastrophically, to prevent it. Their common root lies in the eighteenth century, and this indicates the direction of questions determined by the situation of today.

The eighteenth century witnessed the unfolding of bourgeois

5

society, which saw itself as the new world, laying intellectual claim
to the whole world and simultaneously denying the old. It grew out
of the territories of the European states and, in dissolving this link,
developed a progressive philosophy in line with the process. The
subject of that philosophy was all mankind, to be unified from its
European centre and led peacefully towards a better future. Today
its field of action, a single global world, is claimed in the name of
analogous philosophies of history, but now by two powers at once.
To speak in historico-philosophical terms, today's world unity
turns out — and it is this which makes its fictitious character
apparent — to be a politically dichotomous unity. One half, sworn
to progress like the other, lives by that other's imagined reaction.
The two halves block each other's way, but it is this very fact that
gives them identity. They mutually segregate each other in order to
feign a non-existent unity. Their testimony is therefore one of terror
and fear. The world's Utopian unity reproduces its own fission.

In the eighteenth century, Utopian planning for the future had a
specifically temporal historic function. As the European bourgeoisie externally encompassed the whole world and in so doing
postulated one mankind, it set out inwardly, in the name of the
same argumentation, to shatter the Absolutist order. Philosophers
of history prepared and made available the concepts by which the
rise and the role of the bourgeoisie of that time were justified. The
eighteenth century can be seen as the antechamber to our present
epoch, one whose tensions have been increasingly exacerbated since
the French Revolution, as the revolutionary process spread exten-
sively around the globe and intensively to all mankind. This book
seeks to illuminate that antechamber. The link between the origins
of the modern philosophy of history and the start of the crisis
which, initially in Europe, has been determining political events
ever since 1789, will come within our purview.

This is how the mode of enquiry was narrowed and rendered
historically precise: we shall not question the contents of past
philosophies of history nor their Utopian goals, nor will their
ideological structure be measured, for example, by the economic
rise of the bourgeoisie in those times. Instead, and in order to
illuminate its original link with the beginning of the political crisis,
we shall try to understand the philosophical sense of history by
studying the political situation of the bourgeoisie in the Absolutist
State. The philosophies of history themselves will be left aside, save

for exemplary exceptions; our investigation will focus on the political function which bourgeois thought and endeavour served in the framework of Absolutism. To elaborate the political significance of the Enlightenment, we shall have to look at the structure of the Absolutist State, for this State was the first victim of the great Revolution; its disappearance was what enabled a Utopian modernism to unfold. A primary understanding of Absolutism requires us to look back farther, to the seventeenth century in which the sovereign princely State was perfected. The point of this retrospection is not to construe causalities; suggesting these could only take us back to prehistoric times and to the problems of any beginning — in short, to the questions of a philosophy of history that goes beyond ideology, that resorts to historic reality in order to lay the ground for an historical science which excludes precisely the pseudo-explanations of a *regressus in infinitum*. Such an historical *regressus* would be nothing but progress in reverse, the very thing we are obliged to question.

Our analyses will concentrate on the present that has passed, not on its past. The earlier past will be considered only in so far as it contains conditions relevant to our questions about the eighteenth century. Our theme is the genesis of Utopianism from an historically determined functional context, the context of the eighteenth century. We thus have recourse to political history as far as necessary to establish the value of civic consciousness in the Absolutist system. This simultaneously allows us to view the reverse of our investigation: the nascent political crisis. It is only as a reaction to Absolutist policies that — intentionally or not — Enlighteners' historico-philosophical self-consciousness makes political sense. The State, as it was, demanded a response, and the response was discovered. Derivations from the history of ideas were deliberately waived. The heritage of ideas, already all but completely at the Enlighteners' disposal, was not accepted until a specific situation arose, and not until — this was the novelty — the situation was interpreted in terms of the philosophy of history. In narrowing our enquiry to historic situations we do not, of course, mean to present the people of those days with a moral indictment, to find them more or less guilty. This is self-prohibiting, for man as an historic creature is always responsible, for what he willed as well as for what he did not will, and more often, perhaps, for the latter than for the former.

The method used is thus a combination of analyses from the

history of ideas and analyses of sociological conditions. We emulate thought movements, but only far enough for their political accent to come into view, and we clarify the situations in which the thoughts were conceived and to which they reacted, but only far enough to extract what was politically manifest in the ideas. We do not show either the political course of events as such or the ideas' declension as mere ideas. The general conditions from which the Enlightenment arose and to which it reacted did not change during the eighteenth century. Only particular circumstances changed, though in a manner that brought the Absolutist system's basic difficulties into so much sharper relief. The French State, above all, lost power and prestige; with increasing bourgeois affluence it ran up more and more debts, ceased to score visible successes, lost wars and colonies, until at last the Enlightenment spread to the State's representatives themselves. The Enlightenment became 'a proper ally'.

As for the political premises as such, there can be no doubt that the State's own structure remained unchanged. The sovereign decision continued to lie in the monarch's hands; he chose between war and peace, dismissed Parliament at his pleasure, maintained the standards of his court regardless of all liabilities, until finally the more stubbornly Louis XVI insisted upon his sovereignty the less he found himself able to struggle through to effective decisions. The State had changed; it had become corrupt, but only because it remained Absolutist. The Absolutist system, the situation from which the bourgeois Enlightenment took its departure, remained in force until the outbreak of the Revolution. It constitutes the one constant element of our enquiry, the yardstick which, through a variety of examples, enables us to take successive measurements of the Enlightenment's political development. The Enlightenment acquired a gravity of its own, which came at last to be one of its political conditions. Absolutism necessitated the genesis of the Enlightenment, and the Enlightenment conditioned the genesis of the French Revolution. It is around these two theses that the action of this book takes place.

Sources will be cited only from the period before 1789. No testimonials will be adduced to make personal statements about the authors. Singular events and specific writings are always referred to but are never the issue. The theme remains the unity of the Enlightenment as it happened in the Absolutist State. Each action and each act of thought should direct us towards this event. For our enquiry, all authors remain substitutes. All citations and occurrences could easily be exchanged for others without disturbing the course of the investigation. The notes often contain parallel quotations even though cumulative documentation does not enhance the thesis itself. Great thinkers and anonymous pamphleteers are equally given the floor; it is precisely what they have in common that indicates the unity of the Enlightenment's occurrence, in which anonymity and political import generally coincide. Only a few documents bear the stamp of personality clearly enough — in the cases of Hobbes or Diderot, for instance — to remain unique in the overall flow of events; but even their uniqueness serves to bring out the typical once it is moved into focus.

The heuristic comprehension, meant to clarify the link between the Utopian philosophy of history and the revolution unleashed since 1789, lies in the presupposed connection of critique and crisis. This grasp will prove itself. The fact that the eighteenth century failed to note any connection between the critique it practised and the looming crisis — no literal proof of an awareness of the link could be found — this very fact led to our thesis: that the critical process of enlightenment conjured up the crisis in the same measure in which the political significance of that crisis remained hidden from it. The crisis was as much exacerbated as it was obfuscated in the philosophy of history. Never politically grasped, it remained concealed in historico-philosophical images of the future which caused the day's events to pale — events that became so much less inhibited in heading for an unexpected decision. The basis of this dialectic was the specific manner of critique which the eighteenth century favoured and from which it derived its name. The role of the rising bourgeoisie was determined by the critical practice of the bourgeois intelligentisia and coalesced in the new world.

The entire period under discussion presents the picture of a uniquely powerful process. In the eighteenth century, history as a whole was unwittingly transformed into a sort of legal process. This occurrence, which inaugurates the Modern age, is identical with the genesis of the philosophy of history. 'In critique, history turns automatically into a philosophy of history' (Ferdinand Christian Baur). The tribunal of reason, with whose natural members the rising elite confidently ranked itself, involved all spheres of activity in varying stages of its development. Theology, art, history, the law, the State and politics, eventually reason itself — sooner or later all were called upon to answer for themselves. In these proceedings the bourgeois spirit functioned simultaneously as prosecutor, as the court of last resort, and — due to be of crucial importance to the philosophy of history — as a party. From the outset, progress always sided with the bourgeois judges. Nothing and nobody could evade the new jurisdiction, and whatever failed in the bourgeois critics' judgement was turned over to moral censors who discriminated against the convicted and thus helped to carry out the sentence. 'He who does not recognise this / is to be viewed with contempt.'

In the rigorous process of critique — a process of social ferment at the same time — the bourgeois philosophy of history came into being. All regions touched by criticism contributed to furthering the rise of that philosophy. To begin with, the contrast of ancients and moderns was articulated within the republic of scholars by art and literary critics developing an understanding of time that sundered future and past. A central target of the critical offensive, the Christian religion in its manifold divisions, prepared the charismatic-historical heritage that was subsumed into the future-orientated world-view, in the most varied ways. We know the process of secularisation, which transposed eschatology into a history of progress. But likewise, consciously and deliberately, the elements of divine judgement and the Last Day were applied to history itself, above all in the exacerbated critical situation.

The critical ferment altered the nature of political events. Subjective self-righteousness ceased reckoning with given values. Everything that was historically given, indeed history itself, was transformed into a process — the outcome of which, of course, remained open as long as the categories of private judgement could never catch up with events they had helped to bring about. Eventually, to reach them after all the divine, heretofore impervious plan of salvation was itself transformed: it, too, became enlightened. It was transformed into the morally just and rational planning of the future by the new elite. Since misconceiving the indigenous side of the criticised realms in both religion and politics was a peculiarity of rational critique, it had to look for an escape hatch, the pledge of a tomorrow in whose name today could in good conscience be allowed to perish. To justify itself at all, the critique of the eighteenth century had to become Utopian. Its ultimate object, the Absolutist State, helped in its way to establish the Utopian view of history upheld by the bourgeoisie.

In the political order which it restored by pacifying the areas devastated by religious wars, the state created the premise for the unfolding of a moral world. However, just as soon as their religious bonds are outgrown, the politically powerless individuals will clash with the State: even though morally emancipating them, the State will deny them responsibility by restricting them to a private sphere. Inevitably, citizens will come into conflict with a State that subordinates morality to politics, adopts a purely formal understanding of the political realm and thus reckons without developments peculiar to the emancipation of its subjects. For their goal will be to perfect themselves morally to an extent that will permit them to know, and let every man know for himself, what is good and what is evil. Each one thus becomes a judge who knows, on grounds of his enlightenment, that he is authorised to try whatever heteronomous definitions contradict his moral autonomy. Once implemented by the State the separation of morality and politics hence turns against the State itself: it is forced into standing a moral trial for having achieved something, i.e. to have created a space in which it was possible (for the individual) to survive.

In the course of unfolding the Cartesian *cogito ergo sum* as the self-guarantee of a man who has dropped out of the religious bonds, eschatology recoils into Utopianism. Planning history comes to be just as important as mastering nature. The misconception that history is open to planning is furthered by the technicist State because its political value cannot be made comprehensible to its subject. Politically powerless as a subject of his sovereign lord, the citizen conceived himself as moral, felt that the existing rule was overpowering, and condemned it proportionally as immoral since he could no longer perceive what is evident in the horizon of human finiteness. The dichotomy of morality and politics made morality's alienation from political reality inevitable. The expression of this inevitability is that morality skips the political aporia. Unable to integrate politics, moral man stands in a void and must make a virtue of necessity. A stranger to reality, he views the political domain as a heteronomous definition that can only stand in his way. In consequence, this morality makes men think that in so far as they attain the heights of their destiny they can completely eliminate the political aporia. That politics is fate, that it is fate not in the sense of blind fatality, this is what the enlighteners fail to understand. Their attempts to allow the philosophy of history to negate historical factuality, to 'repress' the political realm, are Utopian in origin and character. The crisis caused by morality's proceeding against history will be a permanent crisis as long as history is alienated in terms of its philosophy.

That crisis and the philosophy of history are mutually dependent and entwined — that ultimately one must indeed go so far as to call them identical — this must, when our enquiry has reached its goal, have become visible at several points in the course of the eighteenth century. Its Utopianism arose from an irrelation to politics that was caused by history, but which was then solidified by a philosophy of history. The critical crossfire not only ground up topical politics; politics itself, as a constant task of human existence, dissolved in the same process into Utopian constructs of the future. The political edifice of the Absolutist State and the unfolding of Utopianism reveal one complex occurrence around which the political crisis of our time begins.

I

The Political Structure of Absolutism as the
Precondition of Enlightenment

CHAPTER 1

The Absolutist State, Raison d'Etat and the Emergence of the Apolitical Sphere (Barclay, D'Aubigné)

Two epochal events mark the beginning and the end of classical Absolutism. Its point of departure was the religious civil war. The modern State had laboriously fought its way out of the religious disorders; not until these had been overcome did it achieve its full form and delineation. A second civil war — the French Revolution — brought the Absolutist State to an abrupt end.

The effective context of both these chains of events touched Europe as a whole, but England's exceptional position is elucidated by the fact that on this island the two happened, as it were, to coincide. Here, the nascent Absolutist State had already been undermined by religious warfare; the struggle for the faith already betokened the bourgeois revolution. On the Continent, on the other hand, as far as one can trace the evolution of the Absolutist State there, it remained the time-bound outcome of the post-Reformation disorders. It was in the locally differing solutions of sectarian conflicts, and in chronologically distinct phases, that the modern State power was established. Its policies were the theme of the seventeenth century; their paths outlined the history of Absolutism. The following period, though marked by the same State form, bore another name: 'the Enlightenment'. It was from Absolutism that the Enlightenment evolved — initially as its inner consequence, later as its dialectical counterpart and antagonist, destined to lead the Absolutist State to its demise.

Just as the Enlightenment's political point of departure lay within

15

the Absolutist system, so that of Absolutism lay in the religious wars. An inner connection links the formal completion of Absolutism with its end, a connection that becomes visible in the role which the Enlightenment was able to play within the confines of the Absolutist State. The Enlightenment reached its zenith in France, the very country in which the Absolutist system had for the first time, and most decisively, overcome the internal religious conflict. The abuse of power by Louis XIV accelerated the process, in the course of which the subject discovered himself as a citizen. In France this same citizen would one day storm the Bastille. The political structure of the Absolutist State, initially an answer to religious strife, was no longer understood as such by the Enlightenment that followed.

The first task of our enquiry is to focus on that connection, to clarify the initial situation of the modern State as far as may be necessary in order to perceive the point of the Enlightenment's political attack on that State. The methodological limitation which this places on any analysis of the political structure of Absolutism — beyond any social or economic questions — is objectively justified. The princely State, supported by the military and the bureaucracy, developed a supra-religious, rationalistic field of action which, unlike its other aspects, was defined by the policies of the State. Socially, the monarchies remained entirely bound by traditional feudal stratification, so much so that in most instances they sought to preserve that stratification. Politically, however, the monarchs strove to eliminate or neutralise all institutions with an independent base. Mercantilism, too, was an economic system subject to political planning and State guidance; similarly, religious and ecclesiastical questions were treated with an eye to their usefulness to the State, whether within the framework of an established Church or under toleration with a purpose. The realm of a political system covering all of Europe constituted the constellation from which the Enlightenment started out.

This realm found its theoretical expression in the doctrine of *raison d'état*. What was made room for here was an area where politics could unfold regardless of moral considerations. 'Dans les monarchies, la politique fait faire les grandes choses avec le moins de vertu qu'elle peut.'[1] When Montesquieu made that statement in

---

1. Montesquieu, *Esprit des Lois*, III, chap. 5.

1748, to characterise the politics of his own day, his formula — apart from its polemical content — had already ceased to be intelligible to the Enlighteners. The historical evidence of the formula was derived from the period of religious wars. In the sixteenth century the traditional order had disintegrated. As a result of the split in ecclesiastical unity, the entire social order became unhinged. Old ties and loyalties were dissolved. High treason and the struggle for the common good became interchangeable concepts, depending on the point of view of the ascendant faction. The general anarchy led to duels, violence and murder, while the pluralisation of the *Ecclesia sancta* fermented corruption in whatever else remained whole: families, estates, countries, nations. Thus, from the second half of the sixteenth century onwards, a problem developed with a virulence which overreached the resources of the traditional order: the need to find a solution to the intolerant, fiercely embattled and mutually persecuting Churches or religion-bound fractions of the old estates, a solution that would circumvent, settle, or smother the conflict. How to make peace? On the greater part of the Continent this epoch-making question found its historic answer in the Absolutist State. And indeed, the State could not be constituted as such until it had found its specific answer to religious civil warfare. What was this answer? What did it mean to the monarch? And to the subject?

While the religious parties drew their energies from sources outside the domains of princely power, the princes could not prevail over them unless they challenged the primacy of religion. It was the only way for rulers to subordinate the various protagonists to the authority of the State. *Cuius regio eius religio* was already a consequence of the fact that even if princes were committed to a particular faith, as rulers they placed themselves above the religious parties. The absolute ruler recognised no other authority over himself than God, whose attributes in the political and historic field he appropriated: 'Majestas vero nec a majore potestate nec legibus ullis nec tempore definitur'.[2]

In his *Argenis*, a *roman à clef* published in 1621, John Barclay supplied a vindication of absolute monarchy that was widely known at the time and translated into almost all European languages. The

---

2. Bodin, *De rep. libri sex*, as quoted by Friedrich Meinecke in *Die Idee der Staatsräson*, ed. W. Hofer, Munich, 1957, p. 72.

author, a humanist learned in the law, had shared the fate of many of his contemporaries; he was the son of a refugee family whose early impressions had been formed by the confrontations with the League and the trauma of the Gunpowder Plot.[3] Alluding to occurrences of that sort, he confronted the monarch with a challenging alternative: 'Either give the people back their freedom or assure the domestic tranquillity for whose sake they relinquished that freedom'.[4] What appears from such passages is the historical mission accorded the monarchy of those days, the mission that was proclaimed as justified[5] by the great majority of Richelieu's generation — against the League, the Fronde, or the monarchomachists. Drawing further on the doctrine of the sovereign contract, Barclay tended towards the Absolutist State, depriving the embattled parties of their rights and transferring those rights — along with all responsibility — to the sovereign alone. *Argenis* was part of Richelieu's constant reading matter; its train of argument, commonplace at the time, recurs in his political testament.[6] Forbearance, it proclaimed, was more dangerous than stringency, more than cruelty even, for the consequences of clemency were bloodier and more devastating than those of instant severity. A monarch who tolerated opposition did indeed relieve himself of responsibility, but he also shouldered the guilt deriving from any unrest that emerged from his tolerance.[7] His postulated monopoly on peace-making enforced the monarch's absolute responsibility, the time-bound expression of which was the notion of his sole responsibility to God.

In his novel, Barclay also showed the direction the King would have to take in order to pacify the country. Either he must subjugate all or no one would be subjugated.[8] The sovereign's absolute responsibility required and presupposed his absolute domination of all subjects. Only if all subjects were equally under the ruler's thumb could he assume sole responsibility for peace and order. Thus, a deep

3. Cf. Richard Barnett, 'Barclay', in *Dictionary of National Biography*, Oxford, 1921–2.

4. John Barclay (*Ioannis Barclaii Argenis*, Editio V, Frankfurt, 1626): 'Aut illos in libertatem restitue, aut domesticam praesta quietem, propter quam libertatem reliquerunt'.

5. Cf. the contemporaries listed by G. Hanotaux, *Histoire du Cardinal de Richelieu*, 5 vols., Paris, 1893 *et seq.*, I, 542ff.

6. Cf. *Argenis*, III, chaps. 4 and 6; and Cardinal de Richelieu, *Testament politique*, ed. Louis André, Paris, 1947, Part I, chap. 5, 2, and Part II, chaps. 5 and 8.

7. Barclay, *Argenis*: 'Nam si rei non fuerunt sumptis armis, certe tu reus in quem illa sumpserunt'.

8. Ibid., p. 261.

breach was laid in the subjects' position. Previously they had their places in a manifold, if loose, structure of responsibilities: as members of a Church, as dependent vassals, in the framework of their own political institutions or of the feudal order of estates. But the more the sense of this pluralistic world was reversed into the senselessness of civil warfare, the more the subjects faced a similarly cogent alternative as that facing the King himself: 'Know then that almost all men have been reduced to this point: to be on bad terms either with their conscience or with the course of the century'.[9] Amidst the toing and froing of persecutors and persecuted, of victims and executioners, the survivor was not he who stood by his faith but he who sought peace for its own sake. These were the theses which Agrippe d'Aubigné, the life-long frondeur, the ostracised and rigorous battler for the faith, put into the mouth of his apostate comrade-in-arms, the politician de Sancy.[10] Conscience and the needs of the situation are reconcilable no longer; hence — d'Aubigné's politician continues — there must be a clean break between the internal and the external. A prudent man withdraws into the secret chambers of his heart, where he remains his own judge, but external actions are to be submitted to the ruler's judgement and jurisdiction. The voice of conscience must never emerge; outwardly it has to be put to sleep. The convert alone survives. 'It is easy to see why; those who are dead wanted to let their conscience live, and it was their conscience that killed them.'[11] An ironical inversion burdened conscience with the guilt of its own ruin. The lines separating murder, manslaughter, and execution were still fluid and indefinite, but in the politician's mind any violent death in a war of religion was tantamount to suicide. He who submits to the sovereign lives by the sovereign; he who does not submit is destroyed, but the guilt is his own. To survive, the subject must submerge his conscience.

Conscience, the intrinsic relationship between responsibility

---

9. 'Sçachez que presque tous les hommes en sont reduits à ce poinct, ou d'estre en mauvais mesnage avec la conscience, ou avec les affaires du siecle . . .' (Agrippe d'Aubigné, *La confession du Sieur de Sancy*, ed. Réaume et Caussade, Paris, 1877, II, 369f.).

10. De Sancy, scion of the Harley family of jurists, had converted in 1597 and become Superintendent of Finances, in which post he could induce all opportunists among his former co-religionists to accept the Edict of Nantes (see A. Garnier, *Agrippe d' Aubigné et le Parti Protestant*, 3 vols., Paris, 1928, II, 255).

11. D'Aubigné, *Sieur de Sancy*: 'La raison en est facile: ceux qui sont morts ont voulus laisser vivre leur conscience, et elle les a tuez'.

and guilt, was forced open. Both elements found a novel co-ordination in the persons of ruler and subject. In the subjects' domain the ruler was freed from all guilt, but he accumulated all responsibility. The subject, on the other hand, was relieved of all political responsibility but threatened, in exchange, with a twofold guilt: externally when acting counter to his sovereign's interest — something the sovereign had the sole right to determine — and inwardly by seeking refuge in anonymity. This fission within the horizon of religious civil warfare paved the way for the 'innocence of power'. The prince alone could claim that innocence, but to maintain it he had to remain aware of the augmented responsibility it entailed. Then, and only then, was he in possession of the authority that guaranteed his power. He came to feel a compulsion to act which continually conjured up new decisions, including decisions involving the use of force; the consequences of inaction could be as serious as those of its opposite, the over-utilisation of power. One risk matched and constantly challenged the other. Indeed, the danger of falling from one extreme into the other was the very source of the evidence of sovereign decisions.

To meet his all-encompassing responsibility, the prince had to seek the measure of his actions in their calculable effect on everyone else. The compulsion to act thus provoked a need for heightened foresight. A rational calculation of all possible consequences came to be the first political commandment.[12] However, in order to keep the consequences of his actions (which, once committed, were not humanly alterable) under his own control as long as possible, the prince was driven further to augment his power, which in turn increased the sources of danger, the risks of abusing or failing to use the accumulated power, that is, of relinquishing its innocence. Louis XIV would succumb to this logic of absolute responsibility, yet obedience to its laws became the art of politics. The scope of the innocence of power remained narrowly circumscribed by the guidelines of a sharpened morality of action. These made up the political rules, rules which to the powerless subject could not but remain essentially alien.

Both politicians and teachers of the secular ethic agreed on this. Not until the eighteenth century were they to divide into two

12. Cf. Richelieu's *Testament politique*, II, chap. 4: ' . . . il est plus important de prévenir l'avenir que le présent . . .'. The aim of all good politics was to anticipate evils rather than have them surprise you.

hostile camps; in the seventeenth they still made common cause
against the theologians. Spinoza continued to maintain that only
theologians believed that statesmen were bound by the same rules
of piety as were private individuals.[13] The exclusion of 'morality'
from politics was not directed against a secular ethic, but against a
religious one with political claims.

The doctrine of *raison d'état* referred so exactly to the sectarian
situation that it did not even confine itself to monarchical Absolutism. On the Continent the doctrine filtered into a tradition of
enhanced royalty, but it gained just as much ground in countries
with a parliamentary — that is, republican — constitution. Every
power which in those days sought to equip itself with authority and
a generally binding nature required this exclusion of the private
conscience in which the bonds of religion or of feudal loyalty were
anchored. Thus the English Parliament in 1640, when it wished to
strip Charles I of his prerogatives, hastily embraced the argument
that every conscience, even the King's, must bow to the interest of
the State. Parliament claimed total sovereignty, to the extent of
forcing the King to act against his good conscience.[14]

Even Spinoza in Holland, far from advocating monarchical Absolutism, deemed it perfectly reasonable to look on every good deed
as sinful if it harmed the State — just as, conversely, sins became
pious works if they served the common weal.[15]

Paradigmatic for the modern State theory's genesis from the
situation of religious civil warfare is Hobbes, whom Spinoza cited.

Hobbes lends himself especially well to a description of this
genesis because he had already dispensed with such traditional
arguments as the God–King analogy. On the contrary, countering
these with the guiding principles of a scientific method, as Dilthey
put it,[16] he wanted to bring the phenomena in all their naked reality

13. Spinoza, *Tractatus Politicus* I, para. 2.
14. Clarendon cites the arguments to which Charles I had to bow so as to legalise
Parliament's proceedings against Strafford. 'That there was a private and a public
conscience; that his public conscience as a king might not only dispense with, but
oblige him to do that which was against his private conscience as a man . . .' 'That the
king was obliged in conscience to conform himself, and his own understanding, to
the advice and conscience of his parliament . . .' 'Which was a doctrine newly
resolved by their divines, and of great use to them for the pursuing their future
counsels', Clarendon adds in retrospect. (Clarendon, *The History of the Rebellion
and Civil Wars in England*, 6 vols., Oxford, 1888, I, 321 and 338ff.)
15. Spinoza, *Tractatus Theologico-Politicus* chap. 19; concerning the connection
with religious civil warfare cf. chap. 16 and *Ethica* IV, 37.
16. Cf. Dilthey, *Gesammelte Schriften*, 5th edn, Stuttgart and Göttingen, 1957, II,
362.

into the field of vision. Moreover, his consistently Absolutist theory of the State already contains the nucleus of the bourgeois notion of a government of laws. The logical next step after looking at the period of religious wars is to turn to the eighteenth century.

CHAPTER 2

Hobbesian Rationality and the Origins of Enlightenment

Unequivocally, Hobbes's doctrine of the State grew out of the historical situation of civil war. For Hobbes, who had experienced the formation of the Absolutist State in France, having been there when Henri IV was assassinated, and again when La Rochelle surrendered to the troops of Richelieu — for Hobbes there could be no other goal than to prevent the civil war he saw impending in England, or, once it had broken out, to bring it to an end.[1] In his old age he still maintained that concerning loyalty and justice nothing was more instructive than the memory of the late civil war.[2]

In the midst of revolutionary turmoil Hobbes continued to search for a fundament on which to build a State that would assure peace and security. While Descartes, in the finished State, shrank from raising such questions as a matter of principle, the situation made them all but central in Hobbes's mind.[3] All theologians, moral

---

1. This is why *De Cive* was published before the methodically arranged systematic physics and anthropology; cf. *De Cive* and *Leviathan*, Part II, chap. 18. He was, according to Hobbes, able to publish Part 3 first because 'praesertim cum eam (partem) principiis propriis experientia cognitis innixam, praecedentibus indigere non viderem'. Hobbes published his first political work, a translation of Thucydides, to allow the Greek example to serve as a warning against the threatening civil war. It appeared in 1628, the year that Parliament won the Petition of Rights from the King (*Works*, VIII).
2. Hobbes, *Behemoth* (1682), ed. Tönnies, London, 1889, V.
3. The conscious renunciation of external innovations put Descartes on the road to inner independence (*Discours de la Méthode*, chap. 2). The first dictate of his 'morale par provision' is obedience to the laws and customs of one's country (ibid., chap. 3). Hobbes polemicised strongly against 'Custome and Example' (*Leviathan*, chap. 11 *passim*) on the grounds that they violated reason. Morality and politics in particular are subject to human intervention: ' . . . politica et ethica, id est scientia

philosophers, and political scientists had failed in their task, he opined, since their doctrines supported the claims of particular parties; in other words, instead of teaching a law above parties, 'non partium, sed pacis studio',[4] they were actually fanning the flames of civil war. To find such a law, Hobbes asks what causes civil warfare. Guiding him in this quest is the idea that the plans and interests of various individuals, parties and churches must be unmasked before one can detect the underlying common cause of civil war. For — understandably, if quite irrationally — a humanity blinded by its hopes and cravings cannot recognise the root of all evils. 'Causa igitur belli civilis est, quod bellorum ac pacis causae ignorantus.'[5] It is along the lines of the *causa belli civilis* that Hobbes works out his rational natural law, which amounts to a theory of the causes of war and peace.

To get to the bottom of civil warfare, Hobbes moves beyond the pros and cons of shifting fronts. He develops an individualistic anthropology, one corresponding to a human nature that has come to view its social, political, and religious ties as problematical. The basic concepts of this nature are termed *appetitus et fuga*, desire and fear,[6] and in an historical perspective they form the elements of a theory of civil war. Yet at the same time Hobbes's entire system is so designed that the end product, the State, is already implied in the premise of civil conflict. From the outset, individuals are described as subjects, that is, as being subject to the sovereign. Without the mediation of an authority they are so fitted into the State order that they can freely unfold as individuals. Hobbes's individualism is the premise for a well-ordered State and at the same time the premise for the uninhibited development of the individual.[7]

---

justi et injusti, aequi et iniqui, demonstrari a priori potest', for, says Hobbes, anticipating Vico, 'justitiae causas, nimirum leges et pacta ipsi fecimus' (*De Homine*, X, 5).

4. *De Cive*, Preface.

5. Ibid.; *De Corpore Politico*, I, 1, 7.

6. *Leviathan*, I, 6. See also Leo Strauss, *The Political Philosophy of Hobbes, Its Basis and Its Genesis*, Oxford, 1936, 15ff.

7. Hannah Arendt has masterfully drawn the radical conclusions from Hobbes's individualistic first steps (*The Origins of Totalitarianism*, New York, 1958, 139ff.). However, in trying to understand Leviathan as a totalitarian society she ignores Hobbes's historical roots. Hobbes deduced absolute sovereignty for the protection of 'man', not property; sovereignty was the emanation of authority, not the vehicle of a 'majority will'. Only under the aegis of the Absolutist State could society as a society of wolves develop so greatly that it could dispense with that State by absorbing it. Despite Hobbes's logical conclusions — and Hannah Arendt's equally logical bent — he did not foresee this development, nor could he foresee it on

To begin with, mankind is ruled by passion, by a ceaseless striving for power which ends only in death.[8] The consequences are strife, war and civil conflict, the *bellum omnium contra omnes*. The constant fear of violent death will not let mankind breathe easier.[9] The longing for peace springs from the same source as the will to power.[10] Man vegetates in continual oscillation between the pursuit of power and the desire for peace; no human being can escape this movement, and raging within it is war. 'Hunc statum facile omnes, dum in es (bello) sunt, agnoscunt esse malum et per consequens pacem esse bonum'.[11] The state of war belongs to human nature, while peace exists only as a desire and a hope.

This difference — that peace is indeed desired as the highest good, but that as a mere wish it does not suffice to guarantee lasting peace — strikes Hobbes as the real moral-philosophical problem.[12]

By posing the problem in this way, he outstripped the type of questioning customary in those days. What discomfited English minds — relations between the sects and the State Church, between Parliament and the King, between the basic laws and the Protector — these Hobbes dismissed as superficial. To us the solution he discovered is interesting in two respects. Firstly, he points to conscience and its role in the sectarian struggles as an ideological value, thus depriving it of its explosive effect. Let me say at the outset that a characteristic of the doctrine of *raison d'état*, the subordination of ethics to politics, is to Hobbes thematically pointless, since reason removes whatever difference may exist between the two domains. The need to found a State transforms the moral alternative of good and evil into the political alternative of peace and war. ✓

Secondly, however, the distinction nevertheless remains relevant. It must be shown, therefore, how, almost against Hobbes's will, the differentiation did appear in ways that marked the constitutional law of Absolutism, demonstrating the inherent logic of the process. The problem, previously avoided in Christian moral philosophy, was now, under a different sign, repeated in the extra-theological area. The entire eighteenth century was dominated by this difficulty.

---

the horizon of the religious civil war.
8. *Leviathan*, I, 11.
9. Ibid., 13; *De Cive*.
10. *Leviathan*, I, 13.
11. *De Cive*, III, 31.
12. Ibid., V, 1.

Ostensibly, Hobbes agrees with the moral philosophers of his time that man is embedded in an eternal and immutable legality.[13] The moral law is universally binding; it compels a man to justify his actions to his conscience (*in foro interno*) not by their effect, but by his own intentions.[14] But, Hobbes continues, laws that oblige nothing but the will, and a sincere and constant will at that, 'are easy to be observed. For in that they require nothing but endeavour; he that endeavoureth their performance, fulfilleth them; and he that fulfilleth the Law, is Just'. With pure intentions it is not hard to be righteous.

The restrained sarcasm with which Hobbes as a twofold emigrant, a participant in both internal and external emigration, reacted to the changing righteousnesses of the civil war parties is significant for a thinker who knew the fatal dialectics of conscience and deed from personal experience. The discrepancy between inner posture and external action had indeed been aggravated to the point of total interchangeability of what was now truly righteous.[15] Was it the state of mind or the action which counted; both at once or only one of the two? And which was more important, state of mind or action? Aware of the dialectic prevailing between the two realms, Hobbes embarks on a fundamental re-examination of their mutual relations, and in doing so encounters the same phenomenon which Shakespeare referred to when he said: 'For that same word, rebellion, did divide/The action of their bodies from their souls'.[16]

Hobbes's first effort, which already made his intention clear, was to do without the customary employment of the word 'conscience'. He removed its fluctuating value and replaced it with a concept bare of any religious significance: the concept of opinion.[17] Conscience,

---

13. *De Cive*, III, 29; *Leviathan*, II, 26. Heaven and earth shall pass away, Hobbes says, paraphrasing Luke 21:33, but natural law, which is moral law, shall not.

14. *De Cive*, III, 30; *Leviathan*, I, 16.

15. 'The names of just, unjust, justice, injustice, are equivocal, and signify diversly ... that when injustice is taken for guilt, the action is unjust, but not therefore the man; and when justice is taken for guiltlessness, the actions are just, and yet not always the man. Likewise when justice and injustice are taken for habits of the mind, the man may be just, or unjust, and yet not all his actions so' (*The Elements of Law*, Cambridge, 1928, I, chap. 16, 4). See also *De Cive*, III, 5; and *Leviathan*, I, 4 and 15.

16. *Henry IV, Part 2*, Act 1, Scene 1.

17. Hobbes was not privy to the present-day distinction between 'conscience' and 'consciousness'. In *Elements of Law* (II, chap. 6, 12), he defines 'conscience' as 'nothing else but a man's settled judgment and opinion ... Men, when they say things upon their conscience, are not therefore presumed certainly to know the truth of what they say ... Conscience therefore I define to be opinion of evidence' (ibid.,

he held, was nothing but a subjective belief, a private view.

The attempt of Presbyterians and Independents to vindicate themselves theologically by divine grace was to Hobbes a mere expression of their passion. For himself, he elaborated an extra-religious, supra-partisan position which in turn enabled him to analyse all parties together, as parties to a common process.[18]

Without illusions, Hobbes acknowledged the disproportion between the various parties' moral-theological goals and the practices whereby they sought to realise these goals. While there might not be any doubt about their good intentions and their will to peace, they were obviously not in agreement about the ways and means which might or might not be conducive to achieving that goal.[19] Moreover, their intent — which, measured by their actions, differed among the various parties — assured them of a generally binding claim.[20] It follows not only that action stood against action, but intent against intent. And the states of mind spurred to more and more radical actions, with the aim of destroying the enemy not just outwardly but inwardly as well.[21] It was a battle of intents whose structure, hidden from the participants themselves, was shown by Hobbes.

---

8). In *Leviathan* (I, 7) he gives us an etymology which testifies to his reluctance to forgo use of the word: '. . . it was, and ever will be reputed a very Evill act, for any man to speak against his Conscience; or to corrupt or force another to do so . . . Afterwards, men made use of the same word metaphorically, for the knowledge of their secret facts, and secret thoughts . . . And last of all, men, vehemently in love with their own new opinions (though never so absurd), and obstinately bent to maintain them, gave those their opinions also that reverenced name of Conscience, as if they would have it seem unlawfull, to change or to speak against them . . .'. Logically, Hobbes practises extreme restraint in his use of the term. Even where he does use it in its basic meaning, as in 'private conscience', he later substituted terms like 'opinion', 'inner thought', 'heart', etc.

18. Cf. *De Cive*, II, 1, in which Hobbes formulated the crucial criterion of his method, impartiality.'Methodus scilicet, qua incipitur a definitionibus et exclusione aequivoci, propria eorum est qui locum contra disputandi non relinquunt'.

19. Cf. *De Corpore Politico*, I, 1, 7: 'Causa autem horum [the evil of civil war] non est quod homines ea velint, voluntas enim nisi boni saltem apparentis est . . .'; and *De Cive*, III, 32: ' . . . quamquam consentiant omnes in laude dictarum virtutum, tamen dissentiant adhuc de earum natura . . .'. Hobbes saw in this the same phenomenon as Augustine when he said 'Non ergo ut sit pax nolunt, sed ut ea sit quam volunt' (*De Civitate Dei*, XIX, 12).

20. Hobbes does not deny the subjective purity and potential usefulness of the various moral teachers, 'sed quae pronunciatae ab illis universaliter, non tamen plerumque universaliter verae sunt'. (*De Corpore Politico*, I, 1, 7).

21. *Elements of Law*, II, 6, 13: 'The truth is apparent, by continual experience, that men seek not only liberty of conscience, but of their actions; not that only, but a farther liberty of persuading others to their opinions; not that only for every man desireth, that the sovereign authority should admit no other opinions to be maintained but such as he himself holdeth'. *De Cive*, I, 5: ' . . . cum maximum sit certamen ingeniorum, necesse est oriri ex ea contentione maximas discordias'.

'Etenim non modo contra contendere, sed etiam hoc ipsum, non consentire, odiosum est. Nam non consentire alicui in re aliqua, est eum erroris in ea re tacite accusare . . . quod ex eo apparere potest, quod nulla acrius gerentur bella quam inter ejusdem religionis sectas et ejusdem reipublicae factiones . . .'[22]

Hobbes's theme was civil war as Rousseau was to describe it a hundred years later along similar lines: ' . . . ils deviennent tous ennemis; alternativement persécutés and persécuteurs, chacun sur tous et tous sur chacun; l'intolérant est l'homme de Hobbes, l'intolérance est la guerre de l'humanité'.[23] A man cannot escape this civil war even if he acknowledges his longing for peace to be a generally valid moral principle.[24] For as the sole purveyor of a legal title to action, his subjectively pure will to peace is precisely what leads to claims of more stringent totality on the part of those who cite their conscience. In other words, since it is in fact a matter of several parties, the pure will leads not to peace but to its opposite, the *bellum omnium contra omnes*. Whoever refers to his conscience wants something, says Hobbes. The hostile parties' claim to exclusiveness rests upon their mental posture, to which Hobbes reduces all religious content; that this posture is common to everyone is the wellspring of civil war. Such a war derives from the poison of rebellious doctrines, one of which deems everyone to be qualified to judge good and evil acts, while the other holds whatever someone does against his conscience to be sinful.[25]

The Reformation and the subsequent split in religious authority had thrown man back upon his conscience, and a conscience lacking outside support degenerates into the idol of self-righteousness. No wonder this very conscience imbued the embattled parties with the courage and energy to keep fighting. Mere conscience which, as Hobbes put it,[26] presumes to mount the throne is not a judge of good and evil; it is the source of evil itself. It was not just the will to power that kindled civil war; those flames — and herein lies the crucial step Hobbes had taken — were fanned equally by appeals to

---

22. *De Cive*, I, 5.
23. This startling formulation, which hints at the subterranean connection between the religious civil war and the French Revolution is contained in the closing passage — omitted from later editions — of Book 4, ch. 8, of *Contrat social* (Manuscrit de Genève, quoted from the edition of M. Halbwachs, Paris, 1943, 448).
24. *De Cive*, III, 27.
25. *Leviathan*, II, 29; cf. *Elements of Law*, II, 8, 5; and *De Cive*, 12, 1ff.
26. *Elements of Law*, II, 7, 2; *De Cive*, 12, 1.

(for)

a conscience without outside support. Instead of being a *causa pacis*, the authority of conscience in its subjective plurality is a downright *causa belli civilis*.

The moral-philosophical reflections in which Hobbes endeavours to fathom the premises of lasting peace take him beyond the traditional realm. He did take up the separation of conscience and action, but only to reattune one to the other.[27] Unlike his contemporaries, he did not argue from the inside outwards but the reverse,

27. The separation of inward and external, or as Hobbes phrases it, or 'externall acts' and 'inward thought', of 'action' and 'habits of mind' (*Leviathan*, I, 15; 1, 38, 40 *passim*) is an integral part of Western tradition. It is rooted in the Christian world-view, and in Augustine's two-world doctrine it was part of the Middle Ages. Thomas Aquinas assumed that man could judge only external acts, that the inner realm was God's (*Summa Theologiae, Prima Secundae*, Qu. 100, Art. 9: 'Homo autem qui est legislator humanae, non habet judicare nisi de exterioribus actibus . . . Sed solius Dei qui est lator legis divinae, est judicare de interioribus motibus voluntatum'). However, external and internal did not clearly contrast so long as the visible institution of the Church held the two together. With the dissolution of the ecclesiastical tie the breach widened. Typical of this are the reformers who rid their conscience of the old Church but then fell back on the State. The contrast of inwardness and externality is essentially the theme of Luther's pamphlet *Von weltlicher Obrigkeit, wie weit man ihr Gehorsam schuldig ist* (1523, W.A. II, 245ff.). Those possessing inner piety, the true Christians, need no law, 'need neither worldly sword nor right' (249). Law, whether the law of the State or the law of the Old Testament, serves external order. The broad mass of people will always be un-Christian, and therefore it is impossible to govern the world according to the Gospels. Consequently the two armies, the truly spiritual that is not subject to worldly rule and the worldly 'that makes external peace and protects against evil deeds' (252), have to be kept apart. Luther's separation of the inward and the external, of the spiritual realm and the world, in which the 'external' office of the rulers is responsible for order and justice, thus seems to lead towards the same goal to which Hobbes aspired. Hobbes believed the absolute and therefore lawful sovereign to be the executor of the law of the Old Testament, which according to Luther was also binding on the princes. Both agree that the inner realm, whether it be that of the Holy Spirit or a religious or moral 'conviction' could not rule this world, for that would create greater conflict and misery than already existed. For man is a 'wild, evil beast', — *homo homini lupus*. For the sake of external peace he needs to be governed, needs laws; his inner self, his beliefs or convictions, are not touched by it. In this respect Hobbes's contrasting of inward and external is in the Christian tradition: Kurt Schilling recently pointed to this connection specifically ('Naturrecht, Staat und Christentum bei Hobbes', *Zeitschrift für philosophische Forschung*, II, 2–3, 1948, 286, 292ff.). Schilling refers to the content of the Hobbesian moral philosophy and its binding conscience. The State was only the necessary condition for 'living freely and openly according to the laws of God, the creator of reason and natural law, and the laws of personal conscience identical with these'. However correct this link of Hobbesian moral philosophy to tradition, and the corresponding, also Augustinian, concept of the Hobbesian State as an institution of external peace, this interpretation fails to note Hobbes's real historical contribution which, given the multiplicity of religious moral teachings, lies precisely in the functionalist reinterpretation of the phenomena of conscience. The separation of inward and external, as well as of conviction and action, thus took on completely new historical meaning, as an allusive comparison with the Reformers makes clear. Luther's separation of inward and external springs from his absolute consciousness of Revelation, his certainty that his inner being was separated from this world. And out of the inner necessity to

from the outside in. In civil war there is no telling unequivocally what is good and what is evil, and the wish for peace is not itself sufficient to cause a flagging of the will to power. How is it possible, then, from the original situation of civil war in which all men are entitled to all things, to develop a legality that allows the wish to become reality? Before a law of nature becomes a real law it requires a guarantee of compliance.[28] A commandment that is anchored in natural law, the commandment to make peace, must be transformed into a law that can be satisfied by concrete execution. The drafting of such a legality is the proper task of moral philosophy; its proper theme is politics. The result is the legitimisation of the Absolutist State in its political structure. The system itself is known.

Hobbes introduces the State as a structure in which private mentalities are deprived of their political effect. In his constitutional

---

proclaim the word of God, objectively audible in his conscience, he encroaches on the external. The separation as a spiritual experience, as Johannes Kühn has shown (*Toleranz und Offenbarung*, Leipzig, 1923, 94), was surmounted by the prophet. Thus the secular realm is subjugated to the spiritual realm in which conscience plays a role; the commonwealth becomes the 'educational institution of the Christian nation', and this is 'unthinkable without intolerance'. Hobbes is 'intolerant' for precisely the opposite reason. He endows the State with all its powers precisely in order to find protection against those prophets of Revelation (*Leviathan*, I, 2 *passim*) who, unlike Luther, believe they can absorb the worldly office completely. In doing so, Hobbes excludes the religious inner realm specifically, so as to analyse it as a political factor. Calvin, like Luther, also saw the contrast of internal and external only from the standpoint of the doctrine of grace (*Institutes of the Christian Religion*, IV, chap. 20, 1–3ff.). Internal and external do not absolutely contradict each other so long as the external institution of the State fulfils its protective role, that is, so long as it is dominated by the Christian inner realm. Internal and external are not identical with Christian and non-Christian; rather, this grace–doctrinal difference can be endured only through a Christian co-ordination of conscience and State. Only in the course of the Reformation did internal and external become simplified into mere contrast: on the one hand, by the Puritans who, being certain of salvation, believed they could do without external supports, and, on the other hand, by the politicians who, in pursuit of politico-religious neutrality, sought to see more and more areas as 'things indifferent'. (Cf. R. Hooker, *Of the Laws of Ecclesiastical Policy*, ed. C. Morris, London, 1954, Book 1, IX, X, Preface, 102: 'This hath bred high terms of separation between such (as the puritans) and the rest of the world; whereby one are named The brethren, The godly, and so forth; the other worldlings, time-servers, pleasers of men not of God, with such like'.) Thus in effect there arose a conflict in which the religious combatants equated the inner realm with their good conscience, and the other with the evil world. Hobbes fought against this sense of self. In his treatment, the contrast between inner and external becomes a heuristic effort to discover the psychological motivations whose laws can make all men, whoever they may be, subject to the laws of the State. In this respect Hobbes also differed fundamentally with the Independents, even though, as Lips has demonstrated (*Die Stellung des Thomas Hobbes zu den politischen Parteien der grossen englischen Revolution*, Leipzig, 1927, 48ff.), he agreed with them on questions of Church–State policy.

28. *De Cive*, III, 27–33; *Leviathan*, I, 15.

law, private states of mind do not apply to the laws,[29] and the laws do not apply to the sovereign.[30] The public interest, about which the sovereign alone has the right to decide, no longer lies in the jurisdiction of conscience. Conscience, which becomes alienated from the State, turns into private morality. 'Auctoritas, non veritas facit legem' — laws are made by authority, not by truth. The prince is above the law and at the same time its source; he decides what is right and what is wrong; he is both law-maker and judge.[31] This law, as constitutional law, is no longer substantially tied to social interests and religious hopes; instead, it designates a formal domain of political decisions beyond any Church, estate, or party. This domain can be occupied by this or that power, only providing it has the authority required to protect the various individuals, irrespective of their interests and expectations. The ruler's political decision takes effect by virtue of that decision.

A State order — in so far as it is secured from above — can only exist if the plurality of parties and individuals also finds itself in a morality that accepts the ruler's absolute political sovereignty as a moral necessity. This morality is Hobbes's morality of reason. To the traditional moral doctrines he opposes one whose theme is political reason. The laws of this morality are fulfilled in the establishment of the State. As rational conclusions they are simultaneously empirical conclusions drawn from the brutal reality — *damnosum experientia* — of civil war.[32] In the war of all against all each individual aims at the destruction of another. This is why a combatant in such a war does not fear any particular thing, or any particular moment, but fears for his entire being; what he feels is the fear of death, the absolute master. But a man in fear of death will flee to the State,[33] and protection is therefore the State's highest moral obligation.

The State, however, can meet its obligation only if all men individually cede their rights to the sovereign who represents them

---

29. *Leviathan*, II, 18.
30. Ibid., 26.
31. Ibid., 18.
32. *De Cive*, Preface, III, 31.
33. *Leviathan*, I, 14; *De Cive*, V, 1: 'sufficitque ad impletionem legis naturalis (id est moralis) ut quis paratus animo sit ad pacem habendam, ubi haberi potest . . .'. The law of reason is equally valid for belief and action: 'Ratio tamen eadem neque finem mutat, quae est pax et defensio, neque media nempe animae virtutes' (*De Cive*, III, 29).

collectively.[34] And not until compliance with this commandment of
reason has been guaranteed by the State will the morality of reason
have the force of law. The subjective wish for peace is, on its own,
insufficient; to become 'moral', it requires the sanction of the State.
Reason beckons the State, but not until the State exists can that
reason be as political as it is moral.

Hobbes's initial point of departure had been a State arising from a
contract pre-ordained in time, so to speak; now he posits the State
in order to make this contract possible. The logical paradox lies in
the fact that the State owes its existence to a contract, and that it
then exists as an autonomous formation. It takes Leviathan to be a
State which is at once the cause and the effect of its foundation.
Thus Hobbes did away with the supposed priority of inner individual resolutions so as to elucidate that each fulfillable morality was
just as originally dependent on the State order. If it was to make
sense, the consistent Absolutist removal of any duality between the
old estates and the new ruler, between the people and their sovereign, had also to ban all distinctions between moral law and political
legality. The civil war that was experienced as a threat to life came to
rest in the State. As an earthly State, this State was a mortal God,
and as a mortal God it safeguarded and prolonged people's lives. At
the same time it remained mortal, however, for it was men's
handiwork and could always relapse into civil war, its native state.

To prevent this, the State must be explained according to the same
rational rules which conditioned its origin. The rationally construed
State was not a pure 'state of reason' like the one looked forward to
in the next century; it was a State for people who would act against
reason as frequently as reason would speak against them.[35] It was
not reason itself that would end the civil war — Hobbes was not a
Utopian — but reason did point the way to the social conditions,
those of peace among men, that may turn the State into a reasonable
'judge' of unreasonable mankind. Peace is guaranteed only if political morality, the quality that makes men cede their rights to the
sovereign representing them, is transformed in the act of state-
founding into a duty to obey.

34. *De Cive*, III, 27 n. 'Breviter, in statu naturae, Justum et Injustum non ex
actionibus, sed ex consilio et conscientia agentium aestimandum est. Quod necess-
ario, quod studio pacis, quod sui conservandi causa fit, recte fit.' The contract of all
with all, and the simultaneous transfer of their rights to the sovereign is thus
established.
35. *Elements of Law*; *Leviathan*, I, 5.

If, and in order that, the necessary protection can be furnished by the State, the decisive moral commandment must be the duty to obey. What makes the State a State is not only the prince's absolute power; it is the interrelation of protection and obedience.[36] Only in the relationship that has arisen between protection and obedience can a neutral status develop in which the laws, however different in substance, can assure peace, safety, and 'contentment' by their legality alone. Reason thus creates a neutral zone of State 'technology' in which there is no law but the prince's will. In such a State only the formal legality of the laws is rational, not their content; therefore the formal commandment of political morality to obey the laws regardless of their content is reasonable. The State is not only a mortal God; it becomes the automaton, the great machine, and the laws are the levers moved by the sovereign's absolute will, in order to keep the State machinery running. Following the paths illuminated by reason the State can be realised only through ending civil warfare and, having ended it, preventing any recurrence. Thus, like the political morality of individuals, the state also corresponds to reason.

For reason, faced with the historical alternative of civil war or State order, 'morality' and 'politics' coincide. It is only in respect of civil war, and of reason's supreme commandment to put an end to this war, that Hobbes's system becomes logically conclusive. Morality bids men submit to the ruler; the ruler puts an end to civil war; in doing so he fulfils morality's supreme commandment. The sovereign's moral qualification consists in his political function: to make and maintain order.

With his unimpeachable sovereignty thus derived from the diverse parties of the civil war claiming legitimacy on moral-theological and religious grounds, Hobbes's answer to the prince's historical position is implied in this derivation. Just as on the Continent the State had overcome the religious wars and acquired its Absolutist form, so in England it was reason which performed this constitutional and moral-philosophical task — the *ratio* which Hobbes knew to be as remote from the confused squabbles of irrational, superstitious, instinct-driven humans as the absolute ruler was from his subjects. To Hobbes, reason was the ending of civil war — a line that can also be reversed in its historic meaning:

36. *Leviathan*, II, 22, and 30, A Review and Conclusion.

34   *The Political Structure of Absolutism*

the ending of the religious civil wars is 'reason'. What manifests itself here is the juncture, still situational, of Absolutism and Rationalist philosophy. Reason, rising from the turmoil of religious warfare, at first remains under the spell of that warfare and founds the State. This is how we are to understand Hobbes's failure to see that the spirit of Enlightenment enables reason to emancipate itself. Hobbes did not know that reason has a gravitation of its own.

For Hobbes, man's rationally derived destiny of rational self-emancipation could not be his historical destiny simply because Hobbes had experienced history as the history of civil wars. In his mind, calling for the State was not progress but simply the need to put an end to civil wars. Not until the State had suppressed and neutralised religious conflict could progressive reason unfold in the newly vacated space. To Hobbes, history was a continuous alternation from civil war to the State and from the State to civil war. *Homo homini lupus, homo homini Deus*[37] — and only when this menacing and simultaneously promising ambivalence is disregarded, that is, when we ignore Hobbes's historic starting point and take his system out of its historically fixed context — only then can the oft-discussed formally logical difficulties of the system enter our field of vision.[38]

37. *De Cive*. The elements of progress in Hobbes's philosophy in no way determine his concept of history. True, Hobbes arrives at 'progress' through the scientific activity of reason and the growing mastery of nature. 'Reason is the pace: Encrease of science the way; and the Benefit of mankind the end' (*Leviathan*, I, 6). Hobbes also endows the light of reason with a strong feeling of superiority over the past, its ignorance and superstitions. Reason and will are directed towards the future, the future of this world, with neither a hereafter nor immortality (*Leviathan*, III, 38). Bliss, however, cannot be achieved in this world; 'ad fines semper ulteriores minime impedita progressio' is the highest good (*De Homine*, 11, 15). Hobbes sees the furthering of progress through experience as a constant, infinite progressive process. If man were able to achieve his goal, he would be contented, 'et non sentire est non vivere'. The development of reason is one of man's tasks, and though it grows out of instinctual nature, it can be achieved only through the regulation of a sensual and affective nature. It can further be helped by a rational education at the universities, whose reform Hobbes supported, or by a monarch using his jurisdiction in an enlightened manner to educate man. But this task of man for progress based on reason is not, however, determined by rational history but by the State. However, the State ultimately is and remains threatened by the natural condition of its genesis to the extent that it has departed from it. 'Nam vita motus est perpetuus, qui, cum recta progredi non potest, convertitur in motum circularem' (*De Homine*, 11, 15). Rosenstock has pointed out that Hobbes, in *Behemoth*, did in fact look on the years from 1640 to 1660 as such a 'revolution', a 'circular motion', which led from the royal sovereignty of Charles I via two usurpers to the sovereignty of Charles II ('Revolution als politischer Begriff der Neuzeit', *Abhandlungen der Schlesischen Gesellschaft für vaterländische Literatur*, Series H. 5, Wrocław, 1931, 90ff.)
38. On the one hand, Hobbes recognises moral laws that are valid without sanction by the State (*De Cive*, III, 28ff.). States living in a natural state are bound by

In view of the achievement of peace, and of its assurance by the sovereign, the sovereign's every command is at the same time a moral command. For people threatened by civil war there is no difference between politics and conscience. But what will happen once peace is secured, once the threat of death has been averted and the citizen is free to develop? This question, which soon disturbed the newly established order, compels us to look more closely at the relationship between morality and politics as characterised by the Absolutist State. And in Hobbes's attempted solution, it can be seen that what ailed his concept of the State, in altered form, was the same dichotomy which he, by means of that State, sought to abolish.

Deliberately disregarding the content of religious or political party programmes, Hobbes did not ask about the structure of a particular state; he asked about what makes the State a State, about its statehood. He did not ask for legal detail, 'legibus speciatim'; he asked: 'Quid sint leges?' What are laws?[39] What interested him was not the substance of laws but their function as warrants of peace. Their legality did not lie in their substantive qualification but in their source alone, in the fact that they expressed the will of the sovereign power. Yet to enable them to be legal in a neutral, supra-partisan, religiously indifferent fashion, Hobbes continuously cited the very difference once derived from historical reality,

---

these laws (*De Cive*, XIV, 4; *Leviathan*, II, 21). Moreover, they permit the individual a basic human right, namely to seek self-protection if the State fails (*Leviathan*, II, 21). In view of these pre-statist laws the State also acts as a vast mechanism safeguarding the fulfilment of natural laws. This is the basis of Hobbes's liberal tradition. On the other hand, he consistently narrows the legal concept to the sovereign expression of will, so that the natural laws — once the State has been formed by them — lose their uniqueness (*De Cive*, III, 33; *De Homine*, XIII, 9; *Leviathan*, I, 15; II, 27). This led Otto Gierke to speak of Hobbes's 'invalidation of natural law by natural law' (*Johannes Althusius und die Entwicklung der naturrechtlichen Staatstheorien*, 3rd edn, Wrocław 1913). The theoreticians of the Absolutist State based themselves on this absorption of natural law by the juridical-political realm. Hobbes resolves every conflict between conscience and command — 'ut tam obedientia nostra, quam inobedientia sit peccatum' (*De Cive*, XII, 2) — in favour of command. But for Hobbes, formal command possesses not only a legal but a moral quality as well. Via the unity of many wills he raises the multiplicity of individual wills into the single will which alone promises peace (ibid., V, 4). The State is not only a vast mechanism, but also an artificial man whose soul is sovereignty. This is the root of Rousseau's democratic theory. Once the highest commandment of peace was perceived as the vanishing point of the Hobbesian system, the various planes could be isolated. Later, as the different directions became independent, they were used against each other.

39. *De Cive*, Preface; *De Homine*, 13, 9: 'Quare etsi actiones quaedam, quae in una civitate justae sunt, in alia sint injustae, justitia tamen, id est non violate leges ubique, ubique eadem est et erit.'

that between inner inclination and outward action; he only used this discrepancy, which according to his analysis would stoke the flames of civil war, so as to make it serve public order.

Hobbes had already thought through the formalisation of the sovereign concept of law; it continued to rest , albeit in constructive revaluation, on the distinction between conscience and action. For this differential alone allowed the substance of an act to be separated from the act itself — the necessary premise of a formal concept of law. In no other way is it possible to call a law legal (regardless of its moral and religious content) and to comply with it at the same time. 'Sovereign' laws could be obeyed only if the subject's frame of mind and course of action — already contradicting one another in civil war — could remain separated from one another, so that he might live in harmony with himself, irrespective of the content of the laws he had to follow. The historic premise of civil war thus became a logically necessary premise for Hobbes's ability to deduce his concept of absolute sovereignty.

Hobbes's cogitative achievement lay in shifting the cleft between conscience and politics, in so far as religiously orientated, so that irrational individuals could not avoid it being removed to a region outside the State machine. The break appears in two places: in the sovereign, who is above the law, and in the individual who is divided into human being and citizen.[40] 'It is true that they that have soveraigne power may commit Iniquitie, but not Injustice . . . .'.[41] An absolute ruler may indeed do wrong, but never legally, only in a moral sense or by violating the utility principle. To prevent this would be to void the premise of peace, Absolute sovereignty, and thus open the floodgates to the misery of new, more unjust actions. The evil at issue here was not determinant for the monarchy but inherent in human nature.[42] Political morality had freed the prince from all bonds; that he would none the less allow a certain equity to

---

40. This separation alone enabled Hobbes to conjoin moral and political laws without having to establish a Utopian identification. In *De Homine*, XIII, 9, Hobbes describes the virtues rooted in beliefs unrelated to the State. In doing so, he ignores so much of traditional moral teachings that he calls 'vis et dolus' the cardinal virtues of pre-statist man: they are the virtues of man as the creature of civil war. 'Justitia et injustitia', on the other hand, are 'qualitates non hominis, sed civis' (ibid.). The later democratic criticism of both Rousseau and Marx opposed this separation. They did take over Hobbes's concept of absolute sovereignty, but put it in the service of 'man'. With this the boundary line to Utopianism was crossed; sovereignty itself became revolutionary.

41. *Leviathan*, II, 18.

42. *De Cive*, VI, 13n.

prevail — by choice, not obligation, let it be said — was to be hoped for, but was not necessary in order for the State to perform as regulator of unreasoning humanity.[43]

Nor was the subject as human being required to identify ideologically with the political laws in order to maintain the State's function as guardian of the peace.[44] For man as citizen, on the other hand, the prime cause of moral laws is no longer to be sought in God, but in the temporal power that puts an end to civil war. These laws are not moral because they correspond to an eternal legality of morals, although they may do this; they are moral because they have originated in a commandment derived directly from the political situation. They are laws of political ethics, on the basis of which decisions are made by the sovereign alone. It is not a frame of mind or a correct measure that makes a virtue out of virtue, but its political foundation.[45] However, for man as a human being it is his frame of mind, his individual conscience, that remains the ultimate criterion of morality. That this, too, will take its bearings from political necessity is also just a hope.

Hobbes's man is fractured, split into private and public halves: his actions are totally subject to the law of the land while his mind remains free, 'in secret free'.[46] From here on the individual is free to migrate into his state of mind without being responsible for it. In so far as conscience participated in the political world it became the controlling authority of the duty to obey. The sovereign command relieved the subject of all responsibility: 'The Law is the publique Conscience — private Consciences . . . are but private opinions'.[47] However, if an individual presumed to a jurisdiction which the State reserved to itself, the individual had to mystify himself, lest he be called to account.[48] The dichotomy of man into private and public

43. *Leviathan*, II, 30, 31.
44. *Elements of Law*, II, 6, 3; *De Cive*, XII; *Leviathan*, III, 32; IV, 46; *Behemoth*, 62: 'A state can constrain obedience, but convince no error, nor alter the minds of them that believe they have the better reason. Suppression of doctrine does but unite and exasperate, that is, increase both the malice and power of them that have already believed them'.
45. *De Cive*, III, 32f.; *Leviathan*, I, 16.
46. *Elements of Law*, II, 6, 3: 'No human law is intended to oblige the conscience of a man, but the actions only.' *Leviathan*, II, 31: 'Private, is in secret free'. Cf. ibid., III, 40.
47. Ibid., II, 29.
48. 'Je me soumettrai à la loi', Diderot was to say a century later, 'et je réclamerai contre elle . . . Mais si cette réclamation, prohibée par la loi même, est un crime capital? . . . Je me tairai ou je m'éloignerai . . .' (Oeuvres Complètes, ed. Assézat et Tourneux, Paris, 1875–9, XI, 122).

spheres was intrinsic to the genesis of the mystery. Later, the mind's inner space would be gradually expanded by the Enlightenment, but any claim to the public domain remained inevitably shrouded in a veil of secrecy. The dialectic of mystery and enlightenment, of mystification and unmasking, was already one of the roots of the Absolutist State. It was the heritage of the religious wars whose consciously accepted duality gained it admittance to the principle of that State.

Reason, interested solely in terminating the civil war, was not concerned with the difference between the moral and political spheres. It had become rational enough, so to speak, to recognise the historic reality of actually different bonds of conscience. One could even afford to recognise that reality; for the formal, technical character of the Absolutist concept of law brought with it an elasticity which bypassed whatever differences between conscience and action might jeopardise public order. Peace and security were thus assured, and the State became a field of moral neutrality, not of political immorality. As a morally neutral space it was an area of genuine exoneration. 'Potentia, si eximia sit, bona est, quia utilis ad praesidium; in praesidio autem securitas.'[49] However, even this space was available only at the price of man's dichotomy, a price that was legal because of Hobbes's conscious acceptance. In his private world man was free; there alone was he human. As a citizen he was the subject of his sovereign; only as a subject was he a citizen.

The exoneration of man placed a burden on the State. That a man was human was his secret; as such he was bound to escape the sovereign's notice. In so far as a subject did his duty and obeyed, his private life did not interest the sovereign. Here, as we shall see, lay the Enlightenment's specific point of attack. It expanded into that same gap which the Absolutist State had left unoccupied in order to end the civil war in the first place. Pressed by the need for a lasting peace, the State conceded to the individual an inner space that did not much impair the sovereign decision; as a matter of fact, it became essential to that decision. It was essential for the State to be politically neutral if it was to preserve its political form. Moral neutrality was the distinguishing mark of the sovereign decision; with the lapse of that neutrality the Absolutist State lost its specific,

49. *De Homine*, XI, 6.

situation-bound presence in the same measure. The State created a new order, but then — in genuinely historic fashion — fell prey to that order. As evident in Hobbes, the moral inner space that had been excised from the State and reserved for man as human being meant (even rudimentarily) a source of the unrest that was originally exclusive to the Absolutist system. The authority of conscience remained an unconquered remnant of the state of nature, protruding into the formally perfected State.

The neutralisation of conscience by politics assisted with the secularisation of morality. Mediatising the ecclesiastical conflicts that accompanied the building of the Absolutist State facilitated the step-by-step expansion of a moral world-view based on nature and reason. A crumbling of the faith in revelation that had necessitated the creation of the State doomed the same State as the old themes recurred in secularised form. A morality striving to become political would be the great theme of eighteenth century. To the extent to which the initial situation, the religious civil war to which this State owed its existence and its form, was forgotten, *raison d'état* looked like downright immorality.

The moral doctrines, as the real heirs of religion, aimed deliberately at life on earth while remaining extra-political in the framework of the Absolutist State. As we have seen, man as a human being had intentionally been omitted from the state structure; it was as a subject alone that he had any public quality.

What the Enlightenment brought about, then, was the distinction between man and subject being no longer understood. Publicly, man was to realise himself as a human being, with the resulting decay of the Absolutist State. That it was the split between morality and politics, of all things, which began and then accelerated the process was something Hobbes could not foresee. Bourgeois humanism inherited from the theologians, and in the political field a verse from the Gospel: 'But he that is spiritual judges all things, yet he himself is judged of no man'[50] — these sentiments would soon be newly and unexpectedly topical.

Summing up, we can say that Hobbes was not an historian, not a

---

50. 1 Cor. 2:15: 'ὁ δὲ πνευματικὸς ἀνακρίνει μὲν πάντα, αὐτὸς δὲ ὑπ᾽ οὐδενὸς ἀνακρίνεται'. 'Ils sont juges,' says Voltaire of the critics, presumably the happiest members of the Republic of Letters, 'et les autres sont jugés' ('Gens des lettres', in the *Encyclopédie*). The Enlightenment was not unaware that it was the successor to the clergy. '[La philosophie] doit tenir lieu de divinité sur la terre', says Raynal in his *Histoire Philosophique et Politique* (1780), XIX, 13.

collector or reporter of past and present facts. As a thinker about history whose purpose was to overcome civil warfare he found an answer beyond his starting-point. An objection already raised by contemporaries was that Hobbes inferred what ought to be from what is, that he had his well-ordered State arise from a state of nature in which men act like wolves towards each other.[51] This objection, which made Dilthey speak of Hobbes's 'impetuous subjectivity', actually proves the historicity of his thinking. History always yields either more or less, and in any event something else, than previously given data; this is just what makes it topical. In fact, Hobbes's thinking was eminently historical when he performed the logically paradoxical leap from the natural state of civil war to the formally perfect State. Hobbes raised the issues that characterised the seventeenth century. What proves the strength of his thinking is its inherent prognosticative element.

51. Richard Peters, *Hobbes*, Harmondsworth, 1956, p. 171; for contemporary criticism see John Bowle, *Hobbes and His Critics*, London, 1951; Dilthey, *Gesammelte Schriften*, 462.

CHAPTER 3

The Exclusion of Natural Law Morality from International Politics and the Concept of War between States as a Precondition of Moral Progress

The supra-sectarian legal order managed not only to pacify the individual States; it left an even stronger imprint on the relations between States. Europe's international law could be effective only because it engendered a new sense of obligation, one that cut across the plurality of faiths. This obligation was political. In staking out a framework of international relations it was analogous to the lines of thought along which Hobbes deduced the State. Nothing but his strict separation of exterior and interior realms could make it possible to core an area of foreign policy out of the welter of religious jurisdictions — a process which against the historic background of sectarian passions amounted all but inescapably to rationalisation.

The secret cabinet politics, the rationalistic calculations which had become routine, would in the eighteenth century be as much a target of the critics calling for publicity as the Absolutist system itself. The universality of an enlightened ethic crossed all the boundaries so painstakingly drawn by politicians. Claiming the same validity from China to America, from Paris to Peking,[1] the enlight-

1. 'Le mot de vertu emporte l'idée de quelque chose d'estimable à l'égard de toute la terre; le vice au contraire', said Vauvenargues in 1746 (*Introduction à la connaissance de l'Esprit humain,*' *Oeuvres,* ed. P. Varillon, Paris, 1929, I, 64, and the Enlightenment concurred with him almost to a man. 'Il n'y a qu'une morale . . . comme il n'y a qu'une géométrie', said his friend Voltaire in the *Dictionnaire*

41

ened ethic blurred every distinction of within and without: those between States[2] and between Europe and overseas[3] as much as the ones between the individual and the State,[4] between man and citizen. The Absolutist policies resting on these separations were questioned on all sides,[5] and so we, too, must ask about the historical import which the European international legal order had

---

Philosophique, ed. J. Benda, Paris, 1954, p. 325. 'On ne peut trop répéter que tous les dogmes sont différents, et que la morale est la même chez tous les hommes qui font usage de leur raison.' On *morale universelle* in Diderot, see also Hans Hinterhäuser, 'Utopie und Wirklichkeit bei Diderot', *Heidelberger Forschungen*, no. 5, 1956, 67, 87; and Paul Hazard, 'Die Herrschaft der Vernunft in *La Pensée Européenne au XVIIIe siècle de Montesquieu à Lessing*, Hamburg, 1949, 235ff. A true critic, says the essay 'Critique' in the *Encyclopédie*, 'doit considérer non-seulement chaque homme en particulier, mais encore chaque république comme citoyenne de la terre . . . il ne doit avoir la société en général, que comme un arbre immense dont chaque homme est un rameau, chaque république une branche, et dont l'humanité est le tronc. Delà le droit particulier et le droit public, que l'ambition seule a distingués, et qui ne sont l'un et l'autre que le droit naturel plus ou moins étendu, mais soumis aux mêmes principes. Ainsi le critique jugeroit non-seulement chaque homme en particulier suivant les moeurs de son siècle et les loix de son pays, mais encore les loix et les moeurs de tous les pays et de tous les siècles, suivant les principes invariables de l'équité naturelle'.

2. Cf. Part II.
3. Cf. Part III.
4. 'Il n'y a qu'une seule morale pour tous les hommes; elle est la même pour les Nations et pour les Individus; pour les Souverains et les Sujets; pour le Ministre et pour le Citoyen obscur . . .' (P.H. von Holbach, *Système social*, London, 1773, II, 131).
5. A history of the concept of politics remains to be written. It is safe to say that in the eighteenth century the term *politique, Politik*, etc., was frequently used in a seemingly neutral, objective sense, as for example Diderot in the *Encyclopédie*: 'La philosophie politique est belle qui enseigne aux hommes à se conduire avec prudence'. It has undergone many changes since Aristotle, so that 'de toutes les parties de la philosophie la politique est celle qui a le plus éprouvé de changements'. However, the key to what the eighteenth century understood by politics, that is, the concept of politics, is to be found in the contemporary — generally universal — moral philosophy. This would exclude the free decision of the prince as the political principle of Absolutism. Accordingly, Diderot divided his essay 'Politique' into two parts. The second meaning of politics was *'faire grâce, faire des grâces'*, etc., and a moral political order excludes this meaning: 'La vertu, principe des républiques, les exclut . . .' (*Oeuvres*, XVI). The following examination of the conflicting concepts of morality and politics adheres to the second meaning and the process connected with it. Politics as the realm of responsible decision moves out of our field of vision to the extent that morality overwhelms the State and thereby turns politics into a symptom of courtly decline.
   A comparison between Bayle at the beginning of the century and Beaumarchais at its close exemplifies this widespread devaluation of politics. Bayle treats a seventeenth-century theme: 'Politica est ars tam regendi quam fallendi homines'. 'Les politiques ont un langgage à part et qui leur est propre; les termes et les phrases ne signifient pas chez eux les mêmes choses, que chez les autres hommes.' (*Diss. sur les lib. diff.*). Bayle comments sarcastically on politics but does not question it as such. Also, Beaumarchais has Figaro voice the widespread feeling that the politician made everything and anything appear mysterious without there really being a secret: all there was was paltriness. Absolutist politics became the victim of enlightened morality.

for the nascent self-comprehension of the bourgeoisie.

The termination of religious civil wars meant the development of vigorous sovereign authorities which would in turn proceed to solve the ecclesiastical problems, each in its own way. It also led to the strict formation of States on a unified plane. By virtue of absolute sovereignty, each State's interior was clearly delimited against the interiors of its neighbours. The conscience of a sovereign was absolutely free, but his jurisdiction was confined to the inner space of the State he represented. The State itself thus became a *persona moralis* confronting other States likewise conceived as *personae morales*, each one free and independent of its inner constitution, whether Catholic or Protestant, monarchical or republican. This delimitation of an independent inner space, a space whose moral integrity was shown by Hobbes to lie solely in its character as a State — this was what it took to effectuate the outward evolution of an inter-state, supra-individual commitment. Vattel, the classic representative of eighteenth-century European international law, accordingly called Hobbes the first 'qui ait donné une idée distincte, mais encore imperfaite du Droit des Gens'.[6]

Hobbes opined that once the state of nature, the war of all against all, had come to an end within a State, it could not continue between individuals either — only between States, which were viewed as *magni homines*.[7] By this personification of entities that had arisen in historic reality, the natural law of individuals antedating the State could be turned into an inter-state law of nations. The *jus publicum europaeum* was based on strict separation of a State's morally inviolate interior from the mutual external and political relations between States. States were absolutely free, and their sovereigns, like Hobbes's men *qua* human beings, were subject to their consciences alone, without submitting like men *qua* citizens to any common, institutionalised higher authority. However, it was precisely in this law-of-nature-type freedom that States, unlike the parties in a civil war, recognised each other politically as free *personae morales*. In this form of mutual recognition the war of all against all did not end exactly like a civil war; instead, it was pared down to a purely inter-state relationship.[8] Each sovereign had the

6. E. de Vattel, *Les Droits des Gens ou Principes de la Loi Naturelle*, London, 1758, Preface, x.
7. Hobbes, *De Cive*, XIV, 4; *Leviathan*, II, 30.
8. Quincy Wright, *A Study of War*, 4th edn., Chicago, 1944, I, 329ff.

jus ad bellum, the same right to make war, and war became a means of princely politics, guided by *raison d'état* and reduced to the common formula of a 'European balance of power'.[9]

With the end of civil war and the internal consolidation of the State, war was diverted to the outside, so to speak, and many Absolutist theoreticians saw it as a permanent institution for the prevention of civil war. The grounds on which they accepted foreign wars were the same rational-psychological reflections beyond any moral frame of mind that might help in mastering religious turmoil. The termination of religious civil war and the confining of war to an affair between States were two corresponding phenomena rooted in the separation of morality and politics, implicit in one case, explicit in the other.[10] What expressed this separation in terms of international law was that states at war — like men in the state of nature — faced each other as equals with the same rights, beyond any question of the moral *justa causa*, and that regardless of the moral grounds of war, solely by virtue of its statehood, each one understood the other as well as itself as *justus hostis*, a rightful enemy.[11]

9. Ibid.
10. 'And Law was brought into the world for nothing else, but to limit the naturall liberty of particular men, in such manner, as they might not hurt, but assist one another, and joyn together against a common Enemy' (Hobbes, *Leviathan*, II, 26). Meinecke cites a number of political scientists (*Die Idee der Staatsräson*, 227f.) who considered war a stable institution for the prevention of feudal or religious schisms. Vico in 1725 said that one of the unique attributes of man is that 'he fights wars so that nations may live securely in peace'. This reasoning was possible only because the differentiation between civil war and war, of external and internal conflict, and thus the 'Principio della "giustizia esterna" . . . delle guerre' (Vico, *Opere*, ed. F. Nicolini, Milan and Naples, 1953, 383, 386), had already established itself. The formal recognition of the adversary differentiates the legal argumentation of the Absolutist era from analogous ideas of earlier times. The awareness that internal peace and external war can exist side by side was demonstrated in Antiquity by the asserted conflict between Greeks and Barbarians (cf. W.W. Tarn, 'Alexander the Great and the Unity of Mankind', *Proceedings of the British Academy*, XIX, 1933, 125), and in the Middle Ages between Christians and heathens. In all these the political conflict had been sparked by a territorial dispute. The establishment of European international law introduced the mutual recognition of the States as adversaries for a common area, namely for Europe itself. Moreover, this could not have happened were it not for Europe directing its energies to the expansion into overseas territories. The total encompassing of the earth apparently eliminated the possibility of external space. To that extent the Marxists reacted logically to the changed situation in considering only the 'internal' war, civil war, necessary and permissible.
11. A war between nations, by virtue of the absolute sovereignty of these nations, is from the outset a *bellum justum*, a 'guerre en forme', conducted 'indépendamment de la justice de la cause' (Vattel, *Les Droits des Gens*, III, 4, para. 68).

Nevertheless, the legal grasp and discovery of a material foreign-political realm beyond moral argument did not constitute a permit for unconscionable acts in war and peace. Instead, like Hobbes's derivation of the State, this point, too, was based on the reflection that an appeal to conscience, which is tied to eternal moral laws, is not a strong enough means to guarantee inter-state order — that in fact it jeopardises such an order. Sovereign nations, said Vattel in 1758, when holding a government post in Saxony and participating in the bitter struggle against the Prussia of Frederick the Great — sovereign nations were free and independent, subject only to their consciences, like men in the state of nature.[12] A nation's conscience, to be sure, was tied to the eternal natural law, which is immutable; to that extent it was always subject to the *jus internum*, the necessary Law of Nations.[13] But how, Vattel asked, could the pure moral law be enforced? 'Mais comment faire valois cette Règle, dans les démêlés des Peuples et des Souverains, qui vivent ensemble dans l'état de Nature?'[14]

The analogous question faced Hobbes during the Civil War, when he asked how something as universally intelligible as the moral requisite of peace might be met. The conclusion reached by Vattel regarding dealings between States was the same arrived at by Hobbes for intra-state ones: namely, that order could be maintained only if the conscience of a sovereign took its bearings not from moral laws alone, but primarily from given political circumstances. This meant that there would always be several forces involved, which in those days meant a number of States in conflict, and though in the sense of eternal morality only one side in a quarrel could be right, in reality all those involved would be acting in good faith, 'dans la bonne foi'.[15] To do justice to this fact, the *Droit des Gens nécessaire* was held by Vattel to be paralleled by a *Droit des Gens volontaire*, a *jus externum* that laid down the rules of an essentially political morality of action between States.[16]

12. Vattel, *Les Droits des Gens*, Preface, para. 4: ' . . . les Nations, ou les États souverains doivent être considérés comme autant de personnes libres, qui vivent entre'elles dans l'état de nature'; II, 1: 'Il appartient à tout État libre et souverain, de juger en sa conscience, de ce que ces devoirs exigent de lui, de ce qu'il peut ou ne peut pas faire avec justice'.
13. Ibid., paras. 7ff.
14. Ibid., III, 12, para. 188.
15. Ibid., 3, para. 40.
16. This is not posited in divine or natural laws binding on conscience; the commitment is only 'external', as in Hobbes's action morality, and with regard to

Both forms of law were based on reason, but on a reality-orientated reason — one that would, if indicated, bid men suspend the moral *jus internum* in favour of the political *jus externum*. To Vattel's mind there was no other way to establish a peaceful order. Subordinating moral law to political necessity seemed plausible when one learned that appeals to moral conscience would not only fail to help put an end to conflict, but would rather, despite all the participants acting in good faith, perpetuate and exacerbate it. 'La décision du droit, de la controverse, n'en sera plus avancée, et la querelle en deviendra plus cruelle, plus funeste dans ses effets, plus difficile à terminer.'[17] Besides, putting a war on a moral plane implies its expansion, for then the neutrals, goaded by an implacable ethic, will feel obliged to intervene. The submission of morality to politics remains in the empirical horizon of religious wars.

Vattel carried on a fierce polemic against Grotius, whom he accused of inferring from any flagrant violation of the moral laws of nature that other States now had a right to intervene, and of being wholly oblivious, in the course of his moral argumentation, of their quite foreseeable results. 'Son sentiment ouvre la porte à toutes les fureurs de l'Enthousiasme et du Fanatisme, et fournit aux Ambitieux des prétextes sans nombre.'[18] The horrors of the Thirty Years War still stood plainly before Vattel's eyes. As prescribed for Central Europe in the Peace of Westphalia, all States were joint guarantors of an order that kept the lid on religious civil war. Accordingly, in a portentous passage, Vattel broke one of his own strict rules: the principle of non-intervention[19] that was to guarantee the intra-state order. He departed from it in the event that a people, in order to escape from a State-imposed reign of religious terror, called for outside help.

In breaching the principle of non-intervention in this way, Vattel took his stand on the borderline between bourgeois-moral and State-political arguments. As a Protestant citizen, he sought to justify William of Orange's landing in England — just as his appeals to the people and for tolerance were already casting doubts on the Absolutist system.[20] Yet at the same time the passage clearly shows

others 'entant qu'on la considère relativement aux autres hommes, et qu'elle produit quelque droit entre'eux' (ibid., para. 17).
  17. Ibid., III, 12, para. 188.
  18. Ibid., II, 1, para. 7.
  19. Ibid., III, 4, paras. 56ff.
  20. Cf. p. 155, n. 43 below.

that the historical premise of the modern State, the end of civil war, had been adopted as the inner premise of States by the inter-state order. If a State endangered its own function as a neutraliser of religious conflict, then it was permissible for other States to violate its sovereignty, if need be. This form of intervention — a rare occurrence by the eighteenth century — would not be based on moral grounds alone; it would mainly serve to safeguard a political order that had to keep fanatical religions from trespassing on the political domain.

The fight against religious despotism found the tenets of a bourgeois lay ethic still aligned with a supra-ecclesiastical State policy.[21] When it came to a parting of the ways, Vattel's knowledge of the cruel consequences of religious Utopianism was what made him subordinate even his 'natural ethics' to politics, to the preservation of the State order. In Vattel's mind, true moral justice could be found only in the Beyond; a morality that took its bearings and political requirements from this world would inevitably displace individual consciences and leanings in so far as they referred to faith or to 'eternal laws of nature'.[22] For all his respect for the moral duties of conscience, which he honoured as an enlightened citizen of his century, Vattel reached the conclusion that, to be a law at all, the law of nations must of necessity be and remain morally imperfect.[23]

The next section will investigate how, by virtue of this particular function, the moral world begins to penetrate invisibly the political sphere of the Absolutist States which is invariably clearly defined. It will emerge how, due to this seemingly non-political process, the

21. Of course the Enlightenment tended to claim that religious tolerance was solely its achievement: 'Si la religion n'enfante plus de guerres civiles, c'est à la philosophie seule qu'on en est redevable' (Voltaire, 'Dieu' in *Dictionnaire Philosophique Oeuvres Complètes* (52 vols., Paris, 1877–85), XVIII, 380); cf. 'Philosophie' in *Dictionnaire Philosophique*, in which Voltaire also calls the end of the religious war in England and the Thirty Years War in Germany an achievement of philosophy.

22. In the effort to create and safeguard an international order, the morally binding *Droit des Gens nécessaire* cannot be adhered to unreservedly. True, a nation 'ne doit jamais perdre de vue le droit nécessaire, toujours obligatoire dans la conscience: Mais lorsqu'il s'agit d'examiner ce qu'il peut exiger des autres États, il doit respecter le droit des gens Volontaire, et restreindre même ses justes prétensions, sur les règles d'un droit dont maximes sont consacrées au salut et à l'avantage de la Société universelle des Nations' (Vatell, *Les Droits des Gens*, III, 12, para. 188).

23. 'On comprendra maintenant sans difficulté, pourquoi le droit est toujours imparfait, quand l'obligation qui y répond dépend du jugement de celui en qui elle se trouve ... Notre obligation est toujours imparfaite par rapport à autrui ...' (ibid., Preface, para. 17). Thus, to him the elimination of inequality in sovereign states does not mean a step which, progressively pursued, would necessarily unite the different nations in a *civitas maxima* (see also Hobbes's analogous ideas in *Leviathan*, II, 17).

State begins to be called into question, as it were, *per negationem*. It will also become clear that it is precisely the system of moral judication that supervises and guides this process in that it encroaches on politics which had hitherto been separated in a dualistic fashion.

From a morality of political reason springs the *Droit des Gens volontaire*, whose distinction from 'natural' international law constitutes the true achievement of Absolutist political thinking. This law 'tolère ce qu'il est impossible d'éviter sans introduire de plus grands maux'.[24]

Aware of human inadequacy — and thereby rationalistically transforming the heritage of the Christian sense of sin — the law of nations voluntarily relinquished all functions of a mental-moral tribunal. Nothing else would allow the members of the international legal community mutually to pledge their freedom to one another. This formal, morally unsubstantial recognition might involve injustices; but to Vattel it was the very primacy of politics that offered an opportunity to meet moral demands as well — by a detour, so to speak, by way of rationalising both war and the State. The premise of this best of all possible orders was the division of international law into the 'necessary Law of Nations', to which only the consciences of sovereigns were subject and which lacked powers of enforcement, and the 'voluntary Law of Nations', which brought with it the rules of a political sphere free from moral arguments.

Thus it was from out of the cruel experience of sectarian civil war that the order of European states unfolded. The name of the law under which that order came into being was the subordination of morality to politics. It left its imprint on the era of wars between States and the great peace treaties: the Peace of Westphalia, Europe's first resolution of religious disputes on an inter-state level, or the Peace of Utrecht, the first formulation of an equilibrium based, among other things, on the prior recognition by all signatories, whether Catholic or Protestant, monarchical or republican, of their

---

24. Ibid. III, 12; cf. Preface, para. 21: ' . . . l'effet de tout cela est d'opérer, au moins extérieurement et parmi les hommes, une parfaite égalité des droits entre les Nations . . . sans égard à la justice intrinsèque de leur conduite, dont ils n'appartient pas aux autres de juger définitivement. . . . Il est donc nécessaire, en beaucoup d'occasions, que les Nations souffrent certaines choses, bien qu'injustes et condamnables en elles-mêmes, parce qu'elles ne pouvroient l'y opposer par la force, sans violer la liberté de quelqu'une et sans détruire les fondemens de leur Société naturelle'.

mutual integrity as States. 'Peace is now kept by an ever-armoured war, and the self-love of one State makes it a guardian of the other's wealth. The society of European States seems to have been transformed into one large family.'[25] With these words, uttered in 1789 at the beginning of the great Revolution, Schiller, in his inaugural lecture at Jena University, summarised the trend of events and succinctly expressed the sense of that political order.

The fundamental constellation of the eighteenth century was the moral world's emergence from a previously secured foundation of political stability. Without the political neutralisation of religious strife, without the limitation of wars to wars waged purely between States, there would have been no social space for the new elite to unfold in. Compared with the past, the bourgeois citizen felt safe and protected in this order. The age of the League and the Fronde, of sectarian turmoil and the Thirty Years War, was over; the civil wars were at an end, and others touched as little as possible on the civilian sphere of the bourgeoisie. Enlightened monarchs became the systematic promoters of their people's happiness. Tied to the prevailing balance was the optimistic hope that war itself might gradually be eliminated, and however exaggerated these hopes might appear in detail, they were not Utopian dreams but the effects and symptoms of the actual order of things. It was against this background of common security that the philosophical faith in the moral progress of bourgeois mankind manifested itself historically.[26] In this context moral progress was a product of political stability. Yet this stability in turn rested on a political constitution to which morality had necessarily to be subordinated.

25. Schiller, *Sämtliche Werke*, Stuttgart and Berlin, 1940, XIII, 3f.
26. The eighteenth century's concern for external peace — given the fanaticism, turbulence and bloodshed of their past — cannot be overestimated. 'Si on n'a pu bannir du monde le monstre de la guerre, on est parvenu à le rendre moins barbare', said Voltaire in 1769 (*Oeuvres Complètes*, XXVIII, 103ff.). 'Nous ne voyons plus les horreurs de la rose rouge et de la rose blanche, ni les têtes couronnées tomber . . .'. Numerous statements bear out that the people abominated war yet thought it civilised. 'Thanks to Providence', said Henry Home, 'war, at present, bears a less savage aspect: we spare individuals, and make war upon the nation only: barbarity and cruelty give way to magnanimity; and soldiers are converted from brutes into heroes' (*Sketches of the History of Man*, II, III). Despite the moral sense Home imputed to war by seeing it as a moral spur to progress, as was not unusual then, his thesis derives its historical justification from war as a means of international politics. Turgot's vision of progress sounds the same note: 'Dans ces balancements tout se rapproche peu à peu de l'équilibre, et quand à la longue une situation plus fixe et plus tranquille . . . la guerre ne désole plus que les frontières des empires (*Oeuvres*, ed. Daire, II, 599). 'Il paraît qu'enfin nos politiques sont parvenus à calculer l'effet qu'a sur eux la réaction de la ruine des nations étrangères et surtout de celles qui leur sont

In the course of its evolution the moral order could not but grow out of the political order, as inevitably as if that had been its base. The path of this departure was predetermined by the separation — once accomplished — of natural law from the realm of free princely decision. To the representatives of a unified and unifying natural law, this separation could now appear as a dual morality that had to be debunked. In the course of the debunking (of the Enlightenment process) the original historical point of the separation — the staking out of a rational realm for political responsibility — also evaporated. The only way to look at politics now was from the perspective of an enlightened conscience.

An enlightened critic summarised his judgement about the international legal order as follows: 'It can be said that as the Kings enlarged their power over their subjects, and as the art of politics linked them with each other by more intimate association, their honour and their consciences went bankrupt'.[27] For the citizen, the indirect relation to politics became the determinant. The citizen remained in a kind of private-sphere reserve that turned the monarch into the person who is guilty of citizen's own innocence. At first it appeared as if the subject was potentially guilty, measured by the innocence of princely power, but now it was the monarch who was guilty from the start, in the measure of the citizens' innocence.

---

voisines', wrote Turgot's assistant, Dupont, to Edelsheim in 1788, when France had to face up to the failure of its Dutch ventures,' which Napoleon claimed triggered the revolution (K. von Baden, *Politische Correspondenz*, Heidelberg, 1888, I, 285). Hertzberg, like Schiller, went so far as to see eternal peace growing out of the balance: 'History will cease to be interesting', he wrote, for the equilibrium turned the hopes of Saint-Pierre into reality (quoted in Dilthey, *Gesammelte Schriften*, III, 195).

The widespread belief that peace also reigned *internally* was in keeping with these testimonials to rational warfare documenting the bourgeois faith in progress. In 1660 'internal peace began', proclaims the *Considérations sur la Population de la France par Mr. Moheau* (Paris, 1778). Cannons are now heard only at festivals; wars are confined to border regions, and most important, those that are fought are 'not civil wars'. 'On the whole', said the *Göttinger Magazin* (II), 'the European nations have become much freer under the growing power of the kings than they were under the despotism of the nobility and clergy in the Middle Ages.' This was said in the English-Hanoverian context, but even the radical Enlightenment agreed with it as far as peace and security were concerned. In his own century, said Helvetius, 'a happy peace has followed the many storms . . . the volcanoes of rebellion have been extinguished everywhere' (*De l'Esprit*, Paris, 1758). In 1740 Frederick the Great even went so far as to say that 'the habit of rebellions and revolution seems to have died out completely in our time' (*Antimachiavell, Oeuvres*, VIII, 243). Even so radical a driving force of the French Revolution as L.S. Mercier in 1783, in the *Tableau de Paris*, still said: 'Une émeute qui dégénerait en sédition est devenue moralement impossible'.

27. Rousset in his comments on Mably's *Le droit public de l'Europe*, 1748, in *Umständliche Geschichte der europäischen Friedensschlüsse . . .*, Frankfurt on Main, 1756, 114.

II

The Self-Image of the Enlightenment Thinkers
as a Response to their Situation Within the
Absolutist State

CHAPTER 4

Locke's Law of Private Censure and its Significance for the Emergence of the Bourgeoisie

The bourgeois intelligentsia set out from the private inner space within which the State had been confining its subjects. Each outward step was a step towards the light, an act of enlightenment. The movement which blithely called itself 'the Enlightenment' continued its triumphal march at the same pace at which its private interior expanded into the public domain, while the public, without surrendering its private nature, became the forum of society that permeated the entire State. In the end society would knock on the doors of the political powers, calling for attention there, too, and demanding admission.

With every step the Enlightenment was shifting the jurisdictional borderline which the Absolutist State had carefully sought to draw between politics and the moral interior. The nascent bourgeois society had already moved this line, with a self-assurance best demonstrated in England — the first country to exemplify the modern bourgeoisie and to serve the Continent as a model. What enters our purview there is the unofficial judgemental activity that was essential for the bourgeoisie, as well as the specific effectiveness of that activity.

John Locke, spiritual father of the bourgeois Enlightenment, began his *Essay Concerning Human Understanding* in 1670, under the rule of the Absolutist Stuarts. He finished the voluminous work in Holland, during his six-year exile, and had it published in England after the fall of James II. In this book, which the following century would rank among the Holy Scriptures of the modern bourgeoisie, Locke also dealt with the laws that citizens live by. Here, he observed, one was treading on ground that had to be examined with special care, in order to avoid obscurity and confusion.[1]

Locke distinguished three kinds of law: first, 'The Divine Law the Measure of Sin and Duty', manifested to man by nature or by revelation; second, 'The Civil Law the Measure of Crimes and Innocence', that is, the law of the State, armed with powers of enforcement and charged with the protection of the citizen; and third, the specifically moral law, termed by Locke 'The Philosophical Law the Measure of Virtue and Vice'.[2]

With these distinctions the relationship between moral and State law, as Hobbes had known it, was already thoroughly revised. Locke's separation of Divine and Civil Law made the religions newly, legally obligatory, and at the same time, by the same separation, the laws of nature and the State (combined by Hobbes so as to vindicate the State) were sundered again. Without dealing with these questions in detail, however, Locke deliberately focused the reader's attention on the third type of law, a type that appeared here as completely novel beside those of the Deity and the State. This was the philosophers' law or, as he also called it, 'The Law of Opinion or Reputation'. According to Locke, this law of public opinion was being discussed and debated more than any other form of law and exerted an astonishing authority, although its origin and significance had not yet become properly known at all.[3] Proof enough of the novelty of the Philosophical Law, the specifically bourgeois law, is the fact that in later editions of his treatise Locke had to defend it time and again from attack.[4]

As he demonstrated quite empirically, the bourgeois moral laws originated in the interior of the human conscience, in the space

1. John Locke, *An Essay Concerning Human Understanding*, ed. C. Fraser, Oxford, 1894, II, 28, para. 4.
2. Ibid., paras. 7–10.
3. In the first edition Locke explains his reason for calling moral law 'philosophical law': ' . . . not because philosophers make it, but because they have most busied themselves to inquire after it, and talk about it . . . which though it be more talked of possibly than either of the others, yet how it comes to be established with such authority as it has, to distinguish and denominate the actions of men, and what are the true measures of it, perhaps, is not so generally taken notice of' (para. 10).
4. Cf. Fraser's comments and the revisions of the Preface published in Locke's lifetime.

which Hobbes had exempted from the realm of the State. Although the citizens, having ceded all their powers to the State, could do no more against any of their fellows than was permitted by the law of the State, 'yet they still retain the power of thinking well or ill, approving or disapproving the actions of those they live amongst and converse with'.[5] The citizens, to be sure, lacked executive power, but they possessed and retained the mental power to pass moral judgements. To this extent Locke was in agreement with Hobbes — but, he went on, it was the citizens' own approval and disapproval which determined what was or was not to be called virtue: 'And by this approbation and dislike they establish amongst themselves what they will call virtue and vice'.[6] In Locke's mind, the citizens' views about virtue and vice no longer remained in the realm of private opinion; rather, their moral judgements themselves had the character of laws. The moral character which Hobbes had extracted from the State was thus broadened in a twofold fashion.

The laws of bourgeois morality existed, as they had for Hobbes, only tacitly and secretly without State authorisation, but they were no longer confined to the individuals as such. Instead, they received their universally obligatory character from an unspoken accord of the citizens, 'by a secret and tacite consent'.[7] The carrier of this secret morality is no longer the individual; it is 'society', a structure taking shape in the 'clubs' in which philosophers, for instance, devote themselves especially to the investigation of the moral laws.[8] The citizens no longer defer to the State power alone; jointly, they form a society that develops its own moral laws, laws which take their place beside those of the State. Thus bourgeois ethics, essentially tacit and secret, moves into the public domain, and appearing at the same time is the second variation to which Locke submits the Hobbesian moral character: that secretly valid bourgeois moral laws are no longer restricted to a human state of mind but determine the moral value of human actions. The citizens themselves do what Hobbes reserved for the sovereign: they set 'the mark of the value'

5. Locke, *An Essay Concerning Human Understanding*, para. 10.
6. This formulation, a crucial one, appears for the first time in the second edition, in which Locke, in the course of the controversies over 'philosophical law' arrived at more concise formulations.
7. Locke, *An Essay Concerning Human Understanding*, para. 10.
8. The law of public opinion is determined by societies, tribes, clubs, sects. Locke stresses the spatial, temporal and personal relativity and the social implications of moral concepts, Hobbes's point of departure in adducing absolute sovereignty, to arrive at the pre-eminence of social forces.

of all acts 'and give the name of virtue to those actions, which amongst them are judged praiseworthy, and call that vice, which they account blamable'.[9]

The legality of the philosophical law is not based on its substantive qualification but on the voluntative action of its source. Yet it is no longer the sovereign who decides; it is the citizens who constitute the moral laws by their judgement, just as merchants determine a trade value. What the citizens of various countries designate a virtue or a vice is not decisive for the legality of a morality; depending on time, place, and circumstances they may declare a virtue to be a vice, and a vice to be a virtue. Rather, the legality of their moral views consists in the citizens' pure judgement itself: ' . . . everywhere virtue and praise, vice and blame go together'.[10] The powers of enforcement which a law requires and which give it public validity also consist of praise and blame: 'Its Inforcement is Commendation and Discredit.'[11] The citizens' every performance of an act of judgement, their separation of that which they find good from that which they find evil, is already legal as the separating act. Their private views rise to the level of laws purely on the strength of the inherent censure. This is why Locke has another word for the law of public opinion: he also calls it 'the Law of private censure'.[12] The private and public domains are not mutually exclusive; as a matter of fact, the public realm arises from the private one. The self-assurance of the moral inner space lies in its ability to 'go public'. The private domain can expand on its own into a public one, and it is only in the public sphere that personal opinions prove to have the force of law.

To his critics, Locke's introduction of this law of private censure seemed to open every door to licence. In a new printing of the *Essay* he therefore attempted a point-by-point defence of the Law of opinion. His essay, he asserted, by no means intended to fix the moral content of the civil laws; its sole purpose was to show the origin and kind of the laws actually prevailing in concrete social life. In substance, he maintained, citizens would as a rule obey the commandments of God and the laws of nature, but these laws received legal validity only from the consent or rejection of bour-

9. Locke, *An Essay Concerning Human Understanding*, para. 10.
10. Ibid., para. 11.
11. Ibid., para. 12.
12. Ibid., para. 13.

geois society. And that, he added, did not surprise him at all, 'since otherwise they would condemn themselves, if they (the private men) should think anything right, to which they allowed not commendation, anything wrong, which they let pass without blame'.[13] If they do not wish to put themselves in the wrong, the citizens must constantly pass judgements of their own, and it is only by their own judgements that they lay down what is morally right in the State and what is not. Obliged to offer a more detailed reasoning, Locke thus hits upon the meaning of moral legislation that is essential for society. Moral turns of mind are here interpreted by him in their social function — but not in order to deduce the State, as Hobbes had done, but to turn them into constant acts of judgement by the rising society. Locke virtually requires citizens to proclaim their private opinions to be generally binding laws, for it is only in their independent judgement that the power of society is constituted, and only in the constant exercise of moral censure will this censure prove to be a law. The oscillating value of the private censures does not argue against their legality. The very fact that they keep overtaking each other makes them legal. Hence an additional term for the 'Law of private censure': it can also be called the 'Law of fashion'.[14]

As in Bayle's works, reason needs the perpetual process of critique to establish itself as supreme authority, so it is only in constant performance of censure that the moral views of Locke's citizens rise to the State of generally binding laws. To the bourgeois consciousness, a critique grouped with reason and a censure grouped with morality become one and the same self-justifying activity.[15] What they have in common is the verdict, the judgement which on the one hand splits the world into domains of good and evil or true and false, but at the same time, in the course of and because of this division, raises the citizenry to the rank of a supreme

13. This significant sentence first appeared in the second version of para. 10.
14. Ibid., para. 12.
15. Sociologically, rational criticism and moral censure may be said to have originated in the world of letters and the world of business. However, in the eighteenth century the two concepts appeared jointly and complementarily: 'censurer et critiquer' (cf. Rousseau, *Oeuvres*, V, 394). Samuel Johnson's *A Dictionary of the English Language* (London, 1755) defines 'to criticise' as 'to censure', a 'critick' as a 'censurer', and Bailly's *English Dictionary* even refers to 'a nice censurer' (5th edn, London, 1731, and also 24th edn, 1782). The *Encyclopédie* treats the two concepts as synonymous (see the essay entitled 'Critique, Censure'), yet it does indicate some distinctions in usage: 'Critique s'applique aux ouvrages littéraires: censure aux ouvrages théologiques, ou aux propositions de doctrine, ou aux moeurs'.

tribunal. Without citing the laws of the State, but also without any political executive power of its own, the modern bourgeoisie unfolded in continuous alternation between moral censure and intellectual critique. 'Not till then,' said Schiller a century later, 'not until we have decided for ourselves what we are and are not — not till then have we escaped the danger of suffering from alien judgements.'[16] The citizens' verdict legitimises itself as just and true; their censure; their critique — these become the executive of the new society.

By his interpretation of the philosophical law Locke gave a political charge to the interior of the human conscience which Hobbes had subordinated to State policy. Public actions were now not merely subject to the authority of the State but at the same time to the moral authority of the citizens. What Locke had thus put into words was the decisive breach in the Absolutist order, the order expressed in the relationship of protection and obedience. Morality was no longer a formal matter of obedience, was not subordinated to the politics of Absolutism, but confronted the laws of the State.

This confrontation renews the question following the mutual relationship of private and State law-making. Which authority decides? The moral authority of the citizens or the political authority of the State? Or both of them jointly? And if both jointly, how do they interrelate? Locke by no means answered these questions; the respective spheres were neither delimited nor clarified by him. Since he did not substantially define the moral laws but merely gave formal descriptions of their origins, it remained entirely possible for their essential concretisms to coincide with the laws of God or the State. Locke could simply allow the various powers to coexist without delimiting one against another. His very failure to perceive them as antithetical is one of the peculiarities of his political theory.[17]

16. Friedrich Schiller, *Sämtliche Schriften*, ed. K. Goedecke, Stuttgart, 1867 *et seq.*, III, 509.
17. Significantly, Locke did not link the concept of politics to courtly life. In England 'moral' and 'political' were not in conflict. Society itself was a 'politic society' that continues even if the government dissolves (cf. *Of Civil Government*, II, 19). Locke does not link the concept of politics to State rule. Conversely, echoing Hobbes, he calls obedience to the laws promulgated by government moral conduct, although he agrees only formally with the theorists of Absolutism, since the specific moral laws, as the passage under discussion shows, are made by society itself. 'There is scarcely any man in England', it says in the *Freeholder* (no. 53), 'of what denomination soever, that is not a free-thinker in politics, and hath not some particular notions of his own by which he distinguishes himself from the rest of the community. Our island, which was formerly called a nation of saints, may now be

Locke's descriptive blueprint furnished the justification for the English form of government as it had come to prevail since 1688, with the rise of the economically determined Whig bourgeoisie. The collusion between that leading social stratum represented in Parliament and the royal executive prevented the systematically demonstrated confrontation from being exacerbated into a domestic political rift.

Of course, if bourgeois moral legislation differs from the legislation of the State in substance and not only in form, then the two will necessarily enter into competition. Translated into the continental world of Absolutist States, therefore, Locke's 'Philosophical Law' assumed an altogether different political role; it was a role already foreshadowed in the divergent impact of the respective powers, as outlined by Locke in the way in which they typically operated in the eighteenth century. To him, the effect of the moral legislation was greater than the State's, but also quite different in kind. For while State laws are directly enforced by State power, the moral legislation works indirectly, through the pressure of public opinion. Direct political power remains a preserve of the State; the Law of opinion is not equipped with the State's means of coercion. However, while the citizens may have ceded their political powers to the State leadership, their 'Philosophical Law' only seems to lack authority.[18] It exists and works by praise and blame alone, but in fact, in the results it achieves, it is much more effective. For from this verdict no man can escape. Not one among tens of thousands can evade the moral judgement of his fellows. 'No man escapes the punishment of their censure and dislike, who offends against the fashion and opinion of the company he keeps.' Thus, beside the authorities of State and religion, the third power proves to be the mightiest, for all citizens are subject to it, 'and so they do that which keeps them in reputation with their company, little regard the laws of God, or the magistrate'. Beyond the English situation Locke thus described the effectiveness peculiar to moral law-making.

The laws of the State work directly, backed as they are by the State's coercive power; moral law-making works within the same State, but indirectly and thus all the more strongly. Civic morality becomes a public power, one that works only intellectually but which has political effects, forcing the citizen to adapt his actions

---

called a nation of statesmen' (quoted in W.E. Lecky, *A History of England in the 18th Century*, London, 1892, I, 75).

18. Locke, *An Essay Concerning Human Understanding*, para. 12.

not just to State law but simultaneously, and principally, to the law of public opinion. Thus, an example of the growing English influence on the Continent opened a new path to the partitioning of morality and politics.

It was in the nature of Locke's differentiation between moral and political law-making that because of their different origins and effects there was no need to visualise a possible overlap, in line with conditions in England. However, when the content of bourgeois morality and State legislation differed, as they did on the Continent, then the 'Philosophical Law' was indeed inescapable as an indirectly effective political factor; directly, however, its political invisibility kept it purely a matter of judgement. The consequence for the citizen, in the event of conflict, was twofold: firstly, an open altercation was superfluous, since the moral law, due to its invisible force and greater reach, was inevitably carried out. Secondly, from the moral viewpoint every conflict was settled in advance, for once the moral law agreed with the philosophers' judgement and with the view of society, then that society — if it only practised its censure — was in the right from the start.[19] The citizens' flexibility in arriving at their private verdicts gave them the assurance of being right together with an invisible guarantee of success. The judgements which continually supersede one another reflect the legality of a process in whose eyes all State law is already obsolete. The flexibility of the moral judges is that of progress itself.

For the citizen of an Absolutist State the premise of the pure authority to pass moral judgements, the demarcation from political rule, came to be an act of judgement itself. That citizen adopted the partition of morality and politics that underlay the Absolutist system, but he transformed it into a specific answer to his situation within the State — a State he saw as confining his own moral domain. Unlike Locke, those citizens did not turn the subordination of morality to politics into a co-ordination or juxtaposition. Instead, they radicalised the antithesis, accomplishing a polarisation that was to become the symptom as well as the instigator of the

19. 'Il arrivera en France', Voltaire wrote to Helvetius in 1763, 'ce qui est arrivé en Angleterre . . . le petit nombre de penseurs se fera respecter. Soyez sûr que tant que les gens de bien seront unis, on ne les entamera pas. C'est l'intérêt du roi, c'est celui de l'É'tat, que les philosophes gouvernent la société'. Not they but the fanatics are the real agitators: ' . . . notre morale est meilleure que la leur, notre conduite plus respectable . . . conservons nos avantages; que les coups qui les écraseront partent de mains invisibles et qu'ils tombent sous le mépris public' (*Oeuvres*, XLII, 570f.).

looming political crises.

We shall have to demonstrate in the next section how the citizens developed their moral realm; how, by polarising morals and politics, they evolved their claim to domination, while at the same time seemingly evading all conflict with the State authority and finally, how they did so either calculatingly or naively, depending on their degree of consciousness.

CHAPTER 5

The Creation of Indirect Countervailing Powers and the Arcanum of Politics

On the Continent there were two social structures that left a decisive imprint on the Age of Enlightenment: the Republic of Letters and the Masonic lodges. From the outset, Enlightenment and mystery appeared as historical twins. Both groups developed a specific style of language and conduct; what they had in common, for all their differences, was exactly what pointed to there being a specific answer to the Absolutist system. This answer, then, was unfolded and elaborated on, and as for seventeenth-century Absolutism, it would not remain without lasting influence on the Enlightenment's further development in the eighteenth century. The political style of the Enlightenment acquired a gravity of its own, one that did not come to be effective until the Absolutist system was already reduced to a mere shell.

In France the zenith of Absolutist power, the age of Louis XIV, was part of the new elite's native constellation. It was made up of the most varied, indeed the most heterogeneous groups — whose common feature, however, was that in the modern State, a State represented solely by the person of the absolute ruler, they found themselves stripped or deprived of any freedom of political decision. In this point of departure lay the common challenge that became the new society's initial bond.[1]

1. Everyone was waiting for the death of Louis XIV, wrote Saint-Simon, 'les uns, en espérance de figurer, de se mêler, de s'introduire, étoient ravis de voir finir un règne sous lequel il n'y avoit rien pour eux à attendre; les autres, fatigués d'un joug pesant, toujours acclabant . . . étoient charmés de se trouver au large; tous en général, d'être délivrés d'une gêne continuelle, et amoureux des nouveautés' (*Mémoires*, ed. St. Beuve, Paris, 1857, XIII, 104). See also Philippe Sagnac, *La formation de la société française moderne*, Paris, 1946, II.

One part of the new stratum that did possess an established political tradition (though the Absolutist State seemed to have lopped it off by dismantling the representative organs of the estates) was the nobility of the Fronde of old, a grouping that was restored to life after the Sun King's death and nourished its autonomy with a new self-confidence. Included in it were individuals like the Duke of Saint-Simon and Count Boulainvilliers — and Montesquieu, too, after a fashion.[2] The nobility always fought the royal monopoly on authority, but how little of a truly independent factor it had become alongside the rising bourgeoisie was demonstrated by the reckless act of political suicide it committed on 4 August 1789.

An entirely contrasting but powerful section within the new society unfolded under the Regency. It was composed of the merchants, the bankers, the tax lessees and other businessmen who had acquired wealth, social prestige and, often, titles of nobility, and who played a leading role in the economy — though none whatsoever in the politics of the State. 'Ses courriers portent ses ordres dans toutes places de l'Europe', so a speaker at the Academy of Marseilles described the merchant prince in 1755, 'et son nom, sur un papier circulant, fait rouler et multiplier les fonds qu'il veut transporter, ou répandre. Il ordonne, il recommande, il protège'.[3] The financiers' self-confidence and social power grew by the extent to which they became creditors to a State whose political control was out of their hands. Without exaggeration, they were kept far from the helm of State — so far in fact they came to feel the distance in the very cash terms that signified the substance of their social power. Many of them, to be sure, made millions in profits from the corrupt tax and tax lease system of the state, but at the same time its secretive and opaque budgeting practices were secured from the grip of the bourgeois moneymen.

Not only did they lack all influence in fiscal matters. Their capital itself was wholly insecure: time and again a royal fiat would arbitrarily rob them of the gains they had worked and ventured for. Following total bankruptcy under law came partial bankruptcies

2. On the role of the aristocracy after 1715, see B. Fay, *La Franc-Maçonnerie et la Révolution Intellectuelle du XVIIIᵉ Siècle*, Paris, 1935, chap. II; and Taine, *Les origines de la France contemporaine*. Taine's characterisation of the nobility culminates in the assertion that 'as clear as they can see their society, so faulty is their vision politically'.
3. M. Guys, *Recueil des Pièces de Poésie et d'Éloquence*. See also Taine, *Les origines* and Sagnac, *La formation*.

and other manipulations in an effort to avoid another collapse of the State household: contracts entered into by the State were suspended on the sovereign's authority, annuity payments were stopped, while the most important political institution in which bourgeois interests were represented, the *parlement* of Paris, was guided by the special wishes of the two higher estates and lacked the power to put a stop to the State's fiscal conduct. The State reserved the right to administer the funds it owned the moneyed aristocracy, and furthermore — quite 'immorally' — it arbitrarily deprived its creditors of their gains. The annual State deficit, risen to some 200 millions by 1788, was thus doubly transformed into a moral capital of society, precisely because all political power was so visibly concentrated in the hands of society's debtor. 'Presque tous les sujets sont créanciers du maître . . . qui est esclave comme tout débiteur' — thus Rivarol apostrophised the situation that set the stage for the French Revolution.[4] A financially powerful society and an Absolutist State confronted one another without being able to close the gap by their attempts at reform. In this interrelation between finance capital — which in society's hands was at the same time a credit balance — and the financial indebtedness of the State, which quite immorally used its political power to conceal or strike out its debts, lay one of the strongest social impulses for the dialectic of morality and politics.

Added to an anti-Absolutist nobility and a financially powerful bourgeois stratum was a third group, an outright object and victim of Absolutist policies: the 400,000 *émigrés* whom the revocation of the Edict of Nantes in 1685 had forced to leave France and pour into Northern and North-Eastern Europe. Eighty thousand of them went to England, where they sided with the Whigs and became ardent defenders of the parliamentary constitution. In the Rain-Bow Coffee-House, a Masonic rendezvous in London, they founded an information centre; from there, via Holland (the intellectual trading post of those days) they flooded all of Absolutist Europe with propaganda in support of the English spirit, English philosophy and, above all, the English Constitution. Desmaizeaux,

---

4. Rivarol, *Mémoires*, ed. M. Berville, Paris, 1824, 2ff. Despite the economic crises of the *ancien régime*, the bourgeoisie continued to prosper, and even in 1789 references to a *Révolution de la prospérité* could be heard. On this, see C.E. Labrousse, *La crise de l'économie française à la fin de l'ancien régime et au début de la Révolution*, Paris, 1944, I, XLVIII *passim*.

the biographer of Pierre Bayle, Pierre Daude, and Locke's friend Le Clerc belonged to this particularly active group.[5]

Intimately connected with the *émigrés*, who ranked as leading spirits of their time, and building upon them, were the philosophers of the Enlightenment. They supplied the troops to wage their innocent war within the *Règne de la Critique*, and they exerted a decisive influence on the character of the bourgeois elite. This free-floating layer of writers and enlighteners, the *philosophes militants* toiling in the cause of moral legality, came mostly from the middle and lower strata — a background that sufficed to leave their social existence bare of any political function.[6] Moreover, there was the growing bourgeois stratum of bureaucrats and judges, about a quarter of a million men who worked in State jobs but whose organisation had also developed its own gravity, so that inwardly they could already detach themselves from Absolutist rule.[7]

A new stratum coalesced from all these highly diverse groups — groups that were socially accepted but politically powerless like the nobility, or economically powerful but socially branded as upstarts like the financiers, or socially without a proper place but of the utmost intellectual importance like the philosophers. It was a stratum which pursued very different, even conflicting interests, but

5. Cf. Weiss, *Histoire des réfugiés protestants de France*, Paris, 1853, I, 272, on the number of refugees. See P. Hazard, *La crise de la conscience européenne*, on the spiritual characteristics. Hazard describes the genesis of the European-bourgeois spirit, but by ignoring the developments unique to England he remains within the European area. The term 'crisis' in particular is the product of the French sense of self, which was formed by the decline of Louis XIV's Absolutist power. In so far as French classicism is used as the primary yardstick, the reference to the 'crise de la conscience européenne' at the turn of the eighteenth century appears justified; but if the *conscience* is put into a concrete political context, then one can speak of a crisis only with regard to the latter half of the century, and then only within a complete, political-existential context that also includes England. On the English influence on Europe, see J. Texte's detailed study, *J.J. Rousseau et les origines du cosmopolitisme littéraire*, Paris, 1895.
6. On the role of the intelligentsia, cf. D. Mornet's seminal work, *Les sources intellectuelles de la Révolutions Française*, Paris, 1933; and Felix Rocquain, *L'Esprit révolutionnaire avant la Révolution*, Paris, 1878.
7. When judicial and administrative reforms appeared likely to be passed by the Assembly of Notables in 1787, Dupont de Nemours wrote to Edelsheim that the administration 'était soumise à un despotisme arbitraire. Cette même administration aura l'organisation la plus parfaite qui a [sic!] encore existé.' There follows a confident account of how henceforth the new generation would take control of commerce, cultural affairs and the police into their own hands. The Absolutist administrative apparatus assured the continuity of the State throughout the Revolution, but at the same time it formed the basis of the modern bourgeoisie. On this, cf. de Tocqueville, *Oeuvres Complètes*, Paris, 1952, II, chaps. 3–5. On the civic role of the German civil service, see Valjavec, *Die Entstehung der politischen Strömungen in Deutschland 1770–1815*, Munich, 1951, I, 2, 77ff.

which shared the fate of being unable to find an adequate place within the Absolutist State's existing institutions. The absolute ruler kept his hand on each and every access to the State's machinery of command — on legislation, the police, the military — and he was further embroiled in a bitter struggle with the remnants of the old estate organisations in which the new elite was represented in part, at least, and could protect some of its interests. Completely closed to it, though, was the field of foreign policy, with its decisions of war and peace.

These men, who determined their country's cultural physiognomy or bore the burdens of the State, were not allowed to decide its fate, for it was intrinsic to the system, to the Absolutist order, that there was nothing at all for them to decide — all were subjects. As far as the Absolutist State was concerned, the sphere of interests that evolved on the grounds of this joint destiny lay outside the State; it was the sphere of society in which the various groups saw their indigenous place. The tension between their socially increasing weight, on the one hand, and the impossibility of lending political expression to that weight, on the other — this tension determined the historical situation in which the new society constituted itself. It was to be crucial to its nature and its evolution. The critical split between morality and politics, noted by the bourgeois intelligentsia, resulted from this difference and exacerbated it at the same time.

Eliminated from politics as a whole, the members of society would meet in wholly 'non-political' localities: at the exchanges, in coffee-houses or at the academies, where the new sciences were studied without succumbing to the State-religious authority of a Sorbonne; or in the clubs, where one could not pronounce judgement but where one could discuss the contemporary judiciary; in the salons, in which *l'esprit* could rule without commitment and did not carry the official stamp it bore in pulpits and chancelleries, or in the libraries and literary societies where one talked about arts and letters, not about the policies of the State. Thus, it was under the protection of the Absolutist State that the new society created its institutions, the tasks of which — whether tolerated or advanced by the State or not — were 'social'. The outcome was an institutionalisation behind the scenes, one whose political strength could not unfold openly, that is, in the paths of princely legislation or in the framework of institutions either set up by the State or still enduring from the feudal order. From the outset, rather, the representatives of society could exert political influence only indirectly, if at all. All institutions of this novel sociable and social stratum acquired a character that was potentially political, and in so far as they already had some influence on policy and on the legislation of the State they turned into indirect political forces.

The State no sooner saw its law-making monopoly threatened from that quarter than it took steps against the new institutions. The fate of the Club de l'Entresol was characteristic. 'C'était une espèce de club à l'anglaise, ou de société politique parfaitement libre', reported its most important member, the Marquis d'Argenson in his memoirs, 'composée de gens qui aimaient à raisonner sur ce qui passait, pouvaient se réunir, et dire leur avis sans crainte d'être compromis, parce qu'ils se connaissaient tous les uns les autres, et savaient avec qui et devant qui ils parlaient.'[8] In this company, which Bolingbroke had inspired,[9] respected scientists, progressive clerics, senior military officers and experienced officials met to collect and discuss news from around the globe; each individual had his speciality, and the most important work centred on questions of domestic and foreign policy. It was there that d'Argenson himself read the first draft of his *Considérations sur le Gouvernement ancien et présent de la France*, a plea for radical administrative reform with the goal of a democratic State Absolutism, handwritten copies of which circulated in France until it was printed in Amsterdam in 1764.

Another member (and dean of the club) was the aged Abbé de Saint-Pierre, one of the new society's first and best-known representatives and critics of the Absolutist State. In 1718 he had published his *Discours sur la Polysynodie ou Pluralité des conseils*, a rather violent attack on the corrupt *vizirat* system; his hope at the time had been that his proposal would help to turn the ministerial councils set up by the Regent into a permanent governmental institution, with significant improvements such as the introduction

8. René-Louis d'Argenson, *Mémoires*, Paris, 1825, p. 230. (On the sources of the memoirs see A. Brette, *La France au Milieu du XVIIIe siècle d'après de Journal du M. d'Argenson*, Paris, 1898, 371ff.).

9. D'Argenson, *Mémoires*, n.95. For a listing of the members, most of them still of the nobility, see pp. 248ff. D'Argenson describes the character of this club thus: 'Nous étions ce qu'on appelle fort communicatifs entre nous, qualité essentielle et qui est l'âme de pareilles sociétés; elle vient de la confiance et de l'estime réciproques, d'une liaison où le coeur a autant de part que l'esprit. Elle tourne au profit commun'.

of a secret ballot.[10] The elite of the nation, represented in parliamentary committees according to each specialisation, should
elaborate a 'Plan général' to reorganise France. Together with this
proposal the abbé combined a political critique whose indirect
method was later characterised by Rousseau:

> Il tourne même avec assez d'adresse en objections contre son propre
> système, les défauts à relever dans celui du Régent; et sous le nom de
> réponses à ses objections, il montroit sans danger et ses défauts et leur
> remèdes. Il n'est pas impossible que le Régent . . . ait pénétré la finesse de
> cette critique.[11]

Probably the Regent did notice the finesse; at any rate, Saint-
Pierre was promptly ousted from the French Academy. He now
hoped to find a new field of action in the private academy of the
Club de l'Entresol.[12]

The company's institutionalisation as a private academy turned
the political criticism that was conducted there into an outwardly
effective political force while circumventing the powers of the State
— that is, into an indirectly effective force. Walpole curried favour
with the club; its deliberations and opinions made the rounds of the
Court in London as well as in Paris; it was already exerting
significant influence on the very public opinion it had helped to
form.[13] What Saint-Pierre, in the sense of his 'polysynodie', would
have liked best, of course, was to see this private company raised to
the rank of an official body charged with the work of political

10. On Saint-Pierre and the Club, cf. Janet, *Histoire de la science politique dans ses
rapports avec la morale*, 2 vols., 3rd edn, Paris, 1887, II, pp. 11ff. The *Polysynodie*
had been founded in the reign of Louis XIV but could not be published in his
lifetime. In his résumé Rousseau summarised the plan: 'Chez tous les Peuples, qui
ont un Roi, il est . . . absolument nécessaire d'etablir une forme de Gouvernement
qui se puisse passer du Roi; et dès qu'il est posé qu'un Souverain peut rarement
gouverner par lui-même, il ne s'agit plus que de savoir comment il peut gouverner
par autrui' (*Oeuvres Complètes*, V, 463). The charge of 'vizierate' was revived in 1787
in the Paris *Parlement* against Calonne and Louis XVI.
11. Rousseau, *Oeuvres Complètes*, 93, 100ff.
12. 'Il se trouvait là comme en un pays que l'on a souhaité long-temps et
inutilement de voir, et où l'on se trouve enfin. Ses systèmes . . . ne respirent que
bureaux de découvertes, que conférences politiques' (d'Argenson, *Mémoires*, 255).
13. 'Il est très vrai que tout le mond savait nos jours', claimed d'Argenson. One
asks: 'Quelle nouvelle? Car vous venez de l'Entresol . . . C'est donc là ce que pense
l'Entresol de tel événement?' (260). Differences of opinion between the Court and
the private sector on questions of foreign policy led to protests by diplomats: 'Qu'est
donc que cet Entresol qui blâme si hautement votre conduite, et dont il sort de
tels mémoires?' This indirect political influence of the Club was the decisive reason
for its prohibition.

planning. However, when he naïvely asked Cardinal Fleury for an
open authorisation of political studies, he received a curt reply: 'Je
vois, monsieur, que dans vos assemblées vous proposeriez de traiter
des ouvrages de politique. Comme ces sortes de matières conduisent
ordinairement plus loin qu'on ne voudrait, il ne convient pas
qu'elles en fassent le sujet.'[14]

While the Marquis d'Argenson (clearly foreseeing this reaction)
had always urged silence and discretion[15] so as to keep the club in
existence at all, Saint-Pierre's attempt to transform the private
company into a public or semi-public organisation received a ban
for an answer. The French Chancellor tolerated neither political
planning nor indirect influence exerted by a society of any kind, and
so the club was forced out of its premises. Nor did attempts to
continue meeting in strict secrecy and at changing locales preserve
its sessions from compulsory closure.

This event, dating from the year 1731, was symptomatic of the
cleft between State and society. Finding its order threatened by the
independent political activity of the new leading social stratum, the
State compelled it to re-emigrate into the underground privacy of its
origin.[16]

---

14. The Chancellor's letter, quoted from ibid., 265.
15. D'Argenson repeatedly asked for discretion: 'Je disais: "Contentons-nous-
en pour nous mêmes, faisons nous oublier" . . . car nous frondions parfois bien
ouvertement. Rien au surplus ne doit être imputé à trahison', (ibid., p. 261).
'L'indiscrétion a tout fait' (ibid., 263).
16. D'Argenson summed up M. le garde des sceaux's arguments justifying the
prohibition thus: 'Que nous étions une Académie politique; qu'il ne convenait pas
qu'un pareil établissement existât sans que le gouvernement y participât, pour en
régler les matières'. Regular work, the large number of members, and above all 'le
bruit que leurs occupations faisaient dans le public' made it impossible to see the
société as private; rather, it was a 'véritable academie politique' and consequently
impermissible without official authorisation (268).
The first prognosis of a revolution in France by d'Argenson and which he
reiterated emphatically dates back to 1731 (see Brette, *La France au Milieu*, 106, 130,
133, 139 *passim*). While d'Argenson still linked his prognoses mainly to current
political developments, Rousseau, a kindred spirit and admirer, was beginning to
summarise the tension between State and society under the concept of crisis. He first
used the term in a political context in 1760, significantly enough in a dispute with a
member of the Club de l'Entresol.
Rousseau's *Jugement de la Polysynodie* contains his criticism of Saint-Pierre's
political criticism. 'Il donne aux Conseils la délibération des matières et laisse au Roi
seul la décision' — thus Saint-Pierre. 'Ne sentoit-il pas', asks Rousseau, 'qu'il falloit
nécessairement que la délibération des Conseils devînt bientôt un vain formulaire ou
que l'autorité royale en fût altérée?' 'Qui regit, rex est', Rousseau says together with
Grotius. Either the expert commissions are mere puppet assemblies, 'des Conseils de
parade', or they spell revolution for the Absolutist State. 'En effet, il n'est rien moins
qu'une révolution dont il est question dans la Polysynodie . . .'. The tension between
the Absolutist State ('un vieillard décrépit et gouteux', as he refers to it here) and the

The only institution of the citizenry that took this claim to Absolutism into account while taking all measures to evade it none the less, was Freemasonry.[17] The Masonic lodges amounted to the formation — typical of the new bourgeoisie — of an indirect power within the Absolutist State. Surrounding them was a self-made veil: the mystery. The silence, for whose breach the Club de l'Entresol had to pay with its dissolution; the taciturnity; the commitment to secrecy were, for the Masons, obligatory determinants of the nature of their society. The mystery, this element that seems so flatly to contradict the spirit of the Enlightenment, needs clearing up, for the Masonic mystery will lead us to the core of the morality–policy dialectic. What the mystery covers — ambivalently, as we shall see — is the political reverse of the Enlightenment.

For what the Masons, from the start and quite deliberately, enshrouded in secrecy and elevated to the level of a mystery was the extra-political intellectual interior which they shared with other bourgeois communities. This act, and the persistent emphasis they placed on it, distinguished them — for all their semi-religious

---

new society seemed so great to Rousseau in 1760 that only a revolution could release it. 'L'ordre politique et l'ordre civil dans les Monarchies ont des principes si différents et des règles si contraires qu'il est presque impossible d'allier les deux administrations'; perhaps the situation 'entre ce qu'on appelle maximes d'État et la Justice et les loix' was altogether irreconcilable. Given this basic difference, Rousseau, despite all the objections raised, prefers a polysynodie to the monarchy since it came closer to a republican constitution, and republican laws and justice. However, if in the existing situation the Kings were to heed Saint-Pierre's proposals, it would mean their 'ruine totale'. Here Rousseau is merely echoing what Cardinal Fleury had touched on thirty years earlier in his letter dissolving the Club de l'Entresol. If society gained power in the sense of Saint-Pierre then, according to Rousseau, there would be turmoil without end, '. . . et nul ignore combien est dangereux dans un grand État le moment d'anarchie et de crise qui précède nécessairement un établissement nouveau' (*Oeuvres Complètes*, V, 485ff.).

17. Except for the quoted sources, the subsequent discussions are based on Eugen Lennhoff and Oskar Posner, *Internationales Freimaurerlexikon*, Zurich, Leipzig and Vienna, 1932, a cosmopolitan-liberal work. On general questions, J.G. Findel, *Geschichte der Freimaurerei*, 3rd edn., Leipzig, 1870, was consulted. On the conflict for and against Freemasonry, Fay, *La Franc-Maçonnerie*, a work of keen perception, proved extremely valuable. The most recent German contribution, by A. Rossberg, *Freimaurerei und Politik im Zeitalter der französischen Revolution*, Berlin, 1942, is based on previously unavailable sources; Rossberg tends to accept hopes as plans, plans as execution and these for *faits accomplis*. Nevertheless, he makes more adequate use of the source material than does R. Le Forestier's *Les Illuminés de Bavière et la Franc-Maçonnerie allemande*, Paris, 1914 (cf. n. 17, Chapter 9 below). F. Runkel's *Die Geschichte der Freimaureren*, 3 vols., Berlin, 1931, cites many sources, but the basic Christian position and anti-English attitude which he projects into the past fail to do justice to the essence of Freemasonry in the eighteenth century. On the rites and background, see W.E. Peuckert, *Geheimbünde*, Heidelberg, 1951; and on the prehistory of the lodges, see Douglas Knoop and G.P. Jones, *The Genesis of Freemasonry*, Manchester, 1947.

pathos and cultic rigidity — from the many newly established
religious communities such as the Pietists, the Methodists, or the
Jansenists, who were also partly persecuted and barely tolerated in
the living of their strictly religious lives.

The essential provisions of the Masonic mystery, the actual
content of the secret work, varied considerably, depending on
doctrinal views. From system to system the mystery differed in
character; conditioned by temporal and social circumstances as well
as by national traits, it could be cast in entirely different moulds.
The one consistent goal of the royal art — to 'polish' the crude
human being, this 'unhewn stone', and lift the brothers into the
regions of light — was pursued in the most varied ways. Moral
purification of low sensuality and sensual pleasure were possible at
the same time, each complementing the other.

The scale of images and hopes that lent substance to the mystery
of the various systems extended from rational plans for social
coexistence to romanticising and mystifying phantasmata. There
were manifold mixtures and shadings; in fact, it is virtually a
characteristic of Masonry that the most contradictory elements
should enter into an indissoluble union. Only the centres of gravity
distinguished factions which ran, to name but a few important ones,
from the English moral-humanitarian association, from 'blue' Masonry and from German Illuminati via knightly orders — such as
the Templars, for instance — to the Swedish Protestant system, and
on to the sectarian Rosicrucian leagues or the French Philaletes who
hoped to illuminate and redeem mankind by means of occult
sciences.

In the secret Masonic organisations, religious and political elements entered into a new kind of union. Rationalistic resurgences
of the myths and mysteries of Antiquity and the unfolding of a
dominant indigenous hierarchy characterised the leagues; as a
whole, however, they were part of neither Church nor State but a
form of organisation peculiar to the new bourgeois society. 'In
essence, Freemasonry is as old as bourgeois society. The two could
not originate otherwise than together — if bourgeois society is not
indeed a mere scion of Freemasonry'.[18] This social-ontological

18. Lessing, *Ernst und Falk: Gespräche für Freimaurer*, 1778, *Sämtliche Schriften*,
XIII, pp. 339f.: 'Freemasonry is not something arbitrary, superfluous, but some-
thing necessary, rooted in the nature of man and in civic society'. Lessing saw
Freemasonry as taking precedence over its historical expressions; the relationship of

statement of Lessing's has retained its historic truth. It was in the lodges and through them that the bourgeoisie acquired a social form of its own. In imitating both, its mystery won a place beside the ecclesiastic mysteries and the arcane politics of States. It was the mystery of a third power, a power living by its self-made law; as in Locke's *Essay* it had stepped as 'Law of private censure' beside the Divine Law and the Civil Law.

The mystery had different contents in different systems, but always the same social function. In the framework of the Absolutist State, the functions of the Masonic mystery were far more import-ant than their real or supposed content. The search for that will mostly be in vain, but an enquiry into the functions will show that it was precisely these which in the framework of the State furnished the true point and proper substance of the arcanum for the moving spirits of society.

At first the lodges were a purely bourgeois creation, but the burghers managed to involve the aristocracy — socially recognised, but politically disfranchised — and thus to consort with the nobility on a basis of social equality. Just as in the salons there was no distinction of rank in the presence of ladies, so the principle of *égalité* prevailed in the lodges as well. There 'noblemen, gentlemen, and working men'[19] all found admission, and the bourgeois citizen found a platform where all distinctions of status were levelled out. This activity of the Masons was indeed an attack on the existing social structure, but it did not as yet bring them into irreconcilable conflict with the Absolutist State. One result of the political equal-ity of subjects was their social equalisation, the removal of old feudal differences; to effectuate this did not yet mean to explode the political system of the Absolutist State itself. However, it was precisely where the social levelling of the feudal hierarchy was most strongly pursued and included in the principles of organisation — in the lodges — that social equality was an equality outside the State. In the lodge the brother ceased to be a subject; he was a man among men, free to think, to plan, and to act in the work of the lodge.

---

the lodges to Freemasonry is like that of 'the Church to piety'. As a historico-philosophical argument this elevation of Freemasonry to a supra-historical force is proof of its specific civic function.

19. This formula is from *The Constitutions of Freemasons 1723*, London, 1923. The referred-to equality only rarely of course encompasses the artisans who were mentioned in the formula because of Masonic tradition.

Le cri de la nature, ami, c'est Liberté!
Ce droit si cher à l'homme est ici respecté.
Egaux sans anarchie et libres sans licence,
Obéir à nos lois fait notre indépendence.[20]

Freedom from the State was the real political appeal of the bourgeois lodges, more than their social equality. Their inner legality, their freedom and independence were possible only in a realm removed not only from the influence of ecclesiastical authority but from political interference by the ruling State power. From the start, therefore, the mystery had a rejecting, protecting function. In 1738 an appendix to the constitution of the Hamburg lodge, the first to be founded on German soil, states explicitly: 'The secrets and the silence are our principal means of self-preservation, and of preserving and strengthening our enjoyment of Masonry'.[21] Protection by the State was replaced by protection from the State.

This protective function of the mystery found its mental correlate in the separation of morality and politics. At the very founding of bourgeois Freemasonry this had been quite consciously laid down. The observance and maintenance of the separation was one of the 'Old Duties' formulated in 1723 under the aegis of Desaguliers, and as the royal art spread over Europe, it determined the direction of the other systems in which the 'Old Duties' were adopted as a working basis. 'A Mason is obliged, by his Tenure, to obey the Moral Law',[22] proclaimed the first article of the constitution. With this obligation Desaguliers laid down a position on two fronts: against the existing States, and against the ruling Churches. Where an individual was previously obliged to join the Church of his country or State, he was now told to submit only to morality, the faith that applied to all men without distinction, the new 'Catholick Religion': 'Yet 'tis now thought more expedient only to oblige them

20. These verses characterising Masonry are in Hazard, *Die Krise*.
21. Quoted in Runkel. *Geschichte der Freimaureren*, I, 106. 'Political and religious pressures are doubtless the most natural impulse of noble souls who stimulate the urge for such undertakings', said Weishaupt, the founder of the Illuminati, barely fifty years later (quoted in Engel, *Geschichte des Illuminatenordens*, Berlin, 1906, p. 56). Therefore, he believed, 'double secrecy' was necessary. 'Their real secret is no other than their origin', said Thomas Paine, 'which but few of them understand.' Even though Paine had already fallen victim to a myth about the source of the 'highest' age, he also said that the fear of persecution was the true reason for the secrecy ('Origin of Free Masonry' in *The Writings*, 4 vols., New York and London, 1894, IV, 290ff.).
22. *The Constitutions*, 49.

to that Religion in which all Men agree . . .'.[23] Hitherto, the Absolutist State had neutralised religious tensions politically; now it was the citizens themselves who wanted to build moral bridges over all distinctions of creed. Masonry was the social realisation of bourgeois moral doctrine. 'Whereby Masonry becomes the Center of Union, and the Means of conciliating true Friendship among Persons that must else have remain'd in a perpetual Distance.'[24]

However, even more important to the union of the social world was an express rejection of the prevailing politics, a politics guided not by laws of a morality outside the State, but by the *raison d'état* of the moment. 'We are resolw'd against **all Politicks**', the Masons declared in Article VI of their constitutions, and they proclaimed that creed throughout the eighteenth century, as they do today.[25]

In England this rejection of politics was initially motivated by a domestic-political purpose — the creation of a new social unity across party lines[26] — but at the same time it was intended to convince the government that the secret society was harmless and deserved toleration. However, while in England the royal art soon entered into close liaison with Hanoverian policy, serving that policy even on the Continent, the separation of moral and political domains as expressed in the Masonic constitutions retained its entire acuity in the Absolutist States. Lacking political authority, the new society made a virtue of necessity: even its secret institution was not understood as 'political', but as 'moral' from the beginning. Reigning in the lodges was a far more deserving sovereign; here it was virtue that wielded the sceptre: 'La vertu a son Trône dans nos

---

23. Ibid.
24. Ibid.
25. Ibid., bold face as in the original. The substance of the work, says Uriot in *Le Secret de Franc-Maçons mis en Évidence* (The Hague, 1744), was 'Architecture, Éloquence, Poésie, Peinture, Musique, Philosophie, Moral, Histoire, Plaisirs délicats et réglés par la Sagesse, voilà les objets de nos entretiens'. Politics and religion were not acceptable 'matières de Controverse' (18). Even today, political and religious matters are not discussed in 'just and perfect lodges' (see Lennhof and Posner, *Internationales Freimaurerlexikon*, 593). To conclude that the non-political character of the lodges was related to the rejection of politics in the eighteenth century is a false conclusion of liberal history, and frequently of Masonic history as well, which misjudges the functional significance of the rejection of politics within the framework of the Absolutist State. The conclusion drawn is based on the experience of post-Revolutionary France.
26. Cf. Raynal's assertion in 1774, testifying to the continuity of this basic position: 'Aujourd'hui l'autorité, devenu plus indépendente, assure aux monarchies des avantages dont un état libre ne jouira jamais. Que peuvent opposer des républicains à cette supériorité redoutable? Des vertus!' (*Histoire, Philosophie et Politique* . . ., The Hague, 1774, I, 257).

loges, nos coeurs sont les sujets, et nos actions le seul encens qu'elle y reçoive avec complaisance'.[27] Time and again the Masons swore that they were not pursuing political ends, that under their common rule in the sign of virtue they had no need of political tricks and external constructs such as the balance of power. The inner union alone guaranteed happiness.[28] Let States cling to power; for the Masons, the mystery bestowed a moral monopoly on their social institution.

As their constitutions stated in so many words, the mystery was the dividing line between morality and politics. It safeguarded and delimited the social sphere in which morality was to be realised.

An evolutionary retrospection shows an imperative resulting from the structure of the Absolutist system: inexorably, the moral inner space could unfold only in secret counter-manoeuvring *vis-à-vis* State policy. The freedom of the secret interior, of the individual citizen's soul, which Hobbes, in order to be able to deduce his idea of sovereignty, had to core out of the Absolutist State; the liberty which Locke then laid down 'by a secret and tacit consent' of the individuals, in a sort of philosophical legislation independent of the State — this civil liberty could be realised in the Absolutist State only so long as it was confined to a secret interior. True, the modern bourgeoisie had outgrown the secret interior of private mental morality and proceeded to consolidate itself in private societies, but these remained delimited by secrecy. The bourgeois Masons were not inclined to do without the secret of the moral interior, for it was precisely there that they found their guarantee of an existence independent of the State. The intellectual fact 'to be in secret free'[29] received its social concretion in the lodges. What the burghers, seeming not even to touch the State, created in their lodges — in that secret inner space within the State — was a space in which, protected by secrecy, civil freedom was already being realised. Freedom in secret became the secret of freedom.

To make freedom a reality, the secret had another consciously developed function beyond its protective one: that of genuinely and intrasocially uniting the bourgeois world as well.[30]

27. Uriot, *Le Secret de Franc-Maçons*, 17.
28. Ibid.: 'Ils ne balancent point à s'unir,' it says, clearly alluding to the existing political situation, 'leur liaison fait le bonheur'.
29. Hobbes, *Leviathan*, II, 31.
30. In English Masonry, the source of all the other systems, the functional significance of the arcanum for all the other systems of thought was a consciously

CHAPTER 6

The Proliferation of Indirect Power and the Schism of Morals and Politics

In advance of its content, the mystery of the lodges lay in the aura it radiated. In secrecy lay the pledge of sharing in a new and better life not known before. The initiation meant 'the discovery of a new world hidden amidst the old'.[1] The eudemonistic citizen, already estranged from Christian revelation, saw in the secret societies an institution 'in which he would find all that he might ever wish for'.[2] Hence there prevailed 'an indescribably widespread drive',[3] and it was virtually a matter of fashion to join one of the secret orders which had been formed, as Frederick the Great once remarked, 'solely by the taste and fashion of the century'.[4] To the initiated,

---

designed feature of the arcanum itself. 'De quelle utilité peut être le mystère d'une chose, qui vraisemblablement n'est rien elle même?' asked an authorised member of the Frankfurt lodges 'de l'Union' and 'de l'Égalité' which were still under direct English influence at the time (1744). 'C'est une précaution nécessaire au bien commun: Nous avons des Loges par toute le Terre, elles sont toutes unies entre'elles aussi étroitement que les Membres d'une seule le sont entr'eux. Voilà le motif de notre exactitude à garder notre Secret' (Uriot, Le Secret des Franc-Maçons, 14). This was written in defence of Masonry and published with the approval of the lodges. The de l'Union lodge was founded by the French envoy who was in Frankfurt for the coronation of the Emperor. The London founding charter is dated 8 February 1742. Cf. Runkel, Geschichte der Freimaureren, I, 153 .

1. Adam Weishaupt, Schilderung der Illuminaten, Gegenstück von Nr. 15 des grauen Ungeheuers, Nuremberg, 1786, 23.

2. Joseph Utzschneider, in [Cosandey, Renner, Utzschneider], Drey merkwürdige Aussagen die innere Einrichtung des Illuminatenordens in Bayern betreffend, Munich, 1786, 36.

3. This remark was made by Nicolai and is quoted in F.J. Schneider, Die Freimaurerei und ihr Einfluß auf die geistige Kultur in Deutschland am Ende des 18. Jahrhunderts, Prague, 1909, p. 111. One had 'enormous expectations' of Masonry, and 'unshakable confidence' in its promises (ibid., 47).

4. Quoted in A. Kohut, Die Hohenzollern und die Freimaurerei, Berlin, 1909.

secrecy brought a new kind of communion. The royal temple was built and held together by the secret; the arcanum acted as the 'glue' of brotherhood. To begin with, joint participation in the same arcanum guaranteed the equality of the brethren; it mediated the differences in estate. The secret linked all the initiates, no matter what they were initiated in; regardless of their position in the existing hierarchy they were now united on a new plane. 'Lorsque nous sommes rassemblées, nous devenons tous Frères, le reste de l'Univers est étranger: le Prince et le Sujet, le Gentil-homme et l'Artisan, le Riche et le Pauvre y sont confondus, rien ne les distingue, rien ne les sépare.'[5] Secrecy separated the brethren from the rest of the outside world and so, by rejecting all extant social, religious, and bureaucratic orders, a new elite evolved, the elite as 'mankind'.

Participation in the mystery kept awake an indefinite distrust, a wariness of all outsiders. A ceaselessly invoked fear of 'betrayal' contributed to an increasing consciousness of one's own new world, and of one's duty to serve it. The mystery also solidified the initiates' sense of superiority, the elite-consciousness of the new society. And within that society the gradation of the arcana into various degrees (which led the high degrees of the Strict Observance into all but pathological excrescences) created a hierarchy *sui generis*, in which bourgeoisie and nobility linked arms.[6] The more the Mason was initiated, the more he gained — or hoped to gain — in influence and prestige. The gradation fostered constant upward mobility,[7] which in turn led to permanent upgrading, and the final arcanum promised a share in enlightenment itself, the source of light.

To satisfy this urge, however, a man had first to subordinate himself. He had to practise obedience, which he did voluntarily,

---

This passage is from a letter of 1777 to Prince Friedrich August of Brunswick-Lüneburg, in which Frederick the Great protests against the interference of Duke Ferdinand of Brunswick in Prussian Masonry (66f.).

5. Uriot, *Le Secret des Franc-Maçons*, 17.

6. '. . . since the First Degree, being the expression of the higher ones, already ennobles, what might yet be expected of the still higher!' (Utzschneider, *Drey merkwürdige Aussagen*, 26).

7. 'All members of a secret society expect something more than they can hear in the world; they rightly expect something excellent and great, something that not everybody knows', said Weishaupt; and because of these high expectations 'all the higher and high degrees were introduced'. (From the address to the *Illuminates dirigentes*, repr. in *Die neuesten Arbeiten des Spartakus* [Weishaupt] *und Philo* [Knigge] . . ., 2nd edn, 1794, 63ff.).

being required to obey only men of the same spirit. In the Strict Observance the disappearance of the leadership into the 'unknown', evolved into a social myth that helped increase the weight of the arcanum and the moral self-control associated with it.[8] The 'great unknown' were always present somewhere, but everywhere at the same time, and, like the 'vanished' of the Illuminati, who secretly sought to occupy that void,[9] they could at any time sit in judgement on the members' conduct and demeanour.[10] In the German lodges the original compulsory secrecy had, as it were, hypostatised itself. It had yielded to a trend towards mystification, promoting faith in an omnipotent, secret, and indirect rule beyond the State. The shrouded summit seemed so far and at the same time so near as the infinite goal of progress, which still regulates things today.

In any case, what developed in the several obediences was an autonomous order of dominion, with the actual leadership stratum assured of superior knowledge by the gradation of the secret. The split between mundane exterior and moral interior was transferred into the society itself and differentiated for leadership purposes. The several degrees of secrecy created a sluicing system that opened inwards into Masonry and upwards within the systems, but not downwards and outwards. The secret become a control mechanism consistently wielded by the Order of Illuminati, for example. The priestly regents of that order began by following Jesuit models and introducing an accurate secret reporting system. Brethren were obliged to file sealed monthly reports about themselves — in moral candour — and about their fellow brethren. 'Thus he must neces-

8. 'I believed that I was under the strictest observation of many persons not known to me; towards this end I sought to fulfil my duties most accurately, because nothing seemed as certain to me as that none of my actions went unnoticed.' Weishaupt was commenting on his entry into a Munich lodge (quoted in Engel, *Geschichte des Illuminaten-Ordens*, 60).

9. Cf. Utzschneider, *Drey merkwürdige Aussagen*, 41, 45, 51. It was Knigge and Bode's plan, according to Knigge, 'to direct everything secretly so as to gain control over the strictest observance without drawing attention to it' (quoted in Engel, *Geschichte des Illuminaten-Ordens*, 138). They thought to establish themselves as the true heads — yet as 'shadows'. 'Through the imperfection and renown of their practices', Freemasonry was 'to serve a better and more clever institution [the order of the Illuminati] as a cover . . . so that the opposition and the government would not mistrust them [the Illuminati]' (*Nachtrag von weiteren Originalschriften . . .*, Munich, 1787, II, 117).

10. 'They welcomed all betrayals by their subjects, in part to gain knowledge of it, in part to keep the traitors living in fear and threaten them with making their betrayal known in case they failed to obey . . . ' (Utzschneider, *Drey merkwürdige Aussagen*, 45).

sarily decipher and compromise himself and others, in writing.'[11] Through these secret controls 'the superiors learn whatever they may wish to learn. And of themselves they can say: We are able to know more than all others, to accomplish more than others.'[12]

For promotion to Illuminatus major, as for original admission, the candidate had to fill out a huge questionnaire which on thirty-two printed pages, put several hundred questions aimed at revealing the applicant in intellectual, moral, social, and economic respects. Here the secret was initially considered a vehicle of moral education, as 'man's leaning toward the hidden and mysterious is used in a way so advantageous to morality',[13] but at the same time it delivered the neophyte to the 'moral regimen', to that 'directorate of tolerance'[14] which on the strength of the secret was already terrorising brethren in the name of morality. Among the countless secret societies, the Illuminati unquestionably represented the German extreme of autonomously structured rule, but in every other respect they were symptomatic. Analogous — if correspondingly earlier — was the founding of the 'Grand Lodge' in England, whose initial purpose was to submit the scattered existing lodges to strict, unified control.[15] In France the process was repeated in 1773.[16]

Originating in the sign of the Masonic mystery was the social framework of a moral International composed of merchants and travellers, philosophers, sailors, and *émigrés* — in short, of cosmopolitans allied with the nobility and the officer caste. The lodges turned into the strongest social institution of the eighteenth-century moral world. That statesmen also used them to gain influence and

11. Ibid., 9. I turn 'everyone into a spy of others, and of all. Afterwards the gifted are selected for the mysteries', said Weishaupt in a letter to Knigge (quoted from the *Originalschriften* in B. Stattler, *Das Geheimnis der Bosheit*, Munich and Augsburg, 1787, 45). The oath of the Rosicrucians also imposed the duty of mutual denunciation by the brothers to their superiors (see Schneider, *Die Freimaurerei und ihr Einfluß*, 137).

12. [Adam Weishaupt], *Schreiben an den Herrn Hofkammerrath Ut[z]schneider in München*, 1786; Appendix, 'Unterricht zu besserer Beurteilung der inneren Einrichtung des Ordens', p. 90. Utzschneider, *Drey merkwürdige Aussagen*, 10, 40. The moral system of rule of the Illuminati is described in Le Forestier, *Les Illuminés de Bavière*.

13. [Bode?], *Gedanken*, 37.

14. The leadership committee of the Illuminati was also known as the morals commission or fiscal office. Von Göchhausen, *Enthüllung des Systems der Weltbürgerrepublik . . .*, Rome (Leipzig), 1786, 376, calls it the 'directorate of tolerance'.

15. Knoop and Jones, *The Genesis of Freemasonry*, 194ff.

16. Albert Lantoine, *Histoire de la Franc-Maçonnerie Française*, Paris, 1925, 70.

pursue political aims only goes to show their great importance. The Kings of Sweden, the Duke of Brunswick as protector of the Strict Observance, the Hohenzollerns and many middle-ranking German princes appear in that list, as does the French Duke of Orléans, the 'Philippe Égalité' of the Great Revolution.

The chaos that broke out in the German fraternal orders in the 1760s could not be removed by the Illuminati either. By way of contrast, the French lodge system experienced a new flowering after the reform of 1773. Most influential in the reorganisation was 'Les Neuf Soeurs', the lodge founded by the philosophers and Encyclopedists in 1769. It was the social link between the representatives of the intellectual *Règne de la Critique* and the Masonic organisation. Under the morally weighty leadership of Benjamin Franklin, Grand Master from 1779 to 1782, this lodge launched a sweeping propaganda offensive for the republican ideals which were just then being realised in America.[17] With the introduction in 1773 of a republican constitution within the Grand Orient of France — the Masons viewed themselves as 'citizens of Masonic democracy' — the number of lodges increased dramatically. In 1772 there were only 164 in France, but by 1789 they numbered 629, 65 of them in Paris alone. On the very eve of the Revolution, Freemasonry had joined the *sociétés de pensée* as an important independent, not State-controlled organisation of the new society. It was not merely an intellectual weapon against the Absolutist State; it also formed a social framework which the Jacobin party machinery could lean on when the radical elements emerged.[18]

Thus it was before and beyond any work of political planning that the mystery, through its twin functions of uniting and protecting the society, signified an intellectual front cutting through the entire world of Absolutist States. Evolving through the mystery and under its protection was a social grouping that acquired the weight of an indirect power, while on the other side of the front the Absolutist State held the high — and in France eventually hollow — ground of a directly ruling power. Already it was the intra-societal

17. Fay, *Benjamin Franklin*, Paris, 1929; idem, *La Franc-Maçonnerie*, 144ff., 226ff.
18. Petion, Brissot, Danton, Rabaut-St. Etienne, Sièyes (not the Robespierres) were members of the Paris lodges, some in the Neuf Soeurs lodge (Fay, *La Franc-Maçonnerie*, 229f.). On the use of social organisations in existence prior to the Revolution to support the Jacobin command structure, see C. Brinton, *A Decade of Revolution: 1789–1799*, New York and London, 1934.

functions that put the absolute sovereignty in doubt, seemingly without even touching the State.[19] The Masonic secret, says de Maistre in 1782, is the fundament of society at large: 'Le secret est le droit naturel parce qu'il est le lien de la confiance, grand base de la société humaine'.[20] The secret is the vinculum of mutual trust that unites the nascent society and this is why it is endowed with the dignity and priority of natural law.

This is also why what de Maistre calls a delicate moral question — can the society keep its plans a secret from the State power? — may also be answered in the affirmative. The secret is a part of the natural law which makes all positive law fade before it. The lodge secret breaks the State power. It can do this, de Maistre adds stereotypically like all Masons, because there is nothing in it that goes against State or Church anyway. But he deliberately makes this his secondary argument: it is not only because of what one tells the State — that the secret does not imperil it — but because and on the very strength of its social function to unite the bourgeois world, that the secret, this obstacle in the path of the State, must remain.

Just how much it was by means of these extra-state, purely intra-societal functions that the society put the State in jeopardy is shown in the ethical–political dialectic which the secret kindled.

In order to guarantee the coalescence of the brethren into an inner community; the unfolding of an autonomous hierarchy; the assurance of superior knowledge; the possibility of an order led by society — to guarantee all this, the secret had to be preserved. Reticence was the foundation and the premise of the social arcanum. The unenforceability of this first basic law of the secret orders, their lack of direct coercive power, evoked a specifically moral jurisdiction. The self-assumed obligation of silence implied a constant self-control of conscience; to the Mason, exercising it meant proving himself virtuous, independent and sovereign. A good Mason 'must become his own judge, must pass judgement on himself'.[21] Accordingly, if he ignored the split in the world that had resulted

19. Freemasonry, proclaimed a German pamphlet in 1742, 'has joined with the noblest princes and sat down with them on the thrones of power and glory' (*Kurze historische Nachricht von dem Ursprung der Freimaurer-Gesellschaft* (1742), repr. in *Des verbesserten Konstitutionsbuches*, 173).

20. De Maistre, *La Franc-Maçonnerie*, 122.

21. [Weishaupt], *Schreiben an den Herrn Hofkammerrath*, 110. The tongue is the key to the secret. Thus the key is 'not of a metal, but', in the words of the ambiguous initiation rite of the apprentice, 'a tongue of good judgement' (*Die entdeckte Heimlichkeit der Freymäurer*, 1779, 36).

from the secret, he was condemning himself; performance of the separation was a worthy act of moral jurisdiction. The creation of a special social space, the critical separation of society and outside world, was thus as original as the moral judiciary which performed and supervised the partition.

The coercive means of that judiciary were indirect, along the lines demonstrated by Locke, and took effect in the form of social pressure.[22] But the gradual development of an intra-societal authority caused the Masons to plan for the direct execution of their moral verdicts. When de Maistre developed his great reform programme for the Strict Observance in France and Germany, the question of treason came up and he declared: 'Dans quelques années nous serons en état de faire taire ce Frère, ou nous serons rien'.[23] In 1782, seven years before the Revolution, the question of how far the symbolically rigorous but only indirectly effective Masonic justice might be wrought directly was already raised as a decisive alternative on which the society's future existence would depend. The direct effect of the social judiciary is clearly visible: as far as its claimed jurisdiction was concerned, the society was already in open competition with the State. The alternative that followed, the 'To be or not to be', was an acute symptom of crisis.[24]

Long before this question became so acute, however, the State had entirely different — to wit, indirect — doubts cast upon it by the moral judiciary. The question was raised, not only inwardly, but outwardly. The act of social self-constitution was always simultaneously an act of passing moral judgement on the State. 'A mesure que le vice s'éleva, la vertu fut abaissée ... et pour n'être point la victime de son cruel antagoniste, elle se fit un azile inaccessible à

---

22. 'Since all the judgements we pass, as well as all our actions betray us' (so said the Illuminati) constant self-control was as essential as the control exercised by the superiors (*Einige Originalschriften des Illuminatenordens*, Munich, 1787, 31). Significantly enough, the betrayal of the secret was punishable — even if only symbolically — by the most cruel torture, including the death penalty (*Des Verbesserten Konstitutionsbuches*, II, 228; *Die entdeckte Heimlichkeit*, p. 25). The secret ritual was betrayed in 1730, but the socially relevant factor, the internal social jurisdiction which the secret work had to protect, persisted.
23. De Maistre, *La Franc-Maçonnerie*, 120.
24. Two years later (1784) the self-jurisdiction of the Illuminati played a crucial part in their dissolution. Upon being inducted, every member of the order had to pledge himself to the *jus vitae et necis* (repr. in *Einige Originalschriften*, 88, 97: 'For the same reason that I hold that the rulers of the world have power over the life and death of man, I gladly pledge myself to my order, which, as the rulers of the world ought to, furthers the best in man').

tout autre qu'à ses fidèles adorateurs.'[25]

What the secret made possible was one's seclusion from the outside world, which in turn led to a form of social existence which included the moral qualification to sit in judgement on that outside world. The medium of the secret widened the private conscience into a society; the society came to be a large conscience, a conscience of the world from which the society voluntarily excluded itself by way of the secret.[26] In their rejection of politics the Masons simultaneously established themselves as the world's better conscience. The separation of ethics and politics implied a moral verdict on the prevailing political system. As long as the politics of absolute monarchy reigned, the secret wrapped the Masons in their cloak of moral innocence and political absence. They did nothing but think, enlighten, embody the spirit, and act as carriers of light. From the soil of the lodges a wholly new value system was deliberately placed next to the existing political order. But since the political reality was regarded as the exact negation of the moral position which in the lodges was already realised — 'La pratique de ce que l'on appelle communément Loy Naturelle fait trois quarts et demy du Maçon'[27] — political absence in the name of morality turned out to be an indirect political presence.

The politicians, it was said in 1744, had unwittingly been fed the maxims of Machiavelli; they feared the worst from the lodges: that their secret concealed a revolution. This was by no means the case, averred the Masons, filled with the pathos of innocence. Rather, they were living by a principle that obviated any revolution: 'La

25. Uriot, *Le secret des Franc-Maçons*, 27. This was cited in a historical survey of the lodges and refers to the era after Noah. It deals with one of the numerous projections of moral dualism into the past which the Masons — armed with the myths of Antiquity — used to legitimise themselves historico-philosophically. By setting themselves apart from the state, the brothers united into an association 'd'honnêtes gens dont le bonheur et la sureté consiste à n'être point confondus avec le Vice' (ibid., 14). We want to build', it continues, 'and all our buildings are either prisons for vices or temples for virtues' (*Kurze historische Nachrichten*, II, 203). This formulation is derived from a French *Ode apologétique* (Uriot, *Le secret des Franc-Maçons*, 39), in which the myth of Astraea, whose return to earth is to spell the beginning of the Golden Age, is revived. This mythological garb straddles the boundary line between allegorical amusement and the almost intentional creation of historico-philosophical myths.

26. The 'most esteemed Order of Freemasons', it says in *Des verbesserten Konstitutionsbuches*, II, 245, 'ranges throughout the whole world'; 'and thus it is . . . with this Order that so long as the secrets remain secret nothing better is to be found than this society; but there is also nothing worse than to let the secret be known to the world' (241).

27. Uriot, *Le secret des Franc-Maçons*, 15.

Religion et l'État n'auroient pas été si souvent la proye des Révolutions les plus sanglantes, si ceux qui les gouvernoient eussent connu et pratiqué comme les Maçons, cette vertu dont on leur fait un crime.'[28] The Masons have nothing to do with politics directly, but they live by a law which — if it prevails — makes an upheaval superfluous. On the one hand, they excise themselves from the State, refrain from ruling and form an indirect power that threatens sovereignty[29] but does so only morally. On the other hand, their

28. Ibid., pp. 10, 14.
29. The anti-statist sentiment of the lodges' conspiratorial planning was detectable as early as 1742, in the *Kurze historische Nachricht von dem Ursprung der Freimaurergesellschaft und deren Geheimnisse mit unpartheiischer Feder vorgestellt*. The anonymous author tells one of the numerous stories about their origin which were current at the time. According to his account, the origin of the Masons coincides with the construction of Kensington Palace. 'When that palace was built, there came into being a conspiracy of the workers against their appointed superiors.' No date is given, but reference is made to Charles I, the 'cause' of the revolt. The government took hold of the situation, discovered the passwords of all the conspirators, not only of the Masons, although they were the largest group and the most secret. Their secret was 'that the supervisors, against whom the attempt was directed, themselves gave cause for the discontent by their wrong administration of justice . . . '. Because of this superiority of the Masons, based on their moral innocence and greater knowledge, the authorities, in order to ward off something still worse, were compelled to issue this statement: 'The Masons are free; namely they are free of the (in the sense of positive but false law) deserved punishment (in the sense of true law), free without the pardon granted the workers (the uninitiated, those still bound to despotism) by an act of grace'.
The morally founded justice of the Masons made the acts of volition and grace of the sovereign princes superfluous; it established a new legitimacy and therefore it meant the beginning of the end of Absolutism. The watchword of Kensington, the author continues, 'which was chosen for the attack, is one of the noblest and greatest secrets which the Freemasons today still must swear to'. In a note, he hastens to point out — in accordance with the constitution that bars Masons from engaging in politics — that the Masons were by no means 'intent to carry out a particular state plan'; rather, they were 'the most honest of men, and do not seek to undertake anything that runs counter to divine, secular, and other laws'. This document makes manifest the ambivalence of the Freemasons, planning the 'attack' from the inside but rejecting all politics outside, so as to be able to plan under the protection of the secret. 'These are respectable concerns that occupy the Freemasons', it goes on to say, ' . . . wherein these consist I will keep secret, and it is also not fitting to say, being that they are secrets'. At any rate, they refrain from 'logical syllogism' and 'pedantry'. 'Their entire existence is directed toward the examination of natural and political matters' (225). They form a 'society which concerns itself with nothing else but how it wants to safeguard itself in this life'. 'Even though most of the members of the society are capable of performing the most important tasks of state, still they are not allowed to volunteer for them . . . everything must remain in its place . . . a capable member must wait until chosen for affairs of importance' (267). And if a moral Mason should achieve a position of leadership he will certainly not be 'Machiavellian'. The pamphlet was published by Multz, in Frankfurt, that is in the same region as Uriot, *Le secret des Franc-Maçons*. The Frankfurt lodge was still under the direct influence of the London Grand Lodge, which, according to Runkel's waspish comment (*Die Geschichte der Freimaurerei*, I, 158), accounts for the radical tenor. The edition cited here appeared jointly with the German Constitu-

virtue does not cease to be a 'crime' — that is, a threat to the State — until they, not the sovereign, determine what is right and what is wrong. Morality is the presumptive sovereign. Directly non-political, the Mason is indirectly political after all. Though morality remains non-violent and peaceful, it is by these very qualities that its polarisation, its diametrical opposition to politics, is jeopardising the existing state.

All lodges were obliged by their constitutions to give protection and refuge to insurgents and rebels if they were morally beyond reproach.[30] The field of action staked out by this provision was not merely extra-State but anti-State.

That the political consequence of the internal moral work, the politically crucial shift from inner moral freedom to outward political freedom, would remain hidden was another function of the arcanum, its specifically political function. This, too, was planned. But that the political significance of the shift was hidden from the bulk of the society as well — this had its roots in the dialectic between ethics and politics that was provoked by the secret. The political secret of the Enlightenment was not to be shrouded just from the outside; as a result of its seemingly non-political beginnings it was concealed from most of the Enlighteners themselves. The remainder of Part II will be devoted to the task of exposing both these concealments, and in the process their internal connections will also become apparent.

---

tion Book of 1783, which was also published in Frankfurt (II, 179ff.). Wolfstieg comments that only a handful of copies of this (undoubtedly frank) pamphlet are extant. Significantly, the year 1783 is given as marking the onset of the growing radicalisation in Germany as well.

30. *Constitutions*, Art. 2, 'Of the Civil Magistrate' (the old designation 'Prince' was discarded in 1723): because of the peaceable nature and loyalty, the Masons have always enjoyed the protection of kings and princes. 'So that if a Brother should be a Rebel against the State', it goes on to say, 'he is not to be countenanced in his Rebellion, however he may be pitied as an unhappy Man, and if convinced of no other Crime, though the loyal Brotherhood must and ought to disown his Rebellion, and give no Umbrage or Ground of political Jealousy to the Government for the time being; they cannot expel him from the Lodge, and his Relation to it remains indefeasible.' This rule was taken over in all countries except in the Republic of Holland.

CHAPTER 7

The Political Function of the Lodges and the Plans of the Illuminati

Lessing's *Conversations for Freemasons between Ernst and Falk* makes clear the political function of the Masonic secret and sheds new light on it. The intellectual elite that saw through and understood the polemical functions of the Masonic conceptual arsenal were few in number. Lessing was the pre-eminent German member of that select group. His skill in allusion was surpassed only by his skill at concealment. His insight into the political nature of the Masonic secret was not the product of a higher level of initiation; on the contrary, he had not passed beyond the third Johannine degree. Deeply and genuinely dismayed by the ineffectiveness of the German Masons, and pained by the inadequacy and importunity of many of his lodge brothers, he deplored the inner strife of the systems. However, what enabled Lessing to allude and conceal so effectively was his astute understanding of the political symptoms; he, as it were, initiated himself into the secret duplicities which were part of the Enlightenment as a political movement. His discriminating conceptual sense gave him insight into the political-moral contradiction of the duplicitous thinking and attitudes of the Enlightenment that had not yet flowered in Germany. His pamphlet on Freemasonry, so eagerly read by the leading German proponents of Enlightenment, attests to this.

The Masons grew, according to Lessing, by their philanthropic and pedagogical activities. The practice of morality was part of their exoterics.[1] 'Their true deeds are their secrets', asserts Falk, the

---

1. G.E. Lessing, *Sämtliche Schriften*, XIII, 349ff., XV, 484ff.

initiate. To begin with, without going into the secret in greater detail, he outlines the sphere of these genuine Masonic accomplishments. They have done 'all the good that still exists in the world — in the *world*, mark you — and continue to work at all the good that will still be done in the world — in the *world*, mark you'.[2] The world, this experimental stage of the Freemasons, harbours three fundamental evils, 'which appear to be the most inexplicable obstacles to providence and virtue'. These are, first, the division of the inhabited world into different States separated from one another by 'chasms' and 'dividing walls', and which because of their conflicting interests repeatedly 'collide' with one another. The second is the stratification resulting from the social distinctions within the States, and the third is the separation of people by religion. With this Lessing has drawn up a schema of the three main points of attack of the cosmopolitan Freemasons: States, social strata, Churches. However, and this is the crucial element of Lessing's thought and proves him to be a political thinker — the enumerated evils, the products of mankind's differences, its boundaries and divisions, are not chance occurrences which can be forgotten or eliminated, but are part of the structure of historical reality. In Lessing's view, mankind's dissimilarities ontologically preceded their historical manifestations — the States, social stratification, and religions. It is not a matter of 'mere man against mere man', but of 'these men against these men'. There exist 'evils without which even the happiest man cannot live', and the State and its governing structure are among the evils man cannot escape. It is the nature of bourgeois society — 'quite against its intention', according to Lessing's paraphrase of optimistic planning — and not simply the fault of the State as such, that 'it cannot unite men without separating them, cannot separate them' without drawing dividing lines and defining distinctions. The same holds true for the constitutions of States: 'It is impossible for all its members to have like relationships among themselves. Even if all of them play a role in the framing of laws, they still do not play an identical role, at least not an identical direct role. There will be more exalted members and lesser members'. The same differences necessarily exist also with regard to property and ownership. 'Well,' Lessing says at the end of his contemplation, 'man can be united only through separation, can maintain unity only through eternal

---

2. Ibid., as all subsequent citations.

separation. That is the nature of things. It can be no other way.'

Lessing sees the differences among men, the boundaries between States and the multiplicity of States as moral evils, but unlike the naïve-Utopian Masons, he does not consider them a manifestation of immoral tyranny but as a part of man's nature. With this presentation of 'inescapable evil' Lessing has also defined the sphere of politics. The conversation between Ernst and Falk then turns to the actual activities of the Masons.

Freemasonry constitutes a focused, powerful counter-movement against that 'inescapable evil', the matrix and subject of State policy. The fundamental role of the Masons is to oppose essentially 'disadvantageous matters' — and not only flaws related to history such as specific constitutions. They are the 'men who voluntarily have taken it upon themselves to work against the inescapable evils of the State'. The initiated Mason recognises the inevitability of States and social differences, and hence also of politics, but his ultimate goal is to prevent the evils brought on by politics 'from making greater inroads than necessity dictates. To render their effects as harmless as possible'. This inevitably brought the Masons into the sphere of national politics, even if theirs was a moral purpose. The same inevitability that made for the evils of politics summoned the Masons to battle against them. Lessing transformed the historical starting-point of the bourgeois secret associations into their historical role. Just as the society developed under the aegis of the State yet at the same time kept itself apart so as to take up its position against it, so according to Lessing's 'ontology' the shortcomings of the world from which the Masons separated themselves dualistically so as to work against it were the root cause of their activities. And these activities become political even, and particularly, when the purpose is purely moral.

The ultimate goal of the Masons — and one Lessing only hints at — was as far as possible to make the state superfluous. The secret dictate of morality demanded that the politically impossible be attempted. The virtuous, perfect bourgeois society which they as brothers personified was, so they believed, nature's ultimate purpose. They, as it were, threw the mantle of moral purpose over the existing state, and that purpose turned the state into a willing tool of bourgeois society, a tool 'for the people'. And it was a self-evident part of their ultimate purpose that the (political) evils that first made possible and necessary the commission of (morally) good deeds had to be overcome. 'The true work of the Freemasons', and that is their secret, 'aims at making the greater portion of everything that is generally referred to as good deeds dispensible.' The Masons thus not only fight ordinary evils exoterically, which is the duty of all decent men, but as esoterics they simultaneously rise above the commonplace sphere of good and evil. Once the motive for good deeds, namely political evils, ceases to exist goodness also loses its significance. When evil disappears, goodness becomes so self-evident that the term becomes superfluous. Although this is an eternally proximate goal, it is *per se* Utopian. In presenting it Lessing outlined the esoteric long-range objective of good deeds. By virtue of untrammelled goodness the arcanum obliged the Masons to work towards the eradication of all evil in the world as well. However, the secret of this esoteric step, in content Utopian, in its function was highly political. And this is precisely what Lessing alludes to. The moral long-term goal, ostensibly beyond suspicion, was sooner or later bound to become the root of all evil, and had from an historical perspective to conflict with the sphere of State policy.

Thus, the critical distinction between morality and politics is also found in Lessing, but beyond it he makes clear its dialectic: on the one hand, the moral activity of the Masons was possible only because of the 'inevitable evil of the State'; on the other, it was directed against it. Awareness of this dialectic constituted the political arcanum of the Masons. The secrecy papered over the fact that their work on behalf of morality would inevitably lead into the political sphere. The purpose of the arcanum, to protect and make possible the moral work of the Masons, was joined by yet another function, that of hiding the indirect political nature of that activity, and in that role it is part of the true content of the arcanum itself.

Lessing thus makes no secret of the objective in terms of the content and ultimate moral purpose of the Masons. Rather, the secret merely hides the political consequence of the moral purpose. Lessing's Masonic programme does not casually propose to make morality into policy, but, being politically astute, he is cognisant of the inevitable effect of moral activity on the political sphere. He knows that virtuous activity aimed at rooting out the evils of the State cannot totally absorb politics. Since human distinctions and differences are ontological facts they can only be 'bridged', not eradicated. To 'eliminate them altogether' would mean 'to destroy the State along with them'. Lessing sees this as an unfulfillable hope,[3] not so much out of patriotism but for reasons of political perception. Thus he outlined not only long-term Utopian goals, as current Masonic literature was wont to do, but he also defined the limits of the moral objective. Ernst's insight is that the initiate knows that in the execution of the moral programme these limits are necessarily overstepped, that morality thus becomes a political factor and that this is better kept secret. This makes him privy to one of the secrets of the Masons which 'he cannot get himself to utter even if possibly he might want to'.

In his pamphlet of 1778 Lessing, as he himself claimed and as Masonic historiography still asserts,[4] outlined 'the true ontology of Freemasonry'. His conversations contain severe criticism of the German Templar system, but they also set out the humanitarian objectives that guided English and French Masonry, and the German Illuminati in particular. The secret does not imply any plans for actual revolt, but it obscures the political consequences of the moral programme directed against the Absolutist State. 'Dignified individuals' must wage war on the States, these inevitable evils of the world, stealthily, invisibly, and silently; that is the secret, the esoteric, of Freemasonry.

Lessing's writings influenced the Illuminati, but they lacked his political acumen. Deficient in political consciousness, they made use of the available literature of the Enlightenment to brew a popular potion. Seen from the European perspective, the Illuminati, as far as Enlightenment was concerned, were on the level of the pre-Revolutionary French; from a regional perspective, given the Bavarian situation, they lagged far behind France, or even Prussia. This discrepancy made for disagreements which were not without a measure of absurdity. Against this limited background Utopian planning seemed like boastful officiousness. Yet it was precisely in

3. Lessing's political wisdom in this instance does not contradict his Utopian philosophy of history which he voiced as a Mason and which he developed, with the beginning third stage of the history of mankind, in the form of a secularised chiliasm. Utopianism and rational planning were neither mutually exclusive; nor since the eighteenth century were they mutually dependent.

4. Thus Lennhoff and Posner, *Internationales Freimaurerlexikon*, in the article on Lessing. The historical data on Lessing's relationship to Freemasonry is found in Runkel, *Die Geschichte der Freimaurerei*, II, pp. 141ff. Runkel's rejection of Lessing does not deal with Lessing's discussion of Masonry in the eighteenth century. Runkel admits that Lessing's analysis is based on the Masonic literature that Lessing, a voracious reader, was familiar with. If the royal art 'never warms Lessing's soul directly' this is not an objection to his structural analysis of Freemasonry.

this caricature, so to speak, that the schema of the century began to take shape. The shift from defence to attack — from the creation of an indirect force to the indirect assumption of power — that took place under cover of the secret, and the reference to the purely moral and non-political character of the society, became demonstrably clear with the founding of the Illuminati in 1776, the year of the American Declaration of Independence. From the day of its inception the order stood in the front line of the fight against Absolutism and the 'religionists'. It was a rallying point for all those who were displeased with Karl Theodor's Bavarian rule; its primary function, as far as its members were concerned, was that of protector, or, as they put it, a 'haven of peace, a refuge for the unhappy, a sanctuary against persecution'.[5]

By means of the secret, they hoped to reserve for themselves a place in which the 'political situation could work no changes'. The rejection of politics was to enable them to introduce a purely moral order.[6] 'All devices of the evil-doers will become ineffective. . . . Men will be judged only by their true, their inner worth',[7] which in turn would be measured only by their convictions, 'so that any disguise becomes ineffective'. The merit of the lower grades lay in the virtuous self-discipline the brothers were admonished to practise, and this required a new type of 'dissimulation'. The shedding of the 'camouflage' inside the order was accompanied by a relentless reminder to preserve it when facing the outside world, a technique which had to be learned with reversed symbols — for the good of the cause.[8] The political skill of obscurement was proof of the degree of political liberation. Consequently the members of the secular confessional hierarchy, under the guidance of their superiors, were taught to become 'useful collaborators', so as to acquire the requisite maturity for the highest purposes.[9]

With regard to questions of state and religion, on the other hand, 'we must still tread carefully with neophytes', asserted the heads of

5. *Schreiben an den Herrn Hofkammerrath*, Appendix: 'Unterricht zu besserer Beurtheilung der inneren Einrichtung des Ordens', 87.
6. See above, pp. 78–9.
7. Weishaupt, *Kurze Rechtferigung meiner Absichten*, Frankfurt and Leipzig, 1787, 50, 86. 'You must judge them by their reasons and objectives. Then all delusion vanishes and the truth emerges.'
8. Cf. the statutes of the Illuminati reprinted in *Einige Originalschriften*, 12ff.
9. *Schreiben an den Herrn Hofkammerrath*, 97ff. 'The society has no use for men as they are; first they have to become that for which they are needed . . .' (*Einige Originalschriften*, 29).

the order. Only after inner testing were the members gradually familiarised with the true and basic goals of the order. 'And at the end came the total revelation of the policy and maxims of the order. The projects for the gradual fight against the enemies of reason and humaneness are drawn up by the supreme council.'[10]

The sanctuary became the headquarters of the attacking force. The moral inner space was not only an institution outside the state; it had a political aspect as well. Parallel to the mystery of superstition and the arcana of politics there was the secret of the Illuminati. 'Why secret societies?' asked Bode, their North German pioneer. 'The answer is simple. It is foolish to play with exposed cards when the opponent covers his hand.'[11] The difference between state and society hardens into clearly drawn battle lines. Unlike most lodges up until then, the Illuminati no longer tried to gain influence by using the direct support of the prince but, on the contrary, sought to bypass him and gain control for themselves. The highest degree revealed 'the greatest of all secrets which so many yearned and vainly looked for, the art of governing mankind, to lead it towards virtue . . . and then to carry out everything that seemed like a dream and appeared possible only to the most enlightened'.[12] Behind the secret there formed not only a power independent of the State, but one that also planned — and this was the arcanum of the higher degrees — the extension of the moral ruling system already existing within the order to the world outside.[13]

10. Third Letter of Spartakus [Weishaupt] to Philo [Knigge], reproduced in *Einige Originalschriften*, 210ff. The initiate is mistaken (declares the induction ceremony) (*Original Schrift*, 72), if he believes that the order intends 'to undermine secular and ecclesiastic rule, to take over the rule of the world'. Yet this is precisely the programme of the upper grades (cf. *Nachtrag von weiteren Originalschriften*, Munich, 1787, II, 93).

11. [Bode?], *Gedanken über die Verfolgung*, 40. Cf. *Einige Originalschriften*, 42. The purpose of the secretiveness of the Brothers is to prevent the 'hindering of their objectives and operations through the presence of ignoble spirits'. Bode (1730–93), editor and translator of English novels, the son of a day labourer who climbed the social ladder, was the sort of active, intelligent citizen who also worked for the political power of the new man. Bode was also responsible for initiating Karl August, Goethe, and Herder into the Illuminati. (The cited pamphlet should probably be ascribed to him at any rate it is among the best published by the Masons. Well written — a rarity at the time — it tersely summarises all then current arguments for and against the secret order.)

12. *Schreiben an den Herrn Hofkammerrath*, 96. (Reprint of the instructions to the chiefs.)

13. The Illuminati sought 'to introduce a worldwide moral regime which would be under their control in every country. This council would decide on all matters concerning pardons, appointments and promotions, as well as rejections *sine appellatione ad principem*. This would give it the unlimited right', said an ex-member,

Education, training, propaganda and enlightenment were in
themselves not enough to achieve the moral objective. Its attain-
ment called for political action, to make virtue triumph over evil.
'Not words, deeds are what is required here.'[14] The 'plan of operation' for fighting the rule of evil was drawn up by the council of
'regents'. The programme of political action called for the indirect,
silent occupation of the State. 'The princely dicasteries and councils'
were gradually to be staffed 'by the zealous members of the order',
that is, the State was to be absorbed from the inside. In this way the
Illuminati would be able to accomplish 'still more', they said, 'than
if the prince himself were a member of the order'.[15] Once the order
held all key positions — in Bavaria they thought that six hundred
members would suffice — than it would 'have gained enough
power . . . to be able, if it so chooses, in a given place, to become
terribly dangerous to those who do not co-operate'.[16] The State is
run from the moral inner space, and the rule of freedom is thereby
protected. At this point the order 'no longer has to fear the government, but on the contrary it holds the government in its hands'.

The phase in which the secret society appeared not only as the
potential but as the actual opponent of the Absolutist State (the
pseudonyms of the Illuminati were referred to as 'noms de
guerre')[17] had been reached. Imperceptibly, the weight and significance of the arcanum shifted into the purely political sphere. Its
protective function became identical with the purely political function of camouflaging the occupation of the State.

Yet in this phase too, the separation of politics and morality
which had already been established within the framework of the
Absolutist State was not discarded. Rather, despite the indisputably
political function of the arcanum, the hypostatised separation of the
two spheres was taken over and intensified. Even apart from the
rather ridiculous and pompous air of von Knigge, who predicted

'to pronounce final judgment over the honesty and usefulness of an individual', the
sort of final judgment they already exercised within the order (Utzschneider, *Drey
merkwürdige Aussagen*, 15).

14. *Schreiben an den Herrn Hofkammerrath*, and *Instruktion für die Oberen*, 88.

15. *Nachtrag von weiteren Originalschriften*, II, 32. Without publicly announcing
the logical consequence (namely, the taking control of the state) the action itself, the
chanelling of Masons into positions of influence, was called the keystone of the 1744
programme in *Secret*, 18.

16. *Nachtrag*, II, 30ff.

17. See Lennhoff, *Politische Geheimbünde*, 25.

that the order would rule the world, and the reticent immodesty that prompted Weishaupt to call himself the modern-day 'Spartacus' — moral dualism proved to be a specific reply to the Absolutist State, a thought process related to indirect action designed to make possible and legitimise the silent conquest of that State.

The conditions for the indirect approach to the seizure of power initially lay in the feeble basis of the new society. The Illuminati, or 'Perfectibilists', as they first called themselves, branched out through Central Europe, with enthusiastic plans for universal happiness and morality. They were zealous in the propagation of these goals, but their actual power to realise them, compared to the power concentrated in the hands of the Absolutist princes, was infinitesimal. 'Making something out of nothing', proclaimed the profound Weishaupt, 'is the masterful accomplishment of politics joined to morality.'[18] Absolutist rule, the greatest obstacle to the realisation of morality and the one that compelled the society to organise secretly could not be eliminated directly. Power was not to be set against power, neither was force to be met by force; on the contrary, the Illuminati called all violent reform reprehensible. The sphere of open political discussion was, however, avoided not only in fact, but also, despite all activist plans, in theory as well. The original response to the Absolutist State turned into a way of thinking that was to remain unpolitical. In the event, anti-statist in origin and intent, the Illuminati retained an apolitical stance. However, it was precisely this which formed the basis for the notion of the indirect assumption of power, which presupposed a non-political position. The sense of powerlessness that was behind the founding of the order combined with a moral innocence and vision that, according to its members, could be found only within it. Thus the brethren, internally untainted by any sort of violence, represented the 'highest and most universal purposes' of mankind, and were 'therefore also able clearly to define the limits and concepts of right and wrong'.[19]

Political powerlessness not only led them to conclude that they possessed a deeper insight and were morally superior; they did not hesitate to demand that these virtues guide the framing of laws. The Illuminati, standing outside the State, also believed they were entitled to stand above it. As with all Masons who sought to impose a

18. *Nachtrag*, II, 46.
19. [Bode?], *Gedanken*, 27.

new governing authority above the various State governments, this conviction originated with the separation of morality and politics; it made possible the inverse logic whereby the most profound power-lessness could lead to the highest plane. By way of the separation of morality and politics the Masons arrived at the stage that endowed them with the moral qualification of political authority. Paradoxi-cally, their claim to political legitimacy grew out of moral inno-cence. That is why the precondition of indirect action, its 'non-political' character, was incorporated into their actual activity.

Without ostensibly encroaching on the State, claim the Illuminati in their guileless naivety, they 'deprive the activities of the State and the Church of their most able minds and workers and . . . thereby undermine the state, even though that is not their immediate purpose'.[20] Beyond its legitimacy, the merely moral purpose also brings the assurance that the requisite action will also be carried out in all good faith. The 'goal' of the moral planners is not the overthrow of the State, yet the State collapses none the less. This makes the political success merely incidental.[21]

So great was the Illuminati's moral sense of self, that is, the abstraction of the political element from the indirect assumption of power, that they believed they could eliminate the state not only here and now, but altogether. As a consequence of their political legitimacy morality becomes an 'art that teaches men to make princes and States dispensible'.[22] This not only serves to hide the political plans, but conceals the fact that these plans are themselves *political*. This concealment proves to be the historical implication of the fight against the sovereign Absolutist State. Within the frame-work of dualistic self-understanding the original camouflage shields the political aspect for the agents as well.

The fact that the choice between the ruling claim of the new society and the rule of the State, which assumed the air of a battle between good and evil, was a political choice thus remained hidden in a double sense: first through the secret, which the State failed to recognise as such. Between the political impotence of the new society and the power it aspires to, the secret is at work. It is the other side of the Enlightenment, and in Germany the Illuminati

20. *Nachtrag*, II, 115.
21. Gaining 'power' was only a 'secondary objective' (*Einige Originalschriften*, 215). See also Chapter 9 below.
22. *Nachtrag*, II, 96.

were the most fervent champions of the Enlightenment. Second, the separation of morality and politics also hides the decisive political question from the society. The internal and fundamental precondition for anti-state activity, namely the moral distancing from politics, becomes transformed into the ostensibly non-political basis of the fight against Absolutism.

The shift towards the political sphere, which, given the moral dualism involved, is also not a shift, thus contained a specific dialectic. The concealment of political action against the State is identical with the growing polemical intensification of the antithesis of State and society. Morally the conflict intensifies but politically it is covered over. This dialectic is part of the dialectic of crisis. It was inherent in the moral antitheses from the beginning of the dispute between State and society: the critical process forced it and the indirect taking of power accelerated it. Under its sign the Absolutist State was destroyed.

The growing importance of the new elite demanded a new political form. On the plane both of the *Règne de la Critique* and of the lodges the bourgeoisie used indirect political methods to bring about a new order.

The emergent society involved the existing State in a dualistic process by remaining aloof from it while at the same time passing moral judgement on it and, as secret executor, seeking to carry out that verdict. The process was moving towards resolution. 'Still', wrote Wieland in his *Secret of the Cosmopolitan Order*, 'the largest and loveliest part of Europe is subjected to a pressure that throttles the noblest forces of mankind . . . Still there are States where instead of universal reason shortsightedness and the arbitrary will of an individual . . . are often the source of law.' The political choice between State and society was inescapable but it had not yet been made. The tension was turning into crisis. 'What has already happened in this respect in the course of our century is known. What is still to happen will perhaps be decided before its end and will have significant consequences. And we can be certain that in all this, the Cosmopolitans will not be idle spectators.'[23]

23. Wieland, *Gesammelte Schriften*, I, 15, 224. In this context, Wieland offers a good description of the new elite which stands apart from the State so as to allow it to attack the State indirectly with greater assurance and deliberateness. The Republic of Letters is 'completely independent of the State . . . so long as it does not act against its principles'. By formally accepting the State, the Cosmopolitans remove themselves from it. 'The Cosmopolitan obeys all laws of the State in which he lives whose

The seeming impartiality of the Cosmopolitans, Wieland assures us, will suddenly become overtly partisan once the issue turns into promoting the 'good cause', and through this they will truly 'make a difference'[24] in bringing about the moral decision through political means as well.

Wieland's prediction was influenced by events in France in 1787, the Assembly of Notables and the imminent convocation of the States General. Yet he was simultaneously taking a stand in the great debate sparked off in Germany by the ban of the Illuminati in 1784. Both developments, the political in France and the organisational in Germany, were acute symptoms of the looming political crisis that closed the eighteenth century without however coming to an end itself.

---

wisdom, justice and value to the community is obvious; as citizen of the world he obeys the remaining ones out of necessity.' This necessity, however, is circumvented, and so the Cosmopolitan, after standing apart from the State, indirectly turns against it. The example of freedom of the press demonstrates this. 'Writings that contain direct insults of individually named or clearly identified persons which are prohibited or taboo in civil law — writings that specifically seek to incite to revolt against lawful authority — writings that are specifically directed against the legal foundation of the State — writings that work specifically towards the overthrow of all religion, morality and civic order — all such writings are undoubtedly as punishable in all nations as high treason, theft, assassination, and so forth. Furthermore, the word "direct" or "specific" is not used idly here; it is so important that the culpability of an indicted publication rests entirely upon it' (ibid., 227). These passages are among the few in which by a spokesman of the Republic of Letters the indirect mode of attack is openly and unambiguously called by name.

24. Ibid., 15, 221. 'Furthermore, the apparent neutrality of the Cosmopolitans in most cases where the State is divided into parties is mere indifference . . . I know of only two instances in which the Cosmopolitans sided with one party against another one.' (In the specific situation which Wieland has in mind the King formed 'one' party and the Notables or the Paris *Parlement*, that is the recently convened but not yet sitting National Assembly, the other.)

CHAPTER 8

The Process of Criticism
(Schiller, Simon, Bayle, Voltaire, Diderot and the 'Encyclopédie', Kant)

The stages of the indirect assumption of power recorded in the annals of the lodge followed the analogous pattern of the Republic of Letters. The social integration of the bourgeois elite in the lodges paralleled the active anti-State litigation in the republic of Letters, litigation which raised and attempted to settle questions of guilt. We find a clear road leading from self-defence to ruling claim, a course that sheds light on the historical significance of the separation of internal and external. If the line drawn between morality and politics was the precondition and expression of the indirect assumption of power, we now find that this very drawing of lines formed the basis of the ostensibly non-political criticism. Just as the Masons, by virtue of the secret, kept aloof from the State, initially in order to elude its influence but later in order, through that very separation, to occupy the State seemingly non-politically, so criticism initially kept aloof from the State so that later, through that very separation it could, seemingly neutrally, extend its reach to the State and subject it to its judgement. Criticism, as we shall see, became the victim of its ostensible neutrality; it turned into hypocrisy.

'The jurisdiction of the stage begins at the point where the sphere of secular laws ends.'[1] Thus Friedrich Schiller in an address to the Palatinate German Society at Mannheim in the summer of 1784 in connection with the question of the moral role of the legitimate

---

1. Schiller, *Sämtliche Werke*, XI, 91.

theatre. Both the theme and the question were in the tradition of eighteenth-century art and dramatic criticism, from Pope's *Essay on Criticism* through Diderot's *l'art pour la morale* to Lessing's *Hamburgische Dramaturgie*.

Schiller's answer — though he was to go further — takes its place alongside these predecessors. Its succinct conclusion states that it was the task of the stage to prepare man for *one* specific emotion, that of 'being human'.[2] The simplicity and clarity of this answer — to which we shall return — is based on a similarly simple and unambiguous antithesis which contrasts existing laws with the new, dramatic jurisdiction acting in the name of human feelings. Schiller draws a conceptual line between the two areas carefully and in such a way as to equate the end of secular laws with the beginning of the new justice. 'It punishes a thousand vices which [secular justice] tolerates with impunity while a thousand virtues kept secret by the latter are acclaimed by the stage.'[3] This is an assertion of mutual exclusion: the Yes on the one side is tantamount to the No on the other, and vice versa. At the same time, the counterpoint makes for the promising conclusion that the actual and spatial conception — the boundary line between stage and State — should also be conceived of temporally: as the replacement of the old jurisdiction by a new, more just dispensation of justice.

This conceptual dualism put Schiller squarely within the framework of his predecessors. Lessing furnished the immediate model when he defended himself against the charge of glorifying vice on the stage. At the opening of the Hamburg Theatre, he had asked:

> If he whom no law punishes or can punish
> The sly wrongdoer, the bloody tyrant,
> If he oppresses innocence, who dares protect it?
> Who? The one who now wields the dagger, the lash,
> Intrepid art . . .[4]

Proclamations of this sort were not apparently confined to the world of the theatre, nor were they an expression of aesthetic concerns; rather, art emerged as the antithesis of contemporary government, a manifestation of the eighteenth-century intellectual

---

2. Ibid., 100.
3. Ibid., 92.
4. Lessing, *Sämtliche Schriten*, IX, 207, 311.

structure which turned the world into a stage of opposing forces.

The series of concepts and counter-concepts that mark the literature of the Enlightenment and its countervailing forces, such as
reason and Revelation, freedom and despotism, nature and civilisation, trade and war, morality and politics, decadence and progress,
light and darkness, can be extended at will without the postulated
concepts losing the characteristic of simultaneously embracing and
excluding their opposites.

Thus Schiller sees the jurisdiction of the stage as being in a
reciprocal relationship to secular laws. 'Precisely this inadequacy,
this precarious nature of political laws,' he asserts, 'determines . . .
the moral influence of the stage.'[5] Its moral jurisdiction is the result
of inadequate political laws, its judgement provoked by politics, just
as on the other hand the inadequacy of political laws first becomes
apparent on the stage. 'Only here do the great men of the world get
to hear' what in their role as politicians they 'never or only rarely
get to hear — truth; that which they never or only rarely get to see
they can see here — man.'[6] The jurisdiction of morality shows them
what their laws really are: they rotate only around negating
duties . . . are smooth and sleek, changeable like moods and
passions'.[7] Thus, in our example, the concept of secular laws is
derived from morality, just as morality is 'determined' via negation
by the politics it seeks to interpret. Not only do moral and political
law confront one another; the political law is at the same time
immoral, just as the moral law is politically 'impotent', and as such
has nothing to do with the prevailing politics. Schiller believes that
the jurisdiction of the secular law does in fact obtain, but unjustly
so, whereas the jurisdiction of the stage does not, although it has
right on its side.

For Schiller the stage is a place of moral jurisdiction where, in
majestic splendour, 'truth incorruptible like Rhadamanthus sits in
judgement',[8] but at the same time moral jurisdiction finds itself in a
dialectical tension because of the division of reality into a sphere of
morality and a sphere of politics. Both phenomena — the moral

5. Schiller, *Sämtliche Werke*, 90.
6. Ibid., 95.
7. Ibid., 90. On Schiller's pejorative use of the term 'political', see his letter to
Dalberg, in which he complains about the 'gentlemen actors' who, in an effort to
undermine him, had maliciously — with 'political cunning' — given a poor performance of his *Kabale und Liebe*.
8. Ibid., 91.

stage and its dialectical relationship to existing laws — show the same political condition, namely, political crisis.

The moral stage provides an exalted view of a world divided into beauty and fear in order to subject politics to its criticism. The stage becomes a tribunal. Its verdict divides the world into two parts by presenting and making tangible the dominant dualisms of the century, 'vice and virtue, happiness and misery, foolishness and wisdom in a thousand guises, and parading them before mankind'. It separates the just from the unjust and in the course of this separation the 'mighty' and 'the rulers,' whose 'justice is blinded by gold and revels in the pay of vice' are vanquished by the more just verdict of the stage. At the point at which the dualistically segregated dominant politics are subjected to a moral verdict, that verdict is transformed into a political factor; into political criticism. From a strictly moral perspective the dualistic play is nothing more than a verdict, but really it is also a criticism of the State evading and failing to execute that verdict. Thus, the dualistic world-view serves and is a function of political criticism.

On the other hand, the division of historical reality into spheres of morality and politics, such as Absolutism accepted, formed the basis of criticism. The stage's moral competence to judge is assured only if it can evade the reach of the secular law. While for Schiller politics 'came to a halt' at the apron of the moral stage, the secular law gave the stage the freedom to become the 'common channel through which the light filters down to the thoughtful, superior portion of the nation'.[9] The light then spreads throughout the State, the stage having kept itself apart so as to be free to subject the state to criticism. Moral art and the sovereign State are pitted against each other to allow the stage to play its part, that of political criticism. In the absence of its own jurisdiction, art takes up 'dagger and lash', or, in Schiller's words, 'sword and scales', forcing the vices of politics to appear 'before the terrible judgement seat'[10] of the separate sphere of the moral stage. The individual, separate jurisdiction of the theatre was conceivable only if administered outside the existing laws, and that meant, so long as it was not effective, that it encompassed criticism of the existing State.

Hence political criticism was contained not only in the moral

9. Ibid., 97.
10. Ibid., 91.

judgement as such but also in the effected separation of moral and political jurisdiction: the moral tribunal became political criticism not only by subjecting politics to its stern judgement, but vice versa as well, by separating itself as a tribunal from the political sphere. This removal already presaged criticism of the State. The stage, by consolidating itself as an independent jurisdiction and positing itself against secular laws, exercised its criticism of the State more incisively and strongly than through the individual verdicts it proclaimed. The dualism of politics and morality in Schiller's assertion thus serves apolitical criticism, yet simultaneously it forms the basis of that criticism. Political criticism is based on this division and is at the same time responsible for it.

This constitutes a genuinely historical-dialectical fact and forms the basis of the political significance of the criticism that gave its name to the eighteenth century.[11] In its historicity the dualistic division of the world into a sphere of morality and a sphere of politics is the precondition and consequence of political criticism. Criticism thus appears not only where it is explicitly voiced; it is the basis of the dualistic world-view that marked that era. The mutual polarisation of all eighteenth-century concepts is given meaning and inner cohesion by the critical function inherent in all dualisms as, conversely, the political criticism could be based only on an historical reality in which morality and politics were separated. Absolutism, which consciously separated the two spheres, gave rise to a criticism which by polemicising about an established situation found the appropriate response to Absolutism.

Schiller's response comes at the end of a long critical process launched by the intellectual stratum of the emergent society against the State. He saw the stage as a social institution that enabled him to subject that 'peculiar group of people',[12] the politicians, to its judgement. 'We must live with these wicked men, these fools',

---

11. 'Criticism' is an eighteenth-century catchword. There are countless volumes with the term 'criticism' or 'critical' in their titles. In 1790, J.G. Buhle, in Göttingen, had this to say on the subject: 'Our age deserves credit to have examined . . . explained and enlightened more critically than previous ages; therefore some have rightly called ours the *critical* age' (*Grundzüge einer allgemeinen Encyklopädie der Wissenschaften*, Lemgo, 1790, p. 39). This contemporary characterisation alone leads to the assumption that the significance of criticism went far beyond the world of learning. The term 'crisis' on the other hand was rarely used in the eighteenth century and certainly cannot be considered a central concept. This fact is not a statistical fortuity; rather there is a specific connection between it and the ascendancy of criticism, a link which this study hopes to illuminate.
12. Schiller, *Sämtliche Werke*, 95.

Schiller exclaimed. But merely unmasking them was not enough; the critical judgements had to be a call to action: 'We must evade them or meet them, we must undermine them or be vanquished by them'.[13] Does the Absolutist State still rule? Or has the new society been victorious? That is the question that arises here. The indirect stance no longer suffices. The critical process is coming to an end. A decision is unavoidable but has not yet been arrived at. The crisis is manifest — it lies hidden in the criticism. But a closer examination of this relationship calls for an analysis of the critical process itself.

It is inherent in the concept of criticism that through it a separation takes place. Criticism is the art of judging; its function calls for testing a given circumstance for its validity or truth, its rightness or beauty, so as to arrive at a judgement based on the insight won, a judgement that extends to persons as well.[14] In the course of criticism the true is separated from the false, the genuine from the spurious, the beautiful from the ugly, right from wrong. 'Criticism'[15] is the art of judging, and the discrimination connected with it

---

13. Ibid.

14. This holds true for the German, English, and French languages. Cf. J. and W. Grimm, *Deutsches Worterbuch*, Leipzig, 1873; J. Murray, *A New English Diction ary*, Oxford, 1888; and Littré, *Dictionnaire de la Langue française*, 1877. The three subsequent notes are in part based on these dictionaries.

15. The word 'criticism' (French *critique*, German *Kritik*) and the word 'crisis' (French *crise*, German *Krise*), both derive from the Greek κρίνω: to differentiate, select, judge, decide; Med.: to take measure, dispute, fight. (The same root, cri–, is found in the Latin *cerno* and *cribrum*, Fr. *crible*: sieve). The Greek usage of κρίνω and κρίσις generally, even if not originally, referred to jurisprudence and the judicial system. 'Crisis' meant discrimination and dispute, but also decision, in the sense of final judgement or appraisal, which today falls into the category of criticism. In Greek, a single concept encompassed today's distinctive meanings of 'subjective' criticism and 'objective' crisis. As judgement, trial and general tribunal, the word κρίσις was used forensically. Thus 'pro and con' were originally contained in the word 'crisis' and the decision was also implicit. When the judge's decision specifically is meant, the term ἀρχὴ κριτικὴ carries the sense of creating order, as Aristotle used it (*Pol.* 1253a; 1275a, b; 1326b). The sovereign and legal order of a community depends on the just decision of the judge. Only he who participates in the office of judge (ἀρχή) is a citizen. The adjectival form κριτικός dating back to Plato refers to this ability and art of judging, of decision-making and arriving at a judgement and, more generally, of the weighing of pro and con, to the 'critical' activity of judgement.

The Septuagint also uses the word κρίσις in the sense of the administration of justice and law which the ruler is called upon to protect and create (*Theologisches Wörterbuch zum Neuen Testament*, ed. G. Kittel, 2nd edn, Stuttgart, 1950). Through the covenant with Israel God proved that He was the true Lord and Judge; in John the word κρίσις takes on the meaning of the Last Judgement. The temporal structure of this judgement, which through Christ's appearance anticipated the still outstanding decision and already is experienced in the conscience of the believers, this meaning in secularised form, would become the accepted one in the eighteenth century. 'Crisis' would not be generally used. The expression 'criticism', of judging, of arriving at a judgement, became prevalent, while 'crisis' in the Greek sense of legal

on the basis of this its general meaning (which it already had in the eighteenth century) is obviously connected with the then prevalent dualistic world-view. This connection can be found in some of the critical documents. To understand the peculiar political significance of criticism in the eighteenth century it is necessary to show the evolution of the critical factor in its conflicting relationship with the State, and then to pursue the gradual development and the growing claim of the critical factor on this State. Such a procedure makes, at the same time, for a temporal classification.

In England and France the word group associated with the

---

order, or in the Christian sense of Judgement Day, disappeared. Based on Hippocrates and Galen's usage of the term ἡ κριτικὴ ἡμέρα, Latin also largely restricted the term 'crisis' to medical usage. The *Encyclopédie* considers this translation an historical fact of the past: 'Galien nous apprend que ce mot crise est un terme du barreau que les médecins ont adopté et qu'il signifie, à proprement parler, un jugement' (essay on 'Crise'). In Latin the crisis of a disease and the medical diagnosis are related concepts, while the concept of crisis is limited to the field of medicine. ('A medicis dicitur subita morbi mutatio novumque indicium, ex quo judicari potest, quid aegro futurum sit'; Forcinelli and Furlanetto, *Lexicon totius Latinitatis*, Patavii, 1940.) Cf. Augustinus 6 conf. I: 'Critica accessio morbi est, ex qua de sanitate aut morte aegrotantis judicium ferri potest'. However, the *criticus* is also — as already in the Greek — a *grammaticus* and art critic. In the Middle Ages the term 'crisis' was limited to medical usage, designating the crucial stage of a disease in which a decision had to be made but had not yet been reached. This is the sense in which the term is still used today.

'Criticism' however has moved away from the originally corresponding word 'crisis' and continues to refer to the art of judging and to discrimination, without implying the weightiness of a decision inherent in the theological, legal or medical sense of crisis. The adverbial and adjectival form 'critical' is of a different order, depending on whether it is used in the modifying sense of crisis or criticism. In 1702 an Englishman (Eng. Theophrast 5, quoted in Murray, *A New English Dictionary*) wrote: 'How strangely some words lose their primitive sense! By a Critick, was originally understood a good judge; with us nowadays it signifies no more than a Fault finder'; and Collier, in *The Great Historical, Geographical, Genealogical and Political Dictionary* (2nd edn, London, 1701) speaks of the presumptuous 'criticks' who made themselves suspect equally to all princes and learned men, Protestants as well as Catholics; in punishment they generally met a violent or ignominious death.

Zedler, who stood in the humanist tradition, in his *Grosses vollständiges Universal-Lexicon* (Halle and Leipzig, 1733) still assigns the same meaning to 'crisis' and 'critic'. Critic means 'judgement' and 'crisis' means 'judgement, reason, thought, therefore one says man has no Crisis, that is, he cannot judge anything'. However, Zedler also gives as the most common meaning of crisis the crucial turning point in a disease, and oddly enough only in the sense of a turning point on the road to recovery. 'Today one calls crisis that curative effect of nature through which the substance of the disease . . . is expelled from the body and the body is thereby freed from its decline and disease.' While Zedler was not yet familiar with the 'critic', his article on 'Critic' uncovers one of the roots of the hypocrisy to which eighteenth-century criticism had degenerated: 'Because criticism indirectly, though not through its direct activity, contributes greatly to true wisdom, still it has happened that the minds that apply themselves to it by taking its indirect effect as direct have fallen prey to great haughtiness, and this includes the office of judge that they have arrogated to themselves . . .'. This encompasses the theme of the century.

concept of criticism was incorporated into the national languages
from the Latin around 1600.[16] The terms *critique* and 'criticism'
(and also 'criticks') established themselves in the seventeenth century. What was meant by them was the art of objective evaluation
— particularly of ancient texts, but also of literature and art, as well
as of nations and individuals. The term was initially used by the
Humanists; it incorporated the meaning of judgement and learned
scholarship, and when the philological approach was expanded to
Holy Scripture, this process too was called 'criticism'. One could be
critical and Christian at the same time; the critical non-believer was
set apart by the sobriquet 'criticaster'.[17]

   Criticism still stood in the service of the religious parties. When
in 1678 Richard Simon published his *Histoire Critique du Vieux
Testament* he used the term 'critique', a term previously used only
by 'personnes scavantes', to describe his reading of the Bible.[18] He
owed both the term and the method to Cappelle, who in 1650, in his
Critica Sacra,[19] had made a comparative philological study of the
original text and translations of the Old Testament. Simon com-
mented that, as a Calvinist, Capelle was not properly aware of the
inevitable consequences of the new method, namely the erosion of
the Protestant principle of belief in Scripture. Simon used the
critical method to attack this fundamental of Protestantism in order

16. Grimm's dictionary calls the word group 'rather recent' in the German
language, stating that it entered the language only in the eighteenth century. While
J.C. Adelung's four-volume *Versuch eines vollständigen grammatischen kritischen
Wörterbuchs der Hochdeutschen Mundart* (Leipzig, 1774ff.) does not yet — or no
longer — contain the word 'crisis', it does list the new terms 'critic' and 'art critic'.
The latter makes a 'business' out of the appraisal of the works of others, and the
expression 'judge of language' and 'hairsplitter' were quite compatible with the
Greek κριτικός for the word is derived from *Kreet, Krit, Zank, Streit, Hader*, etc.
The word group became established in German in the classical era. In England the
usage of the word 'criticism' dates back to 1607; Bacon mentions the literary critic
(*Advancement of Learning*, I, VI, para. 21) and Hobbes uses the term in connection
with philological interpretation and textual comparison (*Works*, VII, 389ff.).
   17. In 1626 reference was made to a 'criticke Scholiast upon the Revelation'
(W. Sclater, *Expos. 2. Thess.*), in 1641 to 'learned and critical Christians' (J. Jackson,
True Evangelists, I, 69), in 1635 to the 'learned Divines and criticke Expositours'
(N. Carpenter, *Geog. Dch.*, II, v. 67). In 1684, after the publication of Spinoza's
Tractatus Theologico-Politicus, an English Bible publisher attacked 'some Jewish
Criticaster' (*N. S. Critical English Edition of the Bible*, VIII, 51). To this day, textual
criticism of Holy Scripture is referred to as 'higher criticism' (Murray, *A New
English Dictionary*).
   18. Richard Simon, *Histoire Critique du Vieux Testament par R.P. Rich. Simon*,
Paris, 1680, Preface.
   19. L. Cappelle, *Critica Sacra, sive de variis quae in sacris Veteris Testamenti libris
occurrunt lectionibus*, Paris, 1650.

to demonstrate the fortuities and overlappings in the Old Testament, to prove via this method the need for an ecclesiastic tradition. In doing so, he referred to the 'veritables Loix de la Critique' which, quite incomprehensibly, were disdained by the theologians but which had the great advantage of being 'claires et évidentes'. The rules governing criticism were unrelated to belief, he argued, together with Spinoza, and hence the Protestants must also abide by them.[20] This assertion put the new art of criticism into the service of the Church, but in fact Simon shifted the criterion of truth from Revelation to the sphere of the clear and rational — and for him this meant critical — thought. Because of this heretical view Simon suffered the same fate that befell his Calvinist adversary Cappelle among the Protestants:[21] the Church anathematised him. So long as the religious controversies dominated, the Humanist and Rational critics found themselves in the same common front as the politicians. The ecclesiastical authorities constituted yet another common opponent, even if viewed from slightly different vantage-points. Therefore, the critics often formed a personal union, like Bodin and Hobbes, who were considered outstanding both as Biblical critics and 'politicians'. Not until the confessional battles of the eighteenth century did the camps diverge: rational criticism also came to embrace the State.

The common reaction of the Churches accorded the term 'criticism' its polemical meaning also; particularly if only textual criticism was involved.[22] The concept was never again to lose this polemical connotation; it was to retain the same meaning throughout the following century.

---

20. Simon, *Histoire Critique du Vieux Testament*, Preface. It is a serious error of Protestants to believe that the Bible was 'claire d'elle mesme'; Therefore the Council of Trent rightly fell back on the tradition of the Church fathers, but it 'n'a pour cela deffendu aux particuliers de chercher d'antres explications lorsqu'il ne s'agit point de la créance. Au contraire . . .'. For that very reason, Simon feels justified in criticising those same fathers: 'Ceux qui recherchent la vérité en elle mesme et sans préoccupation ne s'arrestent point au nom des personnes ny à leur antiquité; principalement lorsqu'il ne s'agit point de la Foy'.

21. For ten years the Protestants successfully prevented the publication of Cappelle's major work until finally, through the intercession of the Oratorians, he was granted the court's permission to publish. He issued his *Critica Sacra* jointly with a pamphlet attacking Buxtorf Jr., *Criticae adversus injustum censorem just defensio*.

22. Protestants and Catholics were in agreement in their opposition to Biblical criticism, as were the two great opponents in the Catholic camp Bossuet, who referred to Simon's 'audacieuse critique', calling it the 'disease and temptation of our time', and Fénelon, who called it 'séditieuse', and consigned the vile critics to Tartarus

Thus, in the context of the textual criticism of Holy Scripture, and from out of the religious conflicts, a new front was formed, remarkable for the novel fact that the spokesmen of the warring Churches were confronted by a common enemy. The line that was drawn between reason and Revelation was of particular significance in the first half of the eighteenth century.[23] Simon, maintaining that the study of philological criticism was essential, 'si l'on veut avoir une connaissance parfaite de la Théologie', was referring to a principle that stood in fundamental contradiction to the idea of Revelation.[24] It was this — even though he was a priest — that made him a precursor of Pierre Bayle, whose *Dictionnaire Historique et Critique* (1695) was the arsenal from which the next generation drew its arms. If initially criticism was merely a symptom of the growing conflict between reason and Revelation, in Bayle it became the factor which divided the two areas.

It was in the literal sense of the term *critique* that Bayle also understood the textual work required for the elucidation of true form and true content. 'La critique est un travail périlleux; car si l'on ignore certains faits particuliers, toutes les autres connaissances n' empêchent pas qu'on ne juge mal des choses.'[25] For him *'la règne de la critique'*, the sphere dominated by the learned philologists, the grammarians of the ancient tongues and their translators, begins — as did art criticism for Pope[26] — with humanism, but in his day this took on an entirely different aspect. At that time, around 1700, heavy tomes were no longer the fashion: 'on s'est tourné vers la justesse du raisonnement, on a cultivé l'esprit beaucoup plus que la mémoire . . . on devient sensible au sens et à la raison plus qu'a tout

---

to suffer a fate worse than uxoricides and parricides — they are to be looked upon as 'que le vulgaire ne croit guère coupables, et que la vengeance divine poursuit impitoyablement' (*Oeuvres complètes*, Paris, 1850, VI, 521, *Télémaque*, I, XIV). 'These monsters, critics', exclaimed Pope in 1709. 'Where Heaven's free subjects might their rights dispute. Lest God Himself should seem too absolute'. He then went on to lecture them on their moral obligations as critics (Alexander Pope, *Collected Poems*, London, 1951, *An Essay on Criticism*, II, 545ff.).

23. In the period under discussion, the problematic age-old tension intensified into the dominant conflict in the world of letters. Cf. D. Mornet, *Les origines intellectuelles de la Révolution française*, Paris, 1933.

24. Richard Simon, *Histoire Critique du Texte du Nouveau Testament où l'on établit la Vérité des Actes sur lesquels la Religion Chrétienne est fondée*, Rotterdam, 1689, Preface.

25. B. Bayle, *Dictionnaire historique et critique*, Rotterdam, 1720, 3rd edn, 'Livineius', p. 1727 b.

26. Pope, *An Essay on Criticism*, 74ff. In Rome the critics for the first time exercised their just authority ('long succeeding critics justly reign'd').

le reste.'[27] By including all areas of human knowledge and history in the critical method and involving them in an infinite process of relativisation, Bayle turned criticism into the essential function of reason. In Bayle, reason forever weighed the *pour et contre* against one another and ran up against contradictions which gave rise to new contradictions; thus reason disintegrated, as it were, into a constant exercise of criticism. If criticism is the ostensible resting point of human thought, then thought becomes a restless exercise in movement.[28] Criticism is the activity that marks reason as a factor of judgement, a constant goad to the process of pro and con. The monumental achievement of Pierre Bayle was to wed the concept of criticism to that of reason.[29] Although in 1709 Vico asserted: 'A critica studia hodie inauguramur ... Etenim critica id nobis dat primum verum, de quo, vel cum dubitas, certus fias', he said this in order to defend himself against a critical approach that ignored probability and the *sensus communis*.[30]

Criticism was not confined to philological, aesthetic or historical concerns but became, more generally, the art of arriving at proper insights and conclusions via rational thought.[31] However, while thinking in terms of pro and con terms stretches to infinity, it tends to evade the aporias of thought. To that extent Kant was the first to bring the Enlightenment process to an end. Until criticism turned

27. Bayle, *Dictionnaire*, 'Alegambe', 155 b; 'Acontius', 66 a. Bayle here deals with the widely discussed question of whether his age was one of decadence or progress. Whereas Simon's criticism leads him to conclude that the present was vastly superior to the past, Bayle expresses scepticism on this as well as on other questions, even though he does admit that progress had been made in the sciences. Today, he said, the world was 'moins savant' but 'plus raisonnable'. Voltaire was to take this up again in the *Encyclopédie* ('Gens de lettres'); among the critics learning has been replaced by the 'esprit philosophique' that permeates all layers of society.

28. 'La raison humaine ... est un principe de destruction, et non pas d'édification: elle n'est propre qu'à former des doutes, et à se tourner à droite et à gauche pour éterniser une dispute ... ' (Bayle, *Dictionnaire*, 'Manichéens', 1900).

29. In the eighteenth century 'critical' and 'rational' were often used interchangeably. Reason becomes a critical process of the search for truth. Cf. Ernst Cassirer, *The Philosophy of the Enlightenment*, trans. F.C. Koelln and J.P. Pettegrove, Princeton, NJ, 1951, 13: 'The whole eighteenth century understands reason in this sense; not as a sound body of knowledge, principles, and truths, but as a kind of energy, a force which is fully comprehensible only in its agency and effects'.

30. Vico, *De nostri Temporis studiorum Ratione* (1709), Godesberg 1947, 20, 26.

31. Criticism as the general medium in the search for truth is often coupled with logic (as in Diderot, *Oeuvres*, III, 465, 1775). This use of 'criticism' to denote methods of developing laws of beauty, their recognition or production — Cassirer even goes so far as to subsume the 'age of criticism' under the aspect of 'basic problems of esthetics' — is characteristic for the genesis of the bourgeois sense of self. Philosophy and art criticism entered into a personal union (Cassirer, *The Philosophy of the Enlightenment*, p. 368).

against reason itself it continued to issue IOUs against the future.

Tracking down the contradictions could alone lead to the discovery of the incontrovertible truth. This is why Pierre Bayle said that a critic 'montre . . . ce que l'on peut dire pour et contre les Auteurs: il soutient successivement le personnage d'un Avocat demandeur, et d'un Avocat défendeur'.[32] It is precisely this dual role of defender and prosecutor that turns the critic into a non-partisan authority, into the advocate of reason. 'Le seul nom même de party m'étant odieux,' said Simon,[33] 'je n'ay aucun interest particulier qui m'engage dans ce qu'on appelle party'. The critic stands above the parties; his task is not to 'destroy' but to 'establish' the truth. He enters into competition with a rational State that sets itself above the religious groupings. Not that he creates a new order here and now; the reign of criticism is non-partisan only in an infinite process of renewal. Thus Bayle's critic also knows only one obligation: his duty towards a future in which truth is found only through the exercise of criticism. The claim to impartiality propelled the process to the same extent that its end was still not in sight. The self-assurance of criticism lay in the connection of the critic to the yet-to-be-discovered truth. Every error discovered, every hurdle overcome reveals fresh obstacles; thus the human compulsion to unravel finds ever more subtle methods to seize on evil and do away with the continuous flow of confusion, until finally there is nothing left for reason to do.[34] Criticism transformed the future into a maelstrom that sucked out the present from under the feet of the critic. In these circumstances there was nothing left for the critic but to see progress as the temporal structure appropriate to his way of life. Progress became the *modus vivendi* of criticism even when — as in Bayle — it was not deemed a forward movement but one of

32. Bayle, *Dictionnaire*, 'Archelaus', 290 b.
33. Simon, *Histoire Critique du Nouveau Testament*, Preface. Pope, who sought to fix criticism to its 'true purpose' by examining 'unerring Nature' sees 'partisanship' as the root of all evil, being an obstacle to natural criticism, while the traditional partisan divisions among the learned would attend to those in the State (Pope, *An Essay on Criticism*, 69).
34. 'En un mot, le sort de l'homme est dans une si mauvaise situation, que le lumières qui le délivrent d'un mal le précipitent dans un autre. Chassez l'ignorance et la barbarie, vous faites tomber les superstitions, et la sote crédulité du peuple si fructueuse à ses conducteurs, qui abusent après cela de leur gain pour se plonger dans l'oisiveté, et dans la débauche: mais en éclairant les hommes sur ces désordres, vous leur inspirez l'envie d'examiner tout, ils épluchent, et ils subtilisent tant, qu'ils ne trouvent rien qui contente leur misérable raison' (Bayle, *Dictionnaire*, 'Takiddin', 2688A).

destruction and decadence.

In every instance the self-made link to the future enabled the rational judge to become a critic of the present. It made available a sphere of absolute freedom in the present to the executor of criticism.

> C'est la liberté, qui règne dans la République des Lettres. Cette République est un état extrêmement libre. On n'y reconoit que l'empire de la vérité et de la raison; et sous leurs auspices on fait la guerre innocement à qui que ce soit. Les amis s'y doivent tenir en garde contre leurs amis, les pères contre leurs enfants, les beaux-pères contre leurs gendres: c'est comme en siècle de fer;
>
> > Non hospes ab hospite tutus
> > non socer a genero.
>
> Chacun y est tout ensemble souverain, et justiciable de chacun.[35]

The critical process for seeking out the truth can be set in motion only under conditions of absolute freedom. In the Republic of Letters everyone is therefore the master of all and subject to the judgement of all. The civil war that unexpectedly did away with the State reappears; and, moreover, in that private inner realm which the State had to grant man as man. There, absolute freedom, the *bellum omnium contra omnes*, reigns; truth is the common goal of all, and criticism — which all engage in and to which all are subject — is the true sovereign in the spiritual conflict. Sovereignty rules relentlessly, and all share in it. Bayle's Republic of Letters, extended to the State, is the total democracy which Rosseau conceived of half a century later.[36] It provides the model of a form of government in which civil war, even if only one of minds, has legitimacy and is the basis of legitimacy.

No obligations exist, for truth will emerge only in the struggle of the critics among themselves. A truth that will not appear until tomorrow absolves the critic of all guilt today. And so the critic, while engaged in his task, wins freedom, absolution from guilt and a part in a forward-looking, non-partisan sovereignty. Beginning with Bayle, this construct explains the important role criticism, (including political criticism) was to play throughout the remainder of the eighteenth century.

To understand the historical significance of criticism one must

---

35. Ibid., 'Catius', 812, a, b.
36. Cf. A. Cochin, *La Révolution et la libre-pensée*, Paris, 1924, 76ff.

also look at its obverse side — the process of pro and con, in the course of which criticism first established its sovereignty. Even though the sceptic Bayle did not believe that the critical function of reason had brought a clear-cut, final answer, in the course of the critical separations a firm boundary line had none the less been drawn: that is, there exists no common ground between reason, religion and revelation. This postulate of Bayle's drew a line which in future made it easier to subject religious belief and Revelation itself to criticism, and thus criticism of institutionalised religion. The judicial function of reason was, on the one hand, based on this delimitation of religion, yet at the same time it instituted this separation so as to criticise religion itself. On the basis of this separation Bayle was convinced of the ultimate absolute dominance of universal critical reason over all types of dualistically separated religions. 'One must necessarily arrive at the conclusion that every single dogma, whether offered as being part of Holy Scripture or otherwise postulated, is false if it is contradicted by clear and distinct rational perceptions, particularly where it concerns matters of morality . . .'.[37]

The spheres of reason and religion were critically separated precisely so as to assure the rule of reason and the pre-eminence of morality over religion. On the other hand, Bayle set another and different limit on those passing judgement, which could not be overstepped, a limit that rational criticism, precisely because it is rational, cannot overstep. This is the boundary line of the State. Regardless of whether a State rules justly or unjustly, it is a crime to rise up against it. 'Tout ce que l'on peut opposer à son injustice, c'est la raison, la soumission, la retraite.'[38] As in Hobbes, reason here still yearns for submission; it proposes turning inward, for there exists no authority able to arbitrate between the State and the individual. Reason, inwardly critical, remains externally loyal to the State.

Pierre Bayle was well aware of the dialectic of a civil war that forced man to a decision against his conscience and his better

---

37. Bayle, *Commentaire philosophique*, Part. I, 2, cited in Hazard, *La Crise*, 136.
38. Bayle, *Oeuvres*, 4 vols., The Hague, 1737, II, 594. This statement comes from *Avis important aux réfugiés sur leur prochain retour en France*, an anonymous pamphlet which Bayle claimed to have written; quoted in R. Raymond, *Pierre Bayle*, Paris, 1948, 218. See also the essay 'Aureolus', I, 399, Note B, in which Bayle discusses the topics State and progress (see Excursus, 186–8 below). Like Hobbes and Spinoza, he still regarded the State as a manifestation of reason, without however considering 'politics' to be a 'rational' thing. 'Le desordre est inevitable dans la Politique', but, 'c'est vain qu'on en chercheroit le remede' ('Bourgogne', 639 b).

judgement. And he clung to this awareness while living in exile. One hopes in vain, he remarked, to get away from the warring camps so as to maintain one's neutrality. In the past one had friends and enemies; now there are only enemies, no friends. 'Sort déplorable de l'homme, vanité manifeste de la raison philosophique.' It was the particular delusion of rational philosophy to believe that its continuing quest for objectivity and neutrality could stealthily be injected into the reluctant world of politics. Certainly forward-looking minds are needed, but they should confine themselves to matters spiritual and intellectual. Once progress enters the world of politics the evils of the civil war that would erupt were certain to be greater than the evils it had hoped to eradicate. Bayle said he wished to be spared the 'terrible benefits' of a civil war. Against the background of that experience, which had its firm roots in the seventeenth century, Bayle drew a sharp distinction between 'critique' on the one hand and 'satires' and 'libelles diffamatoires' on the other. He drew a clear line of demarcation between the judging role of criticism and the political jurisdiction of the State. Within the Republic of Letters the unpolitical quest for truth reigns. In the fight against ignorance and error all means are legitimate:

> Tous les particuliers ont à cet égard le droit du glaive, et le peuvent exercer sans en demander la permission à ceux qui gouvernent. Il est bien aise de connoître pourquoi la Puissance Souveraine a dû laisser à chacun le droit d'écrire contre les auteurs qui se trompent, mais non pas celui de publier des Satires. C'est que les Satires tendent à dépouiller un homme de son honneur, ce qui est une espèce d'homicide civil et, par conséquent, une peine, qui ne doit être infligée que par le Souverain; mais le Critique d'un livre ne tend qu'à montrer qu'un Auteur n'a pas tel et tel dégré de lumière . . . On n'usurpe rien de ce qui dépend de la Majesté de l'État, en faisant connoître au public les fautes qui sont dans un livre.[39]

In making perception its goal, criticism consciously limits its reach to the sphere of human knowledge; man, as 'honnête homme', as 'bon sujet de la République', is not subject to its verdict; he remains the subject of the State. Bayle thus consciously excludes the sphere of criticism from the sphere of the State in order to safeguard the internal laws of criticism within the Republic of Letters. Criticism claims to be non-political; it does not impinge on the State yet it is also not subject to the State. Bayle sees a parallel course: in

39. Bayle, *Dictionnaire*, 'Catius', 812 a, b.

criticism's total claim that all domains of reason be subjected to its judgement and, simultaneously, to its decision, based on an intellectual perception of legitimacy, to refrain from intruding on the political sphere of the State. Bayle himself may have seen the function of criticism as purely 'intellectual' and non-political — considering that his criticism was directed primarily against religious fanaticism — but in fact he consciously completed the crucial separation of the *Règne de la Critique* and the rule of the State which was to lay the groundwork for political criticism. This development becomes clear with Voltaire, who transcended Bayle's experiential horizon.

Voltaire — in agreement with Bayle — also made reference, in 1733, to the difference between 'la critique, la satire et la libelle' to underscore the non-political nature of his criticism. He was engaged in art criticism, but he knew, he felt constrained to point out, 'que les politiques ont regardé cette innocent plaisanterie du Temple du Goût comme un grave attentat'.[40] Having excluded the sphere of criticism from the State, Voltaire made reference to that very separation to overstep, as innocently as Bayle had done, completely 'unpolitically' and 'intellectually', the line dividing it from politics. By engaging in literary, aesthetic and historical criticism Voltaire indirectly criticised Church and State. And with this his criticism took on political significance and, moreover, a quite specific significance, based on the concept of criticism and the corresponding dualistic world.

If initially the belief in Revelation was the central counter-idea of reason, morality and nature, the shift of criticism to the 'sphere of secular laws' was all that was needed further to politicise the intellectual fronts that had opened up. The alliance between reason and the existing State had disintegrated. The policies of the Absolutist States increasingly became the common counterpoint of all dualistic positions. The ruling policies became involved in the critical process. With this, the pro and con of criticism, which had followed its non-political course within the Republic of Letters, turned into a trial between the *Règne de la Critique* and the rule of the State. In this trial the critic was simultaneously prosecutor, supreme judge and interested party. By appealing to the non-partisan sovereignty of criticism but at the same time involving

40. Voltaire, *Oeuvres*, VIII, 551f.

politics in the proceedings, the critics stood above the parties by virtue of their criticism, but as critics of the State they became partisan. Of course, by assuming a superior air, it was always possible to deny partisanship. Intellectual criticism, based on the separation of the non-political Republic of Letters and the political State, now took refuge in this separation and at the same time broadened it so as to extend its intellectual judgement — ostensibly neutral and in the name of impartial truth — to the State as well. Initially, that very criticism was the means used to overstep the self-drawn line between the Republic of Letters and the State. Criticism set itself apart from the State as non-political yet subjected it to its judgement. Therein lay the root of the ambivalence of criticism, an ambivalence that after Voltaire became its historical bench-mark: ostensibly non-political and above politics, it was in fact political.[41]

Criticism was the tenth Muse who had finally come, said Voltaire in 1765, to rid the world of unreason. 'La critique a du bon; je l'aime et je l'honore. Le parterre éclairé juge les combattants, et la saine raison triomphe avec le temps.'[42] Social criticism was still a serviceable weapon for the combatants sitting in the orchestra, who were in league with the actors of the morality play being performed on stage. However, it was at the same time the weapon of those whose criticism — by way of art — encompassed the State. *The Marriage of Figaro* celebrated the union of art and political criticism. Criticism alone was to bring the triumph of reason. Thus it left its earlier designated sphere of art and science and, after Voltaire, the former objects of criticism became the weapons of political criticism.[43]

---

41. On the one hand, Voltaire repeatedly hints that he is offering up a work that 'is saying more than it seems to be saying' — as in his invective against the existing order in the Foreword to *Zadig* (ibid., XXI, 32); and, on the other hand, he is eager to assure the reader of the worth, innocence, and harmlessness of the criticism, as in his essay 'Gens de lettres', in the *Encyclopédie*. He concurs with Bayle that philological criticism no longer seems a necessity; rather, contemporary critics were 'une partie devenue nécessaire . . . leur critique ne s'est plus consumée sur des morts grecs et latins, mais appuyée d'une saine philosophie, elle a détruit tous les préjugés dont la société etait infectée . . . par là ils ont en effet, servi l'État. On est quelquefois étonné que ce qui bouleversait autrefois le monde, ne le trouble plus aujourd'hui; c'est aux véritables gens de lettres qu'on en est redevable' (ibid., XIX, 252).
42. Ibid., XX, 218; cf. X, 428, 1771.
43. 'Critique' in *Dictionnaire philosophique*, ed. Benda, Paris, 1954, 502, 155. In this essay Voltaire no longer deals with the critics of historical sources and philologists but, unlike Bayle, even if at ironic distance, he includes satirists and 'libellistes' among the critics. However, he significantly selects his derogatory example of the 'meat inspectors' and 'toads' who leave their imprint for the succeeding genera-

The march of progress came to encompass the State, and in the same degree to which victory over the religion of Revelation appeared to have been achieved in the middle of the century. Criticism assumed the role Locke had at one time assigned to moral censorship; it became the spokesman of public opinion. Even if it is no longer able to influence private morality, says the essay on 'Critique' in the *Encyclopédie*:[44] 'Il est du moins incontestable qu'elle decide des actions publiques'. The fact that the shift to the exterior had been completed was borne out by Diderot's assertion that one had to distinguish not only between the individual and the citizen, but, together with the critics, between the individual and the author. 'L'équité veut qu'on distingue bien la personne de l'opinion, et l'auteur de l'ouvrage; car c'est bien ici qu'on a la preuve complète que les moeurs et les écrits sont deux choses différentes.'[45] The criticism of the Enlightenment moved beyond the inner sphere of society, the sphere of personal morality. If the distinction between the individual and the subject was basic to the Absolutist order, now — as Bayle had already foreseen — the distinction between the individual and the author became the basis of critical confusion. Criticism granted itself absolution by detaching itself not only from the State but also from its social background. Not only does the author's product hide his true thoughts because official censorship forces him to do so; his writings alienate the individual, who can no longer find himself in them. 'If, without being false, one does not write down everything one does, then, without being illogical, one also does not do everything one writes.'[46] This aphorism of Diderot makes clear the historical shift that has taken place. Criticism has become so sovereign that it continues to rule even without those who initiated it. The depersonalisation of the individual through emancipated criticism finds its expression in the fact that the individual becomes the functionary of criticism. The secrecy, the child of political necessity, initially a genuine arcanum of the Enlightenment,

tion of toads, from among the ranks of officious censors and ex-Jesuits. He still considers Bayle the ideal of the rare, unprejudiced, non-partisan critic.

44. While the essay about the critic still has in mind the editor, commentator, grammarian — in short the textual critic — Marmontel's long essay about criticism itself indicates that by definition criticism had gone far beyond art and letters and already encompassed the State and society. See in particular the section on historical criticism and 'Critique en Morale' (*Encyclopédie*, Lausanne and Berne, 1779, X).
45. Diderot, *Oeuvres complètes*, XIV, 35; 'Cas de conscience', in the *Encyclopédie*.
46. Diderot, *Oeuvres*, IX, 252.

is seized on by the logic of the Enlightenment. By abolishing privilege, the Enlightenment discards all taboos, causing everything to be sucked into the maelstrom of the public gaze. Nothing escapes the embrace of the audience which is, however, to be considered in dialectical terms — that is, everything becomes ideologically alienated to the degree that it becomes public. The yearning for naturalness, for a return to nature, is merely a symptom of this development. The day will come when even the type of trousers worn will assume political significance. The at first politically motivated secrecy gave rise to an uncontrollable and secret power of criticism which alienated all expression of life. It was also a criticism that did not stop before the sovereign. That which Bayle still assigned to the province of satire, the power of death which no guard at the gates of the Louvre could repel, Diderot quite openly — and with an indirect allusion to Bayle — wrote of criticism itself in 1765: 'Tout est soumis à sa loi'.[47] The initiates of the Enlightenment could not fail to understand the substitution of 'criticism' for 'satire' as well as the comparison. Criticism spelled the death of kings.

The extension of the originally drawn boundary between the internal and external spheres thus had unexpected consequences. Although criticism, all-encompassing, reached out into politics, it did not renounce its unpolitical, that is, its rational, natural, moral claim to assure the primacy of truth. Under the guise of universality it continued to resort to polar positions. Every dualistic position as such implied criticism, just as criticism for its part gained its incisiveness (and its seemingly unequivocal character) only through the polarity of ideas. However, when, on the other hand, the attempt was made to take the antithesis seriously, the effort ran foul of the devalued thought structure, and those who nevertheless attempted to restore harmony were accused of illogicality and subjected to still harsher criticism.[48]

---

47. Ibid., X, 237, 'Salon de 1763'. Diderot refers to a pronouncement by Malherbes about death, used by Bayle in his dissertation *sur les libelles diffamatoires* to characterise satire: 'Que la garde qui veille aux barrières du Louvre/N'en défend pas les Rois' (*Dictionnaire*, IV, 2959f.).

48. Typical of this — and highlighting the looming political dispute — is the fate of those theologians who sought to save Revelation, which had become caught in the crossfire of historical and rational criticism, by adapting it to 'reason'. 'We are Christians', Lessing has the 'contemporary theologists' say, 'Biblical Christians, rational Christians. We would like to see the one who can prove that *our* Christianity is in any conflict whatsoever with sound reason.' 'How ticklish it is', comments

Frederick the Great's comment in the Preface of his *Histoire de mon Temps* (1742) typifies the dilemma of those who took the polemical significance of the conceptual position seriously yet were forced, nevertheless, to use the two opposing concepts positively: 'I hope', he wrote, 'that posterity for which I am writing will be able to distinguish between the philosopher in me and the prince, the decent man and the politician'. Frederick was the victim of his era's attachment to dualistic separations. He found it impossible to combine contemporary polar concepts like man and prince or philosopher and politician;[49] the critical function of dualistic conceptions, once one abided by it, implied self-criticism. Frederick was enough of a philosopher to practise it as prince, but too much of a king to allow it to turn into self-accusation.

The critical vortex had a greater impact on the enlightened intelligentsia itself. Something that Voltaire still knew — he handled this ostensibly non-political criticism with sovereign irony and ironic sovereignty — became lost to the following generation of the Enlightenment, namely the use of seemingly non-political yet none the less sharpened weapons in full belief in a sovereignty which in fact it did not possess. Criticism gave birth to hypocrisy. What for Voltaire was still tactical camouflage became habitual practice in the hands of his successors. They became the victims of their own mystification. Strategy became mendacity. Mendacity was the price exacted for their humourlessness, for their inability to use lies as

---

Lessing, 'to pick a quarrel with those who extol and lull reason by denouncing the adversaries of Revelation as the adversaries of common sense! They corrupt everything that aspires toward reason and does not have it'. These kinds of syncretist are the most dangerous enemies of the advocates of reason, and with caustic sharpness and conceptual discrimination Lessing takes up the cudgels against them in his polemical writings (*Sämtliche Schriften*, XII, 432). He is 'certain that the transition from simple rational truths to revealed truths is an extremely hazardous one'. And although he draws a clear line between the two areas he does not by any means disavow Revelation. However, reason clearly enjoys priority. It alone can 'decide' whether Revelation, which surpasses the 'concept' of reason 'can be and must be'.

49. Frederick the Great, *Werke*, Berlin, 1912, II, 2; and *Oeuvres*, Berlin, 1846, II. In each of the three prefaces to his history of the Silesian wars Frederick the Great takes up the question of the relationship of morality to politics. Meinecke analyses this polarity in Frederick's philosophy and political ideas. The King was leading a 'conscious double life as politician and philosopher' (*Idee der Staatsräson*, ed. W. Hofer, Munich, 1957, 326). The question about the relationship of moral legitimacy and actions born of political necessity occupied him throughout his life. However, to see in the theme of 'Macchiavelli and Antimacchiavelli' a 'dualism implanted by Frederick' which subsequently turned into a serious problem for Germany (ibid., 366) transforms the personal part played by the King in this dualism into a guilt where it does not exist. Eighteenth-century moral dualism transcended the individual.

tactical weapons. The essence of that mendacity was the fact that it had no self-insight. It was the price paid for presumption.[50] Voltaire lived long enough to witness the emergence of this new breed and its self-created pathos: 'Il n'y a pas un seul de ces critiques', he wrote in a supplement to his *Dictionnaire philosophique* in 1771, 'qui ne se croie juge de l'univers, et écouté de l'univers'.[51]

The King as ruler by divine right appears almost modest alongside the judge of mankind who replaced him, the critic who believed that, like God on Judgement Day, he had the right to subject the universe to his verdict.

Caught in the web of dualism, the critic failed to see the historical significance of the process he had set in motion. The critic is a leader, the *Encyclopédie* tells us, who knows how to draw distinctions[52] — between truth and opinion, right and authority, duty and interest, virtue and renown. In their dualistic formulation all these concepts circumvented the inherent political problem. Truth, duty, virtue, right — all have already been moved over to one side.

Criticism means drawing distinctions. In the past, to criticise the King meant pointing out his rights to him. Under certain conditions this meant admitting he was right even if the admission was painful. Bayle had done it; his criticism retained an awareness of its political role. To hold the King wrong, on the other hand, meant cancelling all differences. And this is precisely what the *Encyclopédie* did with its network of dualistic concepts. The critic judges all men, 'en homme vertueux, mais en homme'.[53] Critical judgement implies the levelling of everything and everyone, including the King, 'en un mot de réduire l'homme, quel qu'il fût, à la condition de citoyen'. The Enlightenment unmasked, reduced, uncovered, but it failed to see that in the course of this unmasking the essence of the one un-

50. M. Merleau-Ponty, *Phénoménologie de la Perception*, Paris, 1945, distinguishes between psychological hypocrisy, which the person who wants to hide his true feelings is aware of, and metaphysical hypocrisy. The latter deceives itself; by resorting to generalisations it ends up in a condition or situation which, though not fatal, is also not fixed or desired; it is found even among 'serious' and 'candid' persons whenever they pretend unconditionally to be that which they are.
51. Voltaire, *Dictionnaire philosophique*, 502.
52. The reader of history in particular is in need of a moral guide: 'ce guide seroit un critique capable de distinguer la vérité de l'opinion, le droit de l'autorité, le devoir de l'intérêt, la vertu de la gloire elle-même; en un mot de réduire l'homme, quel qu'il fût, à la condition de citoyen; condition qui est la base des loix, la règle des moeurs, et dont aucun homme ou société n'eut jamais droit de s'affranchir' ('Critique', in the *Encyclopédie*).
53. Ibid.

masked becomes dissolved. In the eyes of the hypocritical pro-
ponent of Enlightenment power is identical with the abuse of
power. He fails to see that power can act as an inspiration to those
who wield it. In the view of the political privateer power becomes
force. Hence in the waning days of the Enlightenment it was held
self-evident that a good monarch was worse than an evil one
because he prevented the oppressed multitudes from seeing the
injustice of the Absolutist principle.[54] The Enlightenment unmasked the King as man, and as man he could be nothing but a
usurper. Criticism deprives the historical figure of its significance.
Thus the King, alienated from his element, the political sphere,
becomes a man, and a brutal tyrant at that. And if he is a tyrant,
then the Enlightenment is just in its criticism. The true critic is the
judge not the tyrant of mankind. 'Tel seroit l'emploi d'un critique
supérieur: être enfin le juge, non le tyran de l'humanité.'[55] Criticism
goes far beyond that which had occasioned it and is transformed
into the motor of self-righteousness. It produces its own delusion.

Once the step from the Republic of Letters to the State was taken,
the only function of the dualistic formulation was to put the ruler in
the wrong, to do away with all distinctions. And this involved
putting oneself in the right at the cost of committing an injustice.
Not the King but the critic became the real usurper; and to believe
that this usurpation to be justified was the real self-delusion. Unin-
tentionally, yet not involuntarily, the unmasking created the self-
delusion. By addressing the King on equal terms the subject became
a representative of the nation, an instrument of truth, virtue, and
humanity.[56] The ceaseless unmasking of others led the unmasker
into self-delusion.

Reaching towards infinity, the sovereignty of the critics seemed
to continue its upward climb. Pushing criticism to its utmost limits,
the critic saw himself as the King of Kings, the true sovereign. In

---

54. 'Le gouvernement arbitraire d'un prince just et éclairé est toujours mauvais.
Ses vertus sont la plus dangereuse et la plus sûre des séductions: . . . Il enlève au
peuple le droit de déliberer, de vouloir ou ne vouloir pas, de s'opposer même à sa
volonté, lorsqu'il ordonne le bien . . . ' (Diderot, *Oeuvres*, II, 381). Once again
Rousseau drew the radical conclusion when he said: 'en tout état de cause, un peuple
est toujours le maître de changer ses loix, même les meilleurs; cars s'il lui plaît de se
faire mal à lui-même, qui est-ce qui a droit de l'empêcher?' (*Contract social*, II, chap.
12).
55. 'Critique', in the *Encyclopédie*.
56. Diderot, 'Lettre apologétique de l'abbé Raynal à Mr. Grimm' in *Oeuvres
philosophiques*, ed. Vernière, Paris, 1956, 641.

1758, Diderot, with ironic exaggeration, described this process, the seeds of which had been planted by Bayle: 'L'auteur dit: Messieurs, écoutez-moi; car je suis votre maître. Et le critique: C'est moi, messieurs, qu'il faut écouter; car je suis le maître de vos maîtres'.[57] This upward and forward trend contrasted sharply with the postulated equality of all critics. The *Encyclopédie* divided the *Règne de la Critique*, quite as if it were a lodge, into a hierarchy of three degrees — the *critiques ignorants*, *subalternes* and *supérieurs*.

By overreaching themselves the critics overreached the Enlightenment itself. They were the avant-garde of progress turned into revolution. It is the critics, said Voltaire in 1765, 'qui révoltent un siècle aussi éclairé que le nôtre'.[58] And the result of this situation was that the King began to doubt himself. Something that had not yet happened to Frederick the Great came to pass in France, for the political meaning of the established order of which the king felt himself a part dissipated to the extent to which it lost its function. Louis XVI, when he stood before the Revolutionary tribunal, stood before it not in his role as King but as a man, and Saint-Juste left no doubt about what the man represented: the enemy of humanity.

The critics became the victims of their argumentation to the same extent that the King himself became its victim. The process set in motion by the critics ultimately encompassed them also and duly brought them down. Condorcet eluded it by committing suicide after completing his sketch on eternal progress. Suicide as an alternative to the guillotine is tantamount to the death of hypocrisy. It was left to Rousseau to find self-justification in self-accusation. His confessions are the first modern 'confessions' in which shameless revelations turn truth into lies and make it impossible to tell truth from falsehood.

The change in the relationship of the *Règne de la Critique* to

57. Diderot, *Oeuvres*, VII, 387. Cf. Rousseau's remark in the Foreword to *Emile* (*Oeuvres complètes*, III, 3): 'La Littérature et le savoir de notre siècle tendent beaucoup plus à détruire qu'à édifier. On censure d'un ton maître; pour proposer il en faut prendre un autre, auquel la hauteur philosophique se complaît moîns'. Rousseau's sense of self, as is generally known, fed on the criticism of the reigning philosophers; even so, his comment is characteristic of the *République des Lettres*. Its basic principle was the criticism of criticism. Cf. Simon, *Histoire Critique du Nouveau Testament*, Preface; also Bayle, *Dictionnaire* 978a, 982b, and Voltaire, *Dictionnaire Philosophique* VIII, 305 (1727), XXIII, 47ff., *Mémoire sur la satire*; also Diderot, *Oeuvres*, IV, 296 (1738); X, 177 (1763). The mutual criticism constituted the sovereignty of criticism, and thus for the critics themselves the common non-partisan consciousness of sovereignty.
58. Voltaire, *Dictionnaire Philosophique*, XXIV, 475.

politics only seemed to be a total one. On the eve of the Revolution the roles they had played since Bayle appeared to have changed. In 1781 Immanuel Kant, in the Preface to his *Critique of Pure Reason*, clearly spelled out the claim of criticism to pre-eminence over the State:

> Our age is, in especial degree, the age of criticism, and to criticism everything must submit. Religion through its sanctity and law-giving through its majesty may seek to exempt themselves from it. But they then awaken just suspicion, and cannot claim the sincere respect which reason accords only to that which has been able to sustain the test of free and open examination.[59]

Criticism, which had initially kept itself apart from the State so as to be able to function unimpededly, now, by virtue of its own authority, eradicated the boundary line it had once drawn. In the course of its critical self-justification, the claim of critical reason to pre-eminence over the State also became clearly visible. The dominance of criticism over the public assumed political dignity. 'All true politics is limited to the condition of agreeing with the idea of public law, not contradicting it . . . Consequently true politics must act not only honestly but also openly, not according to maxims that have to be kept hidden.'[60] The Enlightenment and its political secret seemed to have taken over the functions of the State and its arcana. Criticism no longer set itself apart from the State; rather, it advanced so sovereign a ruling claim that State and Church seemed to hide from its judgement, 'both wish to avoid it'. Criticism became so self-confident that it was able to shift the charge of hypocrisy to the State. If the State did not submit to critical reason then it deserved only 'feigned respect'; and it could lay claim to 'unfeigned respect' only by submitting to the judges of the Enlightenment.

This turn changed the heretofore silent and secret role of supreme authority of criticism to a freely and openly proclaimed one. However, the question of sovereignty remained unresolved. So long as the State did not submit to it, critical reason in its historicity continued to be political criticism.

The stages of criticism outlined via Simon, Bayle, Voltaire, Diderot and Kant attest to the growing political importance attached

59. Immanuel Kant, *Kritik der reinen Vernunft*, A 5 Note. After the death of Frederick the Great this note was deleted from the Preface to the 2nd edn, 1787.
60. Kant, *Vermischte Schriften*, ed. Vorländer, Leipzig, 1922, 294.

to the concept of criticism in the eighteenth century. The political import of criticism was contained not in the verbal significance attached to it but grew out of the evolving relationship of the *Règne de la Critique* and the State.

Initially, criticism based itself on this dualism in order to launch its unpolitical process of pro and con against religion. Later, it increasingly involved the State in this process, but at the same time intensified the dualism so as, ostensibly non-politically, to turn into political criticism. Finally, its reach was extended to the State and the legal difference between its own authority of judging and that of the State was negated. Dualistic criticism was by its very nature denied the right to unmask this pretence. Criticism, via counter-criticism, arrived at super-criticism, before finally declining into hypocrisy. Hypocrisy was the veil which the Enlightenment continued to weave and carry and which it never managed to tear apart.

The dualistic 'form of thinking' — in terms of the history of religion and ancient heritage — through its inherently indirect and ultimately direct political criticism became the expression and interpretation of an epochal development: the emergence of the bourgeois world. The bourgeois stratum, growing in strength in social and economic life and with a fresh world-view, saw itself increasingly as the potential holder of political power. However, it was dualistic thought which gave the new elite its sense of self and made it into what it was to become: a group of individuals who, as representatives and educators of a new society, took up their intellectual positions by negating the absolutist state and ruling Church. Eighteenth-century dualism thus opened up an intellectual front which, even though frequently breached, still remained synonymous with criticism. Postulated concepts in turn posited their counter-concepts, which were generally disposed of and 'criticised' in the course of being posited.

The error in which the Enlightenment remained imprisoned, its historical hypocrisy, was that it mistook this negation for a political position. The dualistic division employed by the critics thus turned out to be a paradox: they served as the ferment for eradicating all differences and contrasts, that is, of cancelling the dualistically built-up tensions from which the Enlightenment drew its evidence.

Criticism, in its hypocrisy, led to absurdity. Progress was suddenly interrupted. In Part III we will show how criticism, in its hypocritical stage, experienced, promoted and determined the actual crisis. This will shed light on the inner connection between bourgeois criticism, its indirect assumption of power, and political crisis. The intensification of the crisis will become visible in stages — beginning with the comparatively peaceful situation in Germany and moving on to France and the change from reform to revolution. Yet throughout we will see that the intensification of the crisis corresponded dialectically to the concealing of its political significance. It fell to the bourgeois philosophy of history to obscure the political significance of this concealment. The crisis, even when civil war loomed as a present danger, was made to seem a moral judgement, the logical historical outcome — and the end of the critical process launched by the bourgeoisie against the State.

III

Crisis and Philosophy of History

CHAPTER 9

The Philosophy of Progress and its Prognosis of Revolution

It is in the nature of crises that problems crying out for solution go unresolved. And it is also in the nature of crises that the solution, that which the future holds in store, is not predictable. The uncertainty of a critical situation contains one certainty only — its end. The only unknown quantity is when and how. The eventual solution is uncertain, but the end of the crisis, a change in the existing situation — threatening, feared and eagerly anticipated — is not. The question of the historical future is inherent in the crisis.

In Germany crisis consciousness, the awareness of political tension and its inevitable consequences, gave rise to predictions of the collapse of the existing political order — predictions in themselves symptoms of crisis. Revolution was prophesied. On the other hand, as we have seen, the bourgeoisie failed to appreciate that the decision demanded by the cleft between State and society, the outgrowth of the tension between morality and politics, had to be a political decision. The aspired-to change as revolution, even the mere possibility of revolution, was concealed. At the same time the intensification of the dialectic of morality and politics exacerbated the tension. Concealment and intensification are one and the same process. Its unity is inherent in the philosophy of history of the presumptive elite. The philosophy of history is the other side of the prognosis of revolution. Its reciprocal relation makes the crisis manifest. To illustrate this point we will begin by showing the development of this process in Germany.

The political question of whether the apparatus of Absolutism and its sovereign ruler would continue to govern or whether they would be replaced by the leaders of the new society first surfaced in Germany during the *Sturm und Drang* era. It was debated most ardently among those social exponents of the new bourgeoisie, the secret societies.[1] The polemics surrounding the secret orders, the press war unleashed by the persecution of the Illuminati in Bavaria, gave rise to the political divisions connected with the consciousness of living in a time of latent decisions. Protestants and Catholics, Absolutist officials and proponents of the statist structure, all saw the secret societies as their common enemy, a threat to the existing order.

The mutual claim to exclusiveness which Lessing found both among the champions and foes of Enlightenment was beginning to define the political profile of Germany, as it had for so long in France: 'Thus the one and the other turned his opponent into a monster, so that, if unable to vanquish him, he might at least declare him an outcast'.[2]

The dialectic of morality and politics invested the struggle with a radicalism completely out of proportion to the social position of the German bourgeoisie. The obvious superior power of the State put an end to the secret organisation of the Illuminati. The Illuminati morally indicted the despots 'who put such stress on stupidity and immorality', and charged them with 'continuing to maintain their usurped power'.[3] They, in turn, were persecuted as heretics and vicious rebels, expelled, imprisoned, and finally, under threat of death, prevented from carrying on their activities.[4] Despite the unequal fire-power available to the two camps, which ruled out a direct assault on the State, the situation brought forth a rash of prognoses that anticipated the overthrow of the existing order. These predictions were not based on the actual power of the secret societies but were sparked off by their indirect political role. Alongside the prevailing charge of immorality and anti-religiosity of the anti-Freemasonry polemic, a new, purely political argument was introduced which claimed that the political position of the secret orders presented the threat of revolution. As is generally the case, those under attack were the first to name the direct political factor openly.

1. Cf. Valjavec, *Die Entstehung der politischen Strömungen in Deutschland 1770–1815*, 271ff. On the widespread 'plot theory', see also 430ff.
2. Lessing, *Sämtliche Schriften*, XII, 421.
3. [Bode?], *Gedanken*, 39.
4. After the destruction of the order in Bavaria, the organisation disintegrated rapidly. The last lodge to be closed was the Weimar lodge, in 1785.

The argument focused on the threat to the sovereignty of the princes and — in keeping with the Absolutist concept of the State — it was used to document the illegitimacy of indirect power. Regardless of whether the current prophets in the 'secret leadership' of the Masons were suspected of being Jesuits, atheists, or Calvinists — depending on the religious orientation of the accuser — all agreed that the secret order and its 'heads formed a State within the State, or rather a State above the sovereign States'.[5] And for them consciousness of the existing order was still so obviously bound up with the concept of absolute sovereignty that with the emergence of a different power, outside and above the State, monarchical sovereignty as well as the political order itself seemed to dissolve in the mist of an uncertain future. While the Masons stressed the moral necessity and, consequently, the political possibility of a supra-governmental sovereignty which they themselves were destined to exercise because of their purity,[6] the State's representatives shifted the emphasis from the moral realm to the claim to power of those who appealed to morality. The moral and peaceful intentions of the Masons were considered 'Machiavellian': 'The cunning of the philosophical atheists has invented a ruse imperceptibly to capture the enemy whom they cannot vanquish by their might. They hoist the banner of peace everywhere; they ask only for tolerance and harmony', but under the protection of that toleration they are preparing a 'plan for conquest'. They aim at the overthrow of the churches so as to fan 'the hideous flames of war out of the ashes of tolerance, flames that will not be damped until the basic laws of the land have been abrogated'.[7]

5. *Die entdeckte Heimlichkeit der Freymäurer*, 48. As Valjavec rightly conjectures, this pamphlet was not published in 1779, as the title page indicates, but in 1784, the date given for the appendix. The polemic is clearly directed against the Illuminati, and their programme did not become public knowledge until the 1780s. A comprehensive survey of the literature dealing with the threat to the State posed by the Masons after 1784 is found in Valjavec, *Die Enstehung*, 289ff. The newly appointed regent had to answer these questions: 'Is an association reprehensible that invents a situation that prevents the monarchs of the world from committing evils until such time as the greater revolutions reach fruition? . . . is it not possible that because of this association the states themselves would become stable?' (*Illuminatus dirigens*, Frankfurt on Main, 1794, 134).
6. Cf. [Bode?], *Gedanken*, 32ff. The question whether or not it 'is possible for a secret society to be good for a State' is a major theme of the pamphlets of both camps.
7. M.H.S., 'Die wahre Reformation in Deutschland zu Ende des achtzehnten Jahrhunderts', in *Neueste Sammlung jener Schriften . . . zum Steuer der Wahrheit . . .*, Augsburg, 1785, XVIII. The 'Kritik gewisser Kritiker' was among the

The competing claims to authority of State and society gave rise to the prognostications of revolution which — even if indirectly by way of the French Revolution — were soon to find fulfilment. These and like predictions derived from the political role necessarily played by the secret orders within the States: the weakening of sovereignty. However, what was it that prompted the prognosticators — despite the admittedly minor direct power of the Masons — to conclude that the threat to and endangerment of sovereignty spelled total revolution, to predict a revolution, a 'catastrophe', in the wake of the 'unravelling'?[8] What was the *power* that guaranteed the success of the 'plan of conquest'? Wherein lay the threat that so endangered the state that the predictions continued to be heard long after the Illuminati had been vanquished?

The answer: the *philosophy of history*. The philosophy of history substantiated the elitist consciousness of the Enlightenment. This was the power that the Illuminati possessed, a power they shared with the whole of the Enlightenment. This was the threat: it revealed the plan of conquest to those under attack.

Civic morality could not guarantee that the moral inner space, in itself powerless, could actually come to power. The philosophy of history seemed to bridge the gap between the moral position and the power that was aspired to.

The moral citizen, whether expressly stated or not, was always safe in a philosophy of history which by name alone was an eighteenth-century product. It was largely the successor to theology. Christian eschatology in its modified form of secular progress, Gnostic-Manichaean elements submerged in the dualism of morality and politics, ancient theories of circularity, and finally the application of the new laws of natural history to history itself — all contributed to the development of the eighteenth-century historico-philosophical consciousness. The Freemasons were also in the vanguard of those who sought to supplant theology by the philosophy of history and religion by morality. Their founding statutes,[9] in direct contrast to the Christian doctrine of salvation which Bossuet was still able to detect in the history of the Church triumphant, erected a structure

---

pamphlets in this collection. Augsburg was the publishing centre of the ex-Jesuits under the direction of Aloys Merz (according to Valjavec, *Die Enstehung*, which also contains the subsequent prognoses of the Revolution).

8. Stattler, *Das Geheimnis der Bosheit* (1787), para. 2.
9. *The Constitutions*, 1ff.

of history which shifted true history to the tradition of the royal art. Their history, too, begins with Adam — later expanded by pre-Adamite derivations — but then sees the true turning point not in Christ's birth but in the peaceful rule of Augustus, for under Augustus the royal art spread to Britain, which, as the new 'Mistress of the Earth',[10] was destined to spread the art of peace throughout the world. At first the Christian tenet of salvation was removed voluntarily to a new, self-created past which for its part was to legitimise the plans of international Masonry. The need for and obviousness of these plans, on the other hand, derived from the Newtonian principle. The mathematical and mechanistic harmony of nature was filtered through the moral harmony of the geometrically educated Masons into the realm of human history.[11]

The transformation of Leibnizean theodicy is the German counterpart to this historico-philosophical legitimation of the moral art. The Masons, as the true initiates, take the place of God. Just as God, according to Leibniz, works only in 'secret ways',[12] 'provides for Being, Power, Life, and Reason without making Himself known', so the Masons must hide their secrets, for the beneficence, wisdom and success of their planning is closely linked to the opacity of their plans.[13] For Leibniz the world as it was was the best of all worlds; for the Masons the world could only be the best of all worlds if they disengaged themselves from it through the secret, so as to steer it from the secret backroom of the moral inner space. Leibniz's theological, rational theodicy becomes the rational, historico-philosophical justification of the new man, the 'earth god' who wants to control history. The Masonic order has become the guardian of the rule of harmony in the universe.

While the Masons in this document of 1742 did not yet claim to encompass history totally nor to determine the future, the Illuminati did identify the course of history with their plans, wishes and hopes. Historico-philosophical legitimation was one — and perhaps the most important — aspect of their plan. The ideas of the history

10. Ibid., 48.
11. Cf. I.T. Desaguliers, *The Newtonian System of the World, the Best Model of Government: Allegorical Poem*, Westminster, 1728. See also Fay, *La Franc-Maçonnerie*, 84ff.
12. Leibniz, *Theodizee*, para. 147.
13. According to *Kurze Historische Nachricht*, 241ff. 'Who under these conditions can blame the Freemasons', says Leibniz's *Theodizee* in applying its ideas to Freemasonry, 'that it must hide its secrets, just as God Himself hides the origin of all matter from man.'

of philosophy were a compilation of Rousseauesque concepts of nature, moralising Christianity and generally accepted notions of progress. The draft went back and forth between Weishaupt and Knigge (the supreme head of the order) and the final product became an inherent component of the political programme of action.[14] Both the historico-philosophical lore and the political programme are contained in the same secret. The initiation into the arcanum of indirect power was simultaneously an initiation into the philosophy of history. The Illuminati were the 'archives of nature' in which the course of history had already been outlined.[15] At the dawn of history there existed a condition of total innocence, as in Rousseau, followed by an era of domination and oppression, until the dawn of the morality taught by Jesus, which the secret societies employed to surmount the era of dualism. Superior and inferior, interior and exterior, ceased to be historical phenomena, for the gradual flowering of morality diminished the role of domination and thus of the State.[16] Consequently the Illuminati, being initiates, saw the course of history as the fulfilment of their secret plan to abolish the State. The course of this plan — undermining the State from within to bring about its collapse — was projected temporally into the future in order to assure the peaceful victory of morality, freedom and equality, and with it the achievement of the political objective.

14. On the origin of the programme, cf. 'Kritische Geschichte der Illuminaten-Grade' in *Die neuesten Arbeiten* . . . (1794). The historico-philosophical initiation coincided with the admission to the fifth, the penultimate grade, which was also devoted to political planning. The document is reprinted in *Nachtrag*, Munich, 1787, II, 44–121. After Knigge's defection, Weishaupt, who had formulated the first version (1782), deleted the passages he deemed rebellious because he did not want to find himself in the position of 'one day . . . losing [his] head' (letter dated 28 January 1783, repr. in *Kritische Geschichte*, 41).

15. *Nachtrag*, II, 80. The Illuminati hold the 'key to history' in their hands (ibid., I, 7), to which only the highest grades are admitted, who in turn through secret work achieve 'what hitherto neither effort, nor education, morality, state constitution, even religion, have managed to achieve' (*Schreiben an den Herrn Hofkammerrath*, 97). The secret orders will help 'man recover from his fall, princes and nations will disappear from earth without violence . . . and the world will become the abode of rational beings' (*Nachtrag*, II, 80).

16. Politically impotent, they know themselves to be totally moral, and hence the rule aspired to is morally total. Their task, when they themselves 'rule . . . unobtrusively, with all possible speed and precision . . . is to forge a close union between discrimination and equality, despotism and freedom' (ibid., 46). Their antithesis of despotism and morality will turn into moral despotism, because they believe they are eliminating politics, yet they rule none the less. Weishaupt, incidentally, rescinded this Utopian construction of dictatorship after the break up of his order (cf. 'Kritische Geschichte der Illuminaten-Grade').

Thus the Illuminati were tied to a vision of the future of which they were as morally certain as they were of their actions. The indirect guidance of political events by the internal moral realm determines the course of history.

The heart of the arcanum around which the various functions crystallised — the safeguarding of society, its integration and its victory — was therefore the arcanum of a philosophy of history.

The divine plan of salvation, impenetrable to man, became the secret of the historico-philosophical planners. This gave the Illuminati a very special confidence. Although the divine plan of salvation was secularised into a rational plan of history, it also became the philosophy of history that assured the course of the planned future. The philosophy of progress offered the certainty (neither religious nor rational but historico-philosophical) that the indirect political plan would be realised and, conversely, that rational and moral planning determines the course of history. The assurance that the intention will find realisation is contained in the voluntative act of planning.

What does this identification of indirect political planning with the course of history mean? It shrouds the possibility of revolution yet it conjures up revolution itself.

The moral inner space which initially set itself apart from the State now proclaims the State to be a cover that must be stripped off. The very intention to do away with the State, to topple it, assures the victory of the philosophy of history, for the voluntative act of planning endows the brotherhood with the certainty of the State's collapse. The course of events conformed to their indirect politics and the initiates anticipated the overthrow of the State with the same moral innocence and certainty with which they sought to make the State disappear peacefully. The historico-philosophical reinsurance thus excluded the actual enemy (the ruling State) as the enemy. It was certain to fade away by itself, without any direct declaration of goals by the moral planners. Consequently, they managed to avoid immediate steps towards the objective (that is, the removal of the Absolutist regime) yet retained the certainty of its ultimate achievement. The abolition of the State is planned and indirectly aspired to, but revolution is not necessary, for the State will collapse anyway. The historico-philosophical identification of plan and history made this paradox a self-evident fact. The assurance of victory ruled out the need for direct conflict. The possibility of revolution is concealed. And it is concealed because the revolution is seen only in historico-philosophical terms.

Yet this very historico-philosophical shroud was responsible for the exacerbation of tension. The structure of progress turned the skewed relationship of the secret societies and politics inherent in the dualism of morality and politics into the true meaning of history. The tension between State and society was apparently going to relax in the remote future. However, this shifting of the decision from now to the future gave the Illuminati the needed impetus to occupy the State. 'We console ourselves in our conscience against the charge that we are as little responsible for the toppling and decline of States and thrones as the statesman is the cause of the decline of his country because he foresees it without being able to rescue it.'[17] The necessity for planning posited by the philosophy of history relieved the planners of political responsibility. The Illuminatus was a philosopher of history to the extent that he remained politically not responsible. Thus the revolution was papered over by the structure of historical progress, but this same structure practically mandated the factually revolutionary aspect — the plan to occupy the State and 'do away' with it. The veiling of the political tension, its pseudo-solution sometime in the future, intensified the tension in the present. Thus the Illuminati, basing themselves on their philosophy of history, asserted that they were not rebels, despite their secret efforts to absorb the State, that the danger of overthrow was non-existent, while that same philosophy of history persuaded them that their efforts to abolish the state were bound to succeed. The dualistic weapons of the Illuminati, designed morally to intensify the battle and politically to veil it, were forged in the secret workshop of their philosophy of history. That philo-

---

17. *Nachtrag*, II, 96. The historico-philosophical deflection to the future is the mode of thought that corresponds to the indirect assumption of power, which in turn corresponds to the dualism of morality and politics. To hold that the Illuminati were completely harmless on the basis of a moral self-interpretation that gave them assurance and flexibility of attack is a historical fallacy that still looms on the horizon of the modern history of philosophy. Thus, for example, Le Forestier (*Les Illuminés de Bavière*, pp. 486ff.) denies the thesis that the Illuminati constituted a conspiracy. He is right if by a conspiracy he means the planning of direct action against the State. If, on the other hand, he means that the Illuminati had founded a secret society 'parce que l'histoire nous apprend que les peuples anciens et les plus éclairés ont dû leurs lumières aux Mystères', and if he assumes that, because they claimed to be merely moral and social, that they were also upright citizens, this would mean taking the bourgeois sense of self out of the political context and turning it into a historical truth.

sophy gave them the power they lacked as mere planners. The philosophy of history was simply indirect political power.

Awareness of the political character of the historico-philosophical concealment of political plans associated with the indirect assumption of power highlighted the political significance of the tension between State and society, even if in Germany only of the secret society. The lifting of the historico-philosophical veil from concrete planning brought the Utopian final goal — the abolition of the State — dangerously close. Revolution came into view.

The man who most radically — and most effectively — reduced historico-philosophical planning to its political significance was Ernst August Anton von Göchhausen.[18] Göchhausen's prognosis, based on the historico-philosophical planning of the Masons, stands out not only for its 'unmasking' of political plans but for its conclusive prediction of the coming revolution. He equated philosophy of history with the concealment of revolution.

A former Prussian officer, Göchhausen thought along strict statist lines, while as a Mason he had insight into the ideas of his lodge brothers, demonstrated in his *Enthüllung des Systems der Weltbürger-Republik*.[19] Although he erroneously suspected Jesuit influence behind the Illuminati's 'world citizen plan', his book none the less predicts the rise of the society as threatening 'universal bankruptcy' from the viewpoint of statist ideas of order. He meets the crucial question of social categories head-on: 'World citizen ship. What does it mean? You are either a citizen or you are a rebel. There is no third choice.'[20]

Again and again Göchhausen penetrates the historico-philosophical

---

18. Cf. Valjavec, *Die Enstehung*, 293ff., which also lists the (sparse) secondary literature.
19. *Enthüllung des Systems der Weltbürger-Republik, in Briefen aus der Verlassenschaft eines Freymaurers. Wahrscheinlich manchem Leser zwanzig Jahre zu spät publiziert*, Rome and Leipzig, 1786, is in the form of a dialogue between the Master of the Lodge and Göchhausen, the son of a Prussian officer who has applied for admission into the order. It is a telling account of the Utopian atmosphere of the German lodges. Göchhausen's revelation is based on the Wilhelmsbad Convention proceedings, which prove that Masonry had become a 'tool . . . of very evil hands' (X). Like Bode in his travel diary of 1787 (cited in Rossberg, *Freimaurerei und Politik*, 38), Göchhausen is thinking of the Illuminati, who sought to gain control over the rest of German Masonry. Göchhausen could not yet have been familiar with the most important document of historico-philosophical planning, the *Anrede an die illuminates dirigentes*, published in 1787 by the Bavarian government, but he probably had an inkling of their radical plans, radical, that is, compared to the Templars, largely through Knigge, who tried to recruit him into the Illuminati.
20. *Enthüllung*, 176.

'disguises' of the political course of the secret societies. On the one hand he paraphrases the Utopian plans of the 'world citizens', which — in the words he puts into the mouth of the Master of the Lodge — 'unchains mankind, brings it back to its original rights to inviolable sacred freedom, and restores the Golden Age', but promptly adds: 'From which God, our princes, and . . . their canons may protect us'.[21] Apparently it is reason which 'creates illimitable space' and which will bring about 'the era of spiritual, physical, and political modesty' in a 'land of cold abstraction'; in that event there are only 'two tolerable relationships, that of the ruling and of the ruled human beings', and the Masons — having become 'the censor of the princes and forms of government' — will be the 'highest authority' and the organ of government.[22]

Göchhausen's political concretism of the Masonic plans implies the question — and it runs throughout his book — of the relationship of the world citizen to 'authoritarian order', to the State.[23] The secret of the Masons, he has the Master of the Lodge say in accord with Lessing, does not lie in the ultimate moral goal but in the methods used to achieve that goal, that is, in the indirect approach: '. . . the actual art of influencing mankind and making it happy even against its will lay in hiding that intention from it and from the tyrant. In saying this I have removed one of the locks to the great secret of our order.'[24] Göchhausen does not reveal any of the Illuminati's direct plans for the overthrow of the government, which in fact he could not do, but he relentlessly exposed the political implications of moral objectives whose scope he may not have been aware of, but whose political consequences he was certain of. His view of the indirect plans legitimised in historico-philosophical terms by the Illuminati in their actual political character as sober calculation led him to conclude that the existence of the secret society would lead to the collapse of the existing order

21. Ibid., 216f.
22. Ibid., 309, 247, 388. According to them, the 'proper control' of mankind was 'the business of a few privileged souls' whose 'qualifications' lay in the superiority of their minds (ibid., 247).
23. Göchhausen was a Lutheran. 'The great basic truth on which rests the religious and political existence of society' was 'that human will had to be restricted . . . because it was corrupt' (ibid., 378). Instead of allowing the lodges to turn into 'moral and political plague houses' they should be transformed into 'high schools for citizenship' (ibid., XII, 418).
24. Ibid., 214. The secret is the 'means' for bringing about universal happiness; 'it is not nor must or can it be the ultimate goal' (ibid., 205), a contention quite in accord with Lessing's *Gesprächen*.

regardless of the Masons' intentions. Mankind 'was reeling blindly towards destruction'.[25] His entire book is a warning to the princes, and at the same time a prediction of 'revolutions that are inevitable, that I expect, that I foresee with certainty yet whose onset I cannot fix'.[26]

The political prognosis of revolution and its historico-philosophical concealment are two aspects of a single phenomenon: crisis.

Crisis-awareness had not yet become widespread in Germany; the philosophy of progress served to paper it over. While the progressive bourgeoisie provoked a political decision through its rash criticism and rigorous morality, and at the same time — through the Utopian identification of its plan with history — was convinced of the error of that decision — it masked the crisis. However, it was precisely that concealment that indirectly intensified and brought it on. This was not the case with the spokesmen of the existing order; some of them at least saw the threat in the political reverse side of Utopian planning. They realised that the morally induced decision was a question of political survival, and therefore — unlike society — they were aware of the uncertainty of their future, of the crisis. They expected a political catastrophe. The political decision itself was pre-empted by the French Revolution.

In France the situation had worsened so greatly since the 1770s that the latent crisis had become obvious to all. However, the situation was further intensified by the generally unrecognised dialectic of morality and politics. Among the first to recognise the looming crisis in all its seriousness was a politician who sought to prevent it, yet who, as a spokesman of the new elite, none the less looked down on political developments from the vantage point of a rigorous morality. That man, Anne-Robert-Jacques Turgot, a former physiocrat, held the post of Finance Minister from 1774 to 1776. He was to exemplify the dialectic of dualistic ideas and their revolutionary dynamic.

25. *Enthüllung*, 233.
26. Ibid., VII. The uncertain but universal forecast of revolution is also connected with the fact that Göchhausen — himself very pietistic — saw the Enlightenment as a movement of political liberation. Because of this linkage, the Illuminati, as the social and intellectual pioneers of the German Enlightenment, played a far greater role in the consciousness of the 1780s and 1790s that their social attitude entitled them to. Later, the theses of Abbé Barruel and of Zimmermann and Hoffmann contributed to the continued overestimation of the importance of the Illuminati as the 'inciters of the French Revolution'. However, it was precisely the joint view of the Enlightenment's conception of progress and the plans of the Illuminati that enabled Göchhausen to go beyond the facile charge of 'conspiracy' and arrive at his prognosis.

CHAPTER 10

The Recognition of the Crisis and the Emergence of a Moral Totalism as a Response to Political Absolutism (Turgot)

The discussion of Turgot takes us out of the limited sphere of the Republic of Letters and the lodges. True, as a friend of Marmontel, he was in constant touch with the Encyclopedists and met the brothers of the lodge in the salons of Paris. However, his life was not confirmed to the social sphere. He was also a superb administrator who, at the age of forty-seven held the important post of Finance Minister. Only after his ouster from government did he begin to devote himself exclusively to scholarly pursuits. The intellectual world of this administrator and statesman was the product of the new society. His unquestionably perceptive views had been formed by the categories spawned by the Enlightenment. His friend, the Abbé de Véri, had often pleaded with him to be more conciliatory, more 'political'. Although Turgot was not interested in personal power (which de Véri well knew), he could be unpleasant and overbearing, refusing to take existing circumstances into consideration, and prone to issuing curt judgements.[1] In retrospect, Condorcet said of his mentor that he understood mankind but not the individual man.[2] With Turgot's arrival a moral censor entered the political arena. He stood with one foot in the Enlightenment camp and the other in the State. This dichotomy exemplified the tenuous

1. Abbé de Véri's diary entry about a conversation with Turgot in July 1775, quoted in Douglas Dakin, *Turgot and the Ancien Régime in France*, London, 1939, 221.
2. Condorcet, *Vie de Turgot* (1786), *Oeuvres de Condorcet*, Paris, 1847, V, 189.

nature of the situation, and had he not been a moralist his life would have ended in tragedy.

Turgot was a typical representative of the bourgeois elite which sought to absorb the State indirectly in conjunction with the prince. He was, so to speak, the proclaimer of the philosophy of progress, which corresponded to this intention. But invested with the responsibilities of his office, he did not allow that philosophy to blur his view of the critical situation in which his country now found itself.

While still a student he had come to realise that the Absolutist order did not allow sufficient room for a new society, and that both sovereign and subject were living in a state of constant conflict. 'Tel est le sort des hommes', he wrote in 1753, 'dès qu'ils ne regardent pas religieusement la justice éternelle comme leur loi fondamentale marchant entre l'oppression et la révolte, ils usurpent mutuellement les uns sur les autres des droits qu'ils n'ont pas.'[3] As early as 1731, the interplay between Absolutist 'oppressive' measures and the repeated outbreaks of 'revolts', though insignificant at the time, had prompted Marquis d'Argenson to refer to the threat of revolution, and Turgot saw the danger of civil war lurking in this relationship between the State and the anti-statist movement. His awareness of latent civil war marked his tenure as administrator and statesman. All his measures were designed to ward off the threatening civil war, to prevent open revolution. His plans for the future encompassed an imperial monarchy that would guarantee and secure the liberal bourgeoisie a sufficiently important role to satisfy their demands; with foresight he worked towards this goal in order to spare France, as it were, the decade of 1789–99.[4]

His political programme was directed against two powers: the provincial *parlements*, which he wished to abolish in the name of the law of morality and reason, the same law by which he sought to subject the King to his physiocratic ideas. In the confrontation between monarch and *parlement* he supported the monarch, but his

3. *Oeuvres de Turgot et documents le concernant*, ed. G. Schelle, 5 vols., Paris, 1913–23, I, 421 (1753–4). On Turgot's activities as administrator and minister, cf. Dakin, *Turgot and the Ancien Régime*, and C.J. Gignoux, *Turgot*, Paris, 1945, chap. 3.
4. Cf. de Tocqueville, *L'ancien Régime*, II, 209ff., in which the role of the physiocrats is described thus: 'Toutes les institutions que la Révolution devait abolir sans retour ont été l'objet particulier de leurs attaques; aucune n'a trouvé grâce à leurs yeux. Toutes celles au contraire, qui peuvent passer pour son oeuvre propre ont été annoncées par eux à l'avance et préconisées avec ardeur; ... on trouve en eux tout ce qu'il y a substantiel en elle'. A listing of Turgot's programmes carried out during and after the French Revolution is found in L. Say, *Turgot*, Paris, 1891.

ultimate goal — rooted in an understanding of the state which he derived from natural law — was equally opposed to both. The union between the new elite and the absolute monarch created by the exigencies of the moment (Turgot no longer looked on the sovereign as a lord, a 'maître', but at best as a 'chef'[5] could not conceal the conflict even if, as we shall see, it was covered over.

As a spokesman for the new society, Turgot rejected the existing order and never made any secret of the reason why. In the ministerial council that debated his proposal for abolishing corvée Turgot stated unequivocally that the government was regarded 'comme l'ennemi commun de la société'.[6] Turgot wished to check the hostility between the State and society and thus, as the spokesman of society, took a stand not only against the *parlements* but also against the monarch. Turgot, the champion of tolerance, repeatedly told the King that unless his religious policy heeded the demands of bourgeois society, civil war remained a threat. In one of his memoranda he pointed out that the intolerant Church policy grew out of the same spirit that had led to the St Bartholomew's Day massacre and the League, 'mettant tour à tour le poignard dans la main des rois pour égorger les peuples, et dans la main des peuples pour assassiner les rois. Voilà, Sire, un grand sujet de médiation que les princes doivent avoir cesse présent à la pensée'.[7] Civil war was inevitable if the monarch refused to heed the demands for religious tolerance. On the other hand he warned the King against any show of weakness in his dealings with the feudal *parlements*, and on leaving his ministerial post he predicted that if the King failed in this he would follow Charles I to the scaffold.[8] Behind these warnings loomed the spectre of civil war: 'Tout mon désir, Sire, est que vous puissiez toujours croire que j'avais mal vu, et que je vous montrais des dangers chimériques'.[9]

5. *Oeuvres de Turgot*, I, 283 (1751).
6. Ibid., V, 183 (1776).
7. *Oeuvres de Turgot*, IV, 563 (Projet de mémoire au Roi, June 1775).
8. Ibid., V, 445ff. (letter of 30 April 1776).
9. Ibid., V, 458 (letter of 18 May 1776). Turgot did not consider the general precariousness as a local French phenomenon but rather as a universal one. To him, the question of progress or decadence was no longer one that would be decided within the *République des Lettres* and within the framework of the arts and sciences, as it was put by Bayle, but within the framework of world history, including the political arena. All forces, the moral and political forces of nations, commerce, special interests, forms of government, ' . . . le chemin qu'ils suivent à présent et la direction de leurs mouvements vers un progrès plus grand encore ou vers leurs décadence; voilà la vraie géographie politique' (ibid., I, 257 (1751)). The question of

History has shown that Turgot's fears were by no means groundless. He saw a crisis that cried out for resolution. He wanted to ward off that crisis, and to do so within the framework of a State whose formal structure paralleled that envisioned by Hobbes. Turgot was a champion of enlightened Absolutism. He wanted to do away with the special privileges and trappings of the feudal aristocracy without regard to religious differences and, on the basis of equality before the law of all citizens, build a centralised State[10]

'crisis', meaning crisis world-wide, had already arisen. America, the natural equality reigning there, her freedom and moral purity, was a shining example of the progressive movement of history (ibid., I, 204), and the question whether America would gain political independence was for Turgot a major political problem bearing on the future of the world, one that would determine whether progress or decadence would win out. Already in 1750, Turgot had predicted the independence of the colonies (ibid., I, 222), and he repeated this (ibid., V, 385ff.) in his memorandum of 6 April 1776, in which he counselled the French King against intervening in the War of Independence. Quite apart from France's financial problems, he pointed to the inevitable historical trend which was bound to lead to the collapse of colonial Europe's trade monopoly and to an era of free world trade. Therefore, out of France's colonial interest, he strongly advised against French interference. The absolute independence of the American colonies 'sera certainement l'époque de la plus grande révolution dans le commerce et la politique, non seulement de l'Angleterre, mais de toute l'Europe' (ibid., V, 391). At issue here was a 'révolution totale' (ibid., V, 385) which he prophesied for all colonial powers (ibid., V, 415ff.), above all, backward Spain. Marshalling proofs derived from the history of philosophy, which made the notion of inevitable progress toward a liberal world economy part of the political programme, Turgot argued against a French colonial policy which hoped to compensate for the 1759 defeat in Canada. His fight against traditional national policies contributed directly to his fall the following month and thus, indirectly, to the exacerbation of the domestic tension which he had tried to end by introducing the same liberal economic measures which, from a global viewpoint, he thought of as the progress of history. Turgot suggested granting the American insurgents economic assistance, a proposal overruled by France's subsequent military intervention along the lines proposed by Vergenne. To justify his demand, Turgot once more resorted to an anti-statist argument, advising that the rebels not be recognised as a warring party, for this would compel France to maintain neutrality, 'notre rôle serait la neutralité et refuser de vendre aux Americains' (ibid., V, 410). The world-wide and supra-national outcome which Turgot anticipated enabled him to circumvent the existing international laws which provided for the recognition of warring parties in the case of civil war as well (cf. Vattel, *Les Droits des Gens*, II, chap. 18, para. 291). Consequently, the progressive faction could be helped indirectly via economic assistance. The global nature of the crisis — Turgot used the phrase only parenthetically (*Oeuvres de Turgot*, V, 415ff.) — was also made obvious by his analysis of the unlikely eventuality of an English victory: in that event, the resolution of the critical historical situation would not involve a complete break between republican America and Europe; rather, it would inevitably include the English motherland; the English nation would unite with freedom-loving America and throw off the yoke of the King, 'à secouer le joug de roi' (ibid., V, 389). This may be seen as Turgot's rendition of the French situation of 1789. His example clearly spells out the connection between the European crisis, which was nearing a resolution between the nations and the new society, and the supra-national, historico-philosophically legitimised global unitary conception of that society and its effect on the European crisis.

10. Cf. Condorcet, *Oeuvres*, V, *Vie de Turgot*.

headed by a strong monarch possessing political power. Turgot concurred that political decision-making rested with the sovereign, and as a minister of the Crown he took advantage of this practical maxim, energetically crushing the Paris rebellion and speedily acting to put down the grain riots of May 1775 in the face of the obstruction of the *Parlement de Paris*.[11]

The substance of Turgot's programme stood in complete contradiction to the existing order. The State he visualised was to be an orderly structure headed by a sovereign acting in the interests of a liberal bourgeoisie which asked the State to protect the sanctity of private property and the pursuit of free trade. Turgot's formal acceptance of political absolutism notwithstanding, the new economic order envisioned by him as necessary in order to wipe out the indebtedness of the State meant a complete change in the existing order. Outwardly a defender of the Absolutist State, Turgot in fact sided with the new, emerging society.[12] As a physiocrat and representative of society, he criticised the existing order by applying the yardstick of a natural, moral law above the State, and as a minister of that State sought to end the crisis that elicited his criticism by means of his physiocratic reforms.

How did Turgot create this awareness of the difference between the State and society which as a bourgeois statesman he personified? How did he categorise the two? His ideas — in line with the indirect assumption of power — were rooted in moral dualism. To understand the political role of this dualism, beyond all economic and social planning within the framework of an admittedly critical situation, let us look more closely at Turgot's view of reality. Turgot, thinking dualistically, knew only two forms of law: 'La force, si tant est qu'on puisse l'appeler un droit, et l'équité'.[13] The

11. On the grain riot, cf. Say, *Turgot*, 98ff., and Dakin, *Turgot and the Ancien Régime*, 180ff.

12. Condorcet, *Oeuvres*, V, p. 15, describes how his desire to exercise political influence on behalf of society affected his choice of profession — originally he was a cleric. After deciding to become a civil servant, 'il préféra . . . une charge de maître de requêtes aux autres places de de la robe', he found he was able to exercise considerable influence in the realm of administration and the economy, particularly as 'ministre du pouvoir exécutif dans un pays où l'activité de celui-ci s'étend sur tout . . .'.

13. *Oeuvres de Turgot*, I, 415. Although Turgot did not develop a systematic political theory — like his contemporaries and political allies he was an enemy of all 'systems' — in practice he was guided by certain political concepts which are scattered throughout his writings. His overall political conception is of course rooted in the philosophy of progress; it provided him with the basis of his political ideas and

only limitations of power are those set by another power; Turgot called the law which grows out of that power and is associated with it atheistic, the right of the stronger, of power pure and simple. True, the interplay of forces can create an equilibrium that supports the various interests equally, but this form of right would prove to be basically unjust; the rule of force laying claim to legality is a 'système immoral et foncièrement impie'. Not so the law of *équité* however, for this is rooted in morality, 'la vraie morale connaît d'autres principes. Elle regarde tous les hommes du même oeil.'[14] Turgot thus contrasts two laws — a moral law above the state which is equally binding on all men, regardless of their power and interests, and a law of force that, in unmistakable allusion to the Absolutist system, he saw as the lawful expression of the existing political order.

In the condition of the Civil War Hobbes coupled might and right in so far as they validated the power that put an end to civil war. For Turgot this union broke apart, even though he anticipated the threatening civil war and in practice accepted the absolute sovereign unquestioningly. Furthermore, by polarising might and right he went far beyond Locke, his philosophical mentor. The law of *équité* is the postulated law of society, and opposed to it stands the dominant law of the Absolutist State: despotism, tyranny.[15]

How do the laws thus polarised by Turgot relate to one another? The answer to this question emerges when moral law and political

---

can be fully understood only within that framework. His discussion does not include the historico-philosophical aspect; it deals only with the relationship of morality and politics and the temporal significance of this dualism.

14. Ibid. Although Turgot was stongly influenced by Locke, he does not share Locke's ideas about the relativity of morality. Rather, he believes it is tied to laws equally binding on everyone. On this, cf. the correspondence with Condorcet (C. Henry, *Correspondance inédite de Condorcet et Turgot*, Paris, 1882, 145ff., 155ff.). 'Je ne crois pas la morale en elle même puisse être jamais locale . . . tous les devoirs sont d'accord entre eux, aucune vertu, dans quelque sens qu'on prenne ce mot, ne dispense de la justice . . .'. 'Quand on veut attaquer l'intolérance et le despotisme, il faut d'abord se fonder sur des idées justes' (*Oeuvres de Turgot*, III, 639 (1773), letter to Condorcet).

15. This antithesis puts Turgot squarely into the *Encyclopédie* camp. See Diderot's essay 'Autorité politique' (*Oeuvres*, XIII, 392ff.), which mentions two conflicting sources of authority, 'la force et la violence' and 'le consentement des peuples'. Diderot is more strongly committed to the social contract in the Lockean sense than is Turgot, who believes the 'second' law to be based on an enduring moral law. Both derivations share a claim to exclusiveness. Power loses its legal title when it subordinates itself to morality, to the demands of society: 'Celui qui se l'était arrogée devenant alors prince cesse d'être tyran.' Cf. *Oeuvres de Turgot*, I, 417. On Turgot's negative attitude towards the sect of Encyclopedists, as he called them, cf. Condorcet, *Oeuvres*, V, 25ff.

law come into conflict, a possibility never considered in Locke's counterposing of social and political law, yet one that, given the conditions of the Absolutist State, clearly became a problem, a symptom of the looming crisis.

As to the conflict between the moral dictates of conscience and sovereign commands, Turgot, like Hobbes, did not believe that such a conflict could arise in a government of laws: 'Devoir de désobéir d'un côté, et droit de commander de l'autre, sont une contradiction dans les termes'.[16] The moral imperative of disobedience and the political right to command cannot be antagonistic. The conflict whether — in the eyes of the citizenry — something is harmful to society, or — according to the will of the prince — benefits the State makes clear the true source of law. 'Le droit n'est pas plus opposé au droit que la vérité à la vérité.[17] The criterion for right and wrong no longer resides in the prince's absolute power of command but in the conscience of the individual. 'Tout ce qui blesse la société est soumis au tribunal de la conscience . . .'.[18] Conscience, moral authority rather than the power that rules as such, is the true source of law.[19] In this changed situation Turgot turned Hobbes's intellectual achievement into its polar opposite.

Thus Turgot not only wanted to rid the Absolutist State of its aristocratic–feudal remnants but at the same time, via moral legitimacy, he shattered the specific political system of the State itself. In the Absolutist State the political decision of the prince had the force of law by the power of that decision; the sovereign was consciously excluded from all moral authority so as to create an order politically by concentrating power in the representative of the State. This was

16. *Oeuvres de Turgot*, IV, 561.
17. Ibid., I, 418.
18. Ibid., I, 424.
19. This theory of Turgot's is found in his second letter on tolerance, written in defence of his *conciliateur* to a rigid champion of Absolutism (1753). Turgot begins his letter by saying that freedom of conscience is not able to disturb the external order (*l'ordre extérieur*). However, in justifying freedom of conscience he does not, like Hobbes, stop at limiting it to man's inner sphere; he asserts that it is the right of society. And by this derivation he automatically deprives the Absolutist State of its claim to legitimacy. The subject's duty of obedience applies only when the probability of moral justification is on the prince's side, or if the subject is incapable of making a decision on this. Turgot even acknowledges the contingency of a subject being compelled to carry out an order against his conscience: namely, if the execution of the immoral order protects the innocent segment of society against unrest ('sans troubler cette partie innocent de la société'). The legitimacy of a law thus derives not from morality, at best from the innocent social interest, but never from princely authority.

the crucial point of the Absolutist State as it developed out of the religious civil wars. And the established order interpreted this crucial point — as did Turgot — as a breach, a gap in the political system which had to be closed by natural means either rationally or — as in this instance — morally.[20] A prince who violates morality is committing a crime not only in the eyes of God but before the moral tribunal of society.

Morality deprives the prince's decision of its political character. Obedience is paid not to power, which offers protection, but to a ruler who obeys the dictates of morality. Moral legitimacy is what makes a ruler: 'L'illégimité d'un abus du pouvoir n'empêche pas que l'exercice de ce pouvoir réduit à ses justes bornes ne soît légitime'.[21] The King's legitimacy does not derive from God or from the legality of his power rooted in the King himself; rather it can be seen as legitimate only if the King operates within the limits established by a law based on morality. Certain moral principles may be said to obtain completely independent of the existing order, and they, like enlightened society, seek to assert themselves quite unpolitically. The Absolutist King becomes the executor of an absolute moral law, as Turgot repeatedly told the King, the ministerial council and the *parlement*. Not the King, but moral law was to rule him and through him.[22] This moral view of the political duties of the King deprived sovereign power of its political freedom of decision, that is, its absolute sovereignty. Beyond that, sovereign power was condemned.

Once law is taken out of the political sphere and defined in moral terms, all violations of law that do not conform to morality

20. 'Woe to the oppressed state which instead of virtue has Nothing as its legal code', said Lessing at the opening of the Hamburg theatre (*Sämtliche Schriften*, IX, 207). The moral Nothing, that is to say the prince's political freedom of decision, was to be eliminated, to be supplanted not by the rule of others, the representatives of society for example. When Louis XVI asked the physiocrat Quesnay what he would do if he were in his place, Quesnay answered with the famous words 'I would do nothing'. 'And who would govern?' 'The laws.' (Quoted in Göhring, *Weg und Sieg der modernen Staatsidee in Frankfreich*, Tübingen, 1946, 158.)
21. *Oeuvres de Turgot*, I, 419.
22. In his bill calling for the abolition of corvée, Turgot refers to the resistance of the socially privileged and the difficulties involved in overcoming their opposition: 'mais quand une chose est reconnue juste, quand elle est d'une nécessité absolue, il ne faut pas s'arrêter à cause des difficultés: il faut les vaincre'. In reply to the objection raised at the subsequent meeting of ministers, namely that the king by virtue of his freedom of decision must retain the power to impose emergency work laws, Turgot said: 'Il ne me paraîtrait pas décent, dans un édit où le roi supprime les corvées pour les chemins, d'en annoncer d'autres sans promettre de les payer. Ce serait même une contradiction avec les motifs de justice qui déterminent le roi'.

become acts of pure force: 'de là la distinction du pouvoir et du droit'.[23] However, if such non-political law is valid, then the political decision of the sovereign loses its lawful character in so far as it originates in the political as well as the law-making freedom of decision of the sovereign. The Absolutist source of law, the seat of sovereignty, thus becomes the realm of sheer power. If this power is exercised in a moral fashion it adheres to eternally valid criteria beyond and above politics, and its legitimacy — in the sense of the sovereign power of decision — ceases to be political and becomes purely moral. However, if the power is exercised in violation of accepted moral laws it becomes political in the accepted sense — as the sovereign decision of the ruler — but in its new and newly understood sense it becomes illegitimate, naked power, or, morally speaking, immoral.[24]

The appeal to conscience, the postulated subordination of politics to morality, inverts the foundation of the Absolutist State, but — herein lies the secret of the polarisation of the law of morality and the law of force — without apparently calling the State's external power structure into question. Nothing but 'the law' is supposed to rule. Moral legitimacy is the politically invisible framework along which society, as it were, climbed up. Without itself being able to actuate political influence, this legitimacy of morality is accepted as the true legitimation of the Absolutist State. The prince's power is stripped of its representative and sovereign character, but at the same time the power as function remains untouched, for it is to become a function of society.[25] Being directly non-political, society nevertheless wants to rule indirectly through the moralisation of politics.

The dualistic split of morality and politics circumvents the concrete question of where and how moral law and power coincide, that is, the question about the political form of a moral political system, and ignores it as a categorical political question. From a moral perspective, the King is to rule in the name of morality, that is, of society; but the fact that from a political perspective society

23. Ibid., I, 415.
24. Even if it is not possible politically, from a moral perspective every citizen can lay claim to human rights, 'réclamer les droits de l'humanite'. Toute convention contraire à ces droits n'a d'autre autorité que le droit du plus fort; c'est une varaie tyrannie' (ibid., I, 416 (1753)).
25. Turgot shares this perception with all champions of enlightened despotism (a term which, however, he rejected).

wants to dictate in the name of the King is not and need not be spelled out, since society is after all moral. The political question of who is to exercise sovereignty, which morally has already been resolved, is set aside. This helps to explain why La Harpe was able to say about Turgot: 'Il est le premier parmi nous qui ait changé les actes de l'autorité souveraine en ouvrages de raisonnement et de persuasion'.[26] The intellectual distinction between what is substantially one and the same question — namely, who really rules in the name of morality (the political heart of the bourgeoisie's demand) is concealed. The true representative of sovereignty remains anonymous.

The new elite's absence from the State gave their ideas an acquired political significance. The political secret of the Enlightenment lay in the fact that its concepts, analogous to the indirect assumption of power, were not seen as being political. The political anonymity of reason, morality, nature, and so on, defined their political character and effectiveness. Their political essence lay in being non-political.

Sovereignty also was manifested in a number of non-concretised concepts beyond and above the State: morality, conscience, nation, nature, and so forth. 'On ne peut jamais dire qu'ils [les princes] aient droit en général d'ordonner et de juger sans aucune exception', Turgot remarked, 'et du moment que l'on suppose l'ordre injuste, c'est le cas de l'exception.'[27] The State's legal powers lie in the hands of the prince, but not the prince; rather 'one' decides what is and is not right. Let the King make the decisions; 'one' decides when he does not have to do so. Conscience dictates the exception. The point of convergence between the eternally valid moral laws that govern conscience and the socially concrete representatives of that conscience is not spelled out; the one politically relevant question is sublimated into the anonymous 'one'. Turgot apparently remained committed to the State while, without saying so, dismantling its

26. Quoted in Say, *Turgot*, 108.
27. *Oeuvres de Turgot*, I, 420. Cf. Fénelon's contrary argumentation: 'Il n'y a aucune règle faite par l'homme, qui n'ait ses exceptions . . . Il faut donc qu'il y ait une autorité suprême, qui juge quand il faut changer les lois, les étendre, les borner, les modifier, et les accorder à toutes les situations différentes où les hommes se trouvent' (Fénelon, *Oeuvres*, Paris, 1824, p. 449). Human imperfection led Fénelon to accept the necessity of a supreme state authority, the absolute sovereignty of the princes; Turgot's moral interpretation of the prince — one which Fénelon in his fashion had helped to develop — led him to conclude that, as a result of the imperfection of man, which princes being human are also subject to, conscience must become the ultimate decision-making authority, and that it is subject to the laws discovered by the scholars. Moral 'jurisdiction' takes precedence over political jurisdiction.

political structure.

The division of morality and politics — and herein lies the
ideological impact of this polarisation — deprived the Absolutist
State of its political base while simultaneously shrouding this fact.
Loyalty to the State and patriotism are — equally — criticism and
disavowal of the existing order.

In practice this ambivalence meant that the spokesmen of bourgeois society were able to change the respective area of debate in
accordance with the probable effect, without renouncing the ad-
vantages of dualistic conceptualisation. In Turgot this process can
be observed even in insignificant locutions. Turgot alternately appealed to the prince and the man in his sovereign to help him reach
the desired social objective. The dualism of man and prince, an
expression of the vast dualism of morality and politics, contained a
revolutionary explosive force. The confrontation began with the birth
of Absolutism and was used by Catholic political theorists to make
the sovereign princes, in their role as human beings, subject to the
indirect authority of the Holy See. However, during the flowering
of Absolutism this confrontation was resorted to only to remind the
prince of his moral duty, always presupposing that the realm of
politics was necessarily superior to the moral realm.[28] Later, bourgeois society returned to the confrontation of man and prince, and
turned it into a powerful and effective weapon.[29] Turgot's behaviour, as we shall see, bears this out.

28. Fénelon was a typical defender of Absolutism, yet at the same time he
appealed to the 'man' in the prince to commit him to moral duties.
29. According to H. Sée, the first country that put the moral reduction of the
prince to man to political use was England. It was Bolingbroke who coined the
saying 'Un roi, c'est un homme, qui est coiffé d'une coronne'; Pope's *Essay on Man*
(Epistle IV, Section VI) played a highly significant part in popularising this conception of the ruler. Based on Bolingbroke, and supported by the Masons Ramsey and
Warburton, this notion began its triumphal march across the Continent. The effects
of this reinterpretation of the sovereign are alluded to fairly overtly in the essay
'Souverains' in the *Encyclopédie* (Diderot, *Oeuvres*, XVII): 'Le chevalier Temple
disait à Charles II qu'un roi d'Angleterre, qui est l'homme de son peuple, est le plus
grand roi du monde; mais s'il veut être davantage, il n'est plus rien. Je veux être
l'homme de mon peuple, répondit le monarque'. A very good presentation of the
range of the changing concept of the sovereign, from absolute ruler to first servant of
the State and thence to mere man, according to the geographic location, is found in
Briefwechsel meist historischen und politischen Inhalts, IV, Göttingen, 1779, 206ff.
The listing of related titles is contained in the essay entitled 'Varianten in der
politischen Terminologie': 'Political science has its own terminology ... In the
enlightened parts of Europe there is largely agreement on its major concepts, but
there are still differences in the presentation of these concepts. Moreover, these
differences are far more important in politics than in any other science'. The private
citizen, 'for his own sake should keep a list of geographic-political variations', and

In 1775 Turgot, who as a pioneer of toleration, had incurred the displeasure of the Court of Louis XVI, demanded in his role as minister an edict of toleration. A glance at the map of the world reveals a great many different religions, he wrote to the King, and each sees itself as the sole possessor of the true faith. However, religious belief pertains to the after-life; it is purely a matter of conscience and concerns only the private individual in the isolation of his soul. To attempt to prove this is probably a waste of time but the opposing viewpoint, that of intolerance, continues to cause bloodshed and profound misery. In matters of religion man must never be subjected to the political control of the prince. To persuade the King of this, Turgot posed the dual aspects of the sovereign, man and prince, against each other. 'Déplorable aveuglement d'un prince d'ailleurs bien intentionné, mais qui n'a pas su distinguer ses devoirs comme homme de ses droits comme prince.'[30] A Catholic prince, Turgot conceded, was doubtless subject to the Church, 'mais c'est comme homme dans les choses qui intéressent sa religion, son salut personnel. Comme Prince, il est indépendant de la puissance ecclésiastique.' The Church can command only the man in the prince; as prince he is not subject to its dictates. Turgot as spokesman of 'man' appealed to the 'prince' in the prince, because the man in the prince is not one of his kind, being a Catholic and intolerant.[31] He appeals to the sovereign possessing the power of decision, who as prince stands above the parties, and thus remains within the limits of the State. Religious tolerance, by dint of the prince's authority, would become a realm of neutrality within the State, and thus the ultimate symbol of the State which ended the

---

the essay proposes to do just that. The basic question which the private citizen must be able to answer correctly for the sake of his own well-being is whether the prince is simply a prince or also a man or both. An anthology of all moral reductions of prince to man was offered at the turn of the century by F.C. von Moser, *Politische Wahrheiten*, Zurich, 1796. His instructive collection of quotations is at the end of the chapter on the 'psychic diseases of kings and princes' (ibid., 209ff.). Even though Moser's ideas were feudal-conservative, Heidelberg University accused his book *Herr und Diener* of *lèse-majesté*; without direct polemical intent but with moral rigour, Moser reduced his view to the following formula: 'Man does not lie hidden in the king, the king lies hidden in man, and as is man, so is the King.'

30. *Oeuvres de Turgot*, IV, 565 (June 1775).

31. Intolerance reigns only when 'les hommes déjà intolérants' hold power: 'ceux au contraire qui sont convaincus des avantages de la tolérance, n'en abuseront pas' (ibid., I, 387f.). With misgivings Turgot listened to his friend de Véri tell him that the King was by no means enlightened enough to be persuaded by the force of Turgot's arguments.

religious civil war.[32]

When protection against religious persecution within the State was at issue, he appealed to the prince in the prince. However, when the issue was the State itself, its political and social structure, not the after-life and eternal justice, we find a change of emphasis. The non-political man for whom toleration is asked of the State is suddenly transformed into a humanitarian authority, completely outside religious-ecclesiastical tolerance but rather in the area of political demands. The dualistic concept endows the political demand with the pathos of moral dignity and the political emphasis of this claim remains hidden behind the generality of humanitarian demands. The representative of man, then, no longer appeals to the 'prince' in the prince, but to the 'man' in the prince. When he assumed his ministerial post, Turgot wrote to the King: 'Votre Majesté se souviendra que ... c'est à elle personnellement, à l'homme honnête, à l'homme juste et bon, plutôt qu'au Roi, que je m'abandonne'.[33] The reference to humanitarianism — moral as it is — questions the absolute sovereignty without apparently alluding to it, by stressing not the (political) prince but the (moral) man. As absolute prince, the prince can be either tolerant or intolerant without impairing his sovereignty by any one decision; rather, he manifests his sovereignty through a particular decision. As a man, the prince was defined; he could be only one thing, namely the humane executant of humanitarianism. If his decision should fail to accord with his position as spokesman of humanitarianism, then the prince could fall back on his role as prince, but in that event his decision would no longer be seen as the decision of a prince by the tribunal of humanity but as that of a despot, a tyrant, or from the humane perspective, as inhumane.[34]

32. 'Cette affaire du jansenisme et du molinisme est en quelque sorte une guerre civile'; both parties, moreover, were subject to the same ecclesiastical authority, which called for other types of official intervention than in the case of the Protestants (ibid., 564f.).

33. Ibid., IV, 113 (24 August 1774). One might interject that Turgot arrived at this formulation because he wanted to find a truly confidential position with the King to back him against the feudal orders in his fight for tax reform. As far as Turgot's moral consciousness is concerned that may be so, but this was made possible by the fact that the Masons, the philosophers and Encyclopedists had long before prepared the ground for these concepts and moral arguments.

34. Göchhausen (*Enthüllung*, 238) claims that it was the propagandistic aim of the Freemasons to make nobility and man, prince and despot, religion and superstition, synonymous in the public mind. 'If princes are nothing more than men then their aura is gone.' Rousseau undertook the most radical reduction of ruler to man. He has

If the princes none the less cling to their righteous absolute sovereignty, they not only prove the charge of being the negation of the moral position, but become a blot on the moral world of society. Thus, the dualistic world-view associated with the indirect assumption of power affects even insignificant locutions. Invisibly and corrosively, slowly yet lethally, the bourgeoisie — whether consciously or unconsciously — destroyed the Absolutist structure from within. Once the prince as the representative of the State was reduced to the moral category of man, the dialectic inherent in the moral dualism turned this moral category into a political factor, even if it did not label it as such. The political function of the prince as prince was directly transferred to the 'man'.[35] With the introduction of moral legitimacy the political power of decision previously reserved for the sovereign alone was potentially made available to all members of society, to all men. Given this universality, society responded to the absolutist system by keeping that power politically anonymous. The political power of decision was so unambi-

---

nothing but disdain for a king who clings to and appeals to the power of his throne: 'je vois qu'il n'existe que par sa couronne, et qu'il n'est rien du tout s'il n'est roi'. And, by contrast, the King who renounces his throne gains in esteem: 'il monte a l'état d'homme' (*Oeuvres*, II, 348; *Emile*, 1, III).

35. When the people emerged from their political anonymity and took political control of the State it became obvious that the prince as the object of moral consideration was not a 'man' but the prop of a political power that had to be toppled, that is, a political enemy. 'L'unique but du Comité fut de vous persuader que le roi devait être jugé en simple citoyen; et moi, je dis que le roi doit être jugé en ennemi, que nous avons moins à le juger qu'à le combattre' (Saint-Just, 'Sur le Procès de Louis XVI', 13 November 1792, in *Oeuvres*, ed. J. Gratien, Paris, 1946, 120). With these words, Saint-Just at the trial of Louis XVI rent the moral veil behind which the eighteenth-century bourgeoisie had assembled and behind which it ultimately concealed its political plans. Saint-Just left the area of moral jurisdiction and openly proposed a political verdict, largely because the political adversaries themselves began to make use of moral categories to evade the verdict: 'Je dis l'homme quel qu'il soit; car Louis XVI n'est plus en effet qu'un homme, et un homme accusé'. This was the basis of Raymond Desèze's summation in defence of the King (*Défense de Louis XVI par R. Desèze*, Leipzig, 1900, 1). With the victory of the Revolution, the antithesis of man and prince lost its real purpose, namely to deprive the prince indirectly of his sovereignty. Once the prince is deposed, the humanitarian battle position, politically speaking, becomes so insignificant and so variable that with the appeal to the man, a political enemy can be put on the defensive by labelling him a monster. Moral dualism, that political expression of the indirect assumption of power, which in the eighteenth century could still be used by one camp in all good conscience of political innocence, afterwards became the weapon of all parties. The dualism of morality and politics, the intellectual weapon that helped bring on the Revolution, subsequently turned into the dialectical reality of the civil war itself; its staying power can be gathered from the almost inevitable employment of ostensibly moral categories for political purposes. In using the weapons appropriate to the eighteenth century, all parties became the victim of a mutually intensifying and compulsory resort to ideology which has characterised the modern age ever since.

guously concentrated in the hands of the monarch that every intention to moralise that authority took on political, and moreover oppositional, as well as near-revolutionary significance. However, the historical dictate of the developing situation, the necessity of constituting itself in political anonymity, compelled a response, through the moral dualism, in keeping with this situation, which put the State indirectly, though fundamentally into question.

Once the bourgeoisie was established in its position above the State, then the State's superior weapons, particularly in this area, accrued to them. Moral totality and the consequent claim to exclusiveness are the specific reply to the Absolutist system they had shattered and which subsequently were to mark political life itself.

The examination and invocation of established laws of morality, of nature, of common sense, meant the assumption of an absolute, untouchable, immutable intellectual position, which in society assured the same qualities the Absolutist prince laid claim to in the political realm. 'True is that which does not tolerate contradiction.' The exponents of the moral positions may be politically powerless, but they do gain an overwhelming power of exclusiveness. By the yardstick of the laws of the moral world, social and political reality is not only incomplete, limited, or unstable but also immoral, unnatural and foolish. The abstract and unpolitical starting point allows a forceful, total attack on a reality in need of reform.

The totality of the politically neutral claim of a fixed, eternally valid morality necessarily turns political acts and attitudes, once they are subjected to a moral test they cannot pass, into total injustice. Moral totality deprives all who do not subject themselves to it of their right to exist. An immoral government, according to Dupont, Turgot's deputy, becomes 'la partie adverse de chacun'.[36] This locution, 'the party against all', was employed by bourgeois society in its criticism of the government. The moral approach turns the government into a party, a power sector with 'special interests' — that in substance was the criticism levelled by society against the representative of State power — and at the same time into a party with no place within the moral totality of society. The government becomes a party against all, in other words, a party that by definition cannot be a 'party'. The very articulation of the criticism

36. *Oeuvres de Turgot*, IV, 582. (This formulation is contained in the municipality plan.)

constitutes a condemnation, an attack on the existing State. Thereby the apparently self-evident consequence has been drawn from the Absolutist system. By the judgement of this levelling criticism the prince, as representative of all, turns into the 'party against all'.

Political Absolutism found itself dialectically opposed by a wholly moral adversary who totally questioned it morally. Once the morally polarised existing powers were subjected to moral judgement, the State became an area of personally non-binding yet moral claims to totality. The eighteenth-century moralisation of politics was tantamount to the politicisation of the intellectual realm without making it appear so.

The latent political crisis — the question of the pre-eminence either of the State or the 'spirit' of society — hovered in the background of the overt tension between morality and politics. Yet when moral criticism and its claim to primacy entered the political arena, when a man committed to this morality, in league with the sovereign, fought for a new order, the King backed off. Turgot's rigid moralism, the reason why so many men of the Enlightenment put their hope in him, was also the reason that Galiani prophesied his early fall. Turgot would soon go or have to go, he wrote in September 1774,[37] 'et on reviendra une bonne fois de l'erreur d'avoir voulu donner une place telle que la sienne dans une monarchie telle que la vôtre, à un homme très vertueux et très philosophe'. And so Turgot had to go. During the brief tenure of this uncompromising, rigid moralist, the basic yet veiled problem of who was to govern — the laws of society of the Absolutist king battling with his *parlement* — came to the fore. Implicit in the solution of the grave economic situation was the prevention of civil war as well as the morally legitimated rescue from financial bankruptcy, the dismantling of the political structure of the State. The feudal *parlement* and the court camarilla undoubtedly suspected this, as did the King when he rid himself of Turgot's moral tutelage[38] and returned to the fold of the *parlement*, a move that in effect exacerbated the crisis.

Turgot's dismissal also spelled the failure of the only attempt to meet society's demands indirectly, that is, formally within the framework of the Absolutist State and in union with the King.[39]

37. Galiani to Mme. d'Épinay, 17 September 1774.
38. Cf. Turgot's letters to the King in *Oeuvres*, V, 445ff.
39. Necker tried to push his reforms through together with the *Parlement* and the

Turgot's departure coincided with the American Declaration of
Independence, which was widely disseminated in France by a
rapidly growing Freemasonry.[40] Subsequently the political postulates of society, its desire for a 'constitution', consolidated themselves increasingly behind its economic demands. The tension
Turgot had tried to ease indirectly intensified into a direct conflict
between the bourgeoisie and the Absolutist State, and led to civil
war.

Civil war, this unexpected end to the enlightened century, had
long been justified. The explosive revolutionary force inherent in
moral dualism legitimated the civil war, if not overtly then certainly
indirectly. Even Turgot, who in his role as practical statesman had
tried to prevent that war, as philosophical citizen took an appropriate position towards it.

Absolutism maintained that the subordination of morality to
politics was the ordering principle to end and neutralise the civil
war, while Turgot saw this same principle as the beacon of civil war.

The sovereign's actions in violation of the laws of moral conscience, against human rights, are now labelled 'se préparer un titre
pour dépouiller à son tour l'autorité légitime'.[41] Unlike Hobbes,
Turgot did not believe that the subordination of conscience to the
dictates of politics would prevent civil war. On the contrary, it
seemed to conjure it up: 'S'opposer à la voix de la conscience, c'est
toujours être injuste, c'est toujours justifier la révolte, et par
conséquent toujours donner lieu aux plus grands troubles'.[42] Turgot's assertion that conscience is binding on ordinary men and
princes alike is linked to a dual observation. To act contrary to the
voice of conscience, to be morally unjust, justifies and at the same
time precipitates civil war. Both conclusions, which Turgot drew
from conscience and applied to the political situation, are addressed

---

orders; politically he tended to oppose the Absolutist State, as was made evident by
the convocation of the Provincial Assembly, the cause of his break with the Court. In
doing so he took a much more overt and direct position against the Absolutist State
than Turgot, who opposed any division of power. Turgot, according to de Véri, saw
the convocation of the Provincial Assembly as a step towards legitimising civil war.
To the extent that he was an Absolutist, he none the less referred to a 'legitimate civil
war', something Dakin (*Turgot and the Ancien Régime*, 279) finds incomprehensible.
Yet given the internal division which Turgot fairly embodied, it is easily understood.
    40. Cf. B. Fay, *L'esprit révolutionnaire en France et aux États-Unis à la fin du
XVIIIᵉ siècle*, Paris, 1925, chaps. 2 and 3.
    41. *Oeuvres de Turgot*, IV, 563 (1754).
    42. Ibid., I, 412 (1754).

to the sovereign lord, and in both instances Turgot took cognisance
of the increasing demands of society. To ignore a morally concerned
society was bound to pave the way for conflict and disorder, bound
to endanger the State. Turgot, who was able to see the social
structure more clearly than most, was talking about the actual
significance of society, and the State's failure to recognise that
importance threatened its own existence. However, even before that
— through the appeal to conscience — it meant granting moral
legitimacy to every revolt, and revolt breaks out precisely when the
sovereign does not subordinate himself to conscience. To be immoral is not only to be 'always unjust'; immorality as such justifies
revolt. With this equation Turgot, who in his official function
sought to prevent civil war, proved to be a revolutionary philosopher. The dualism of morality and politics assures complete innocence to the citizen if the State fails to subordinate itself to morality,
and if 'in consequence' a 'revolt' breaks out.[43]

The actual moment of the revolt by the man of conscience may

43. Vattel, *Les Droits des Gens*, exemplifies the threat posed, even if indirectly, to
Absolutist sovereignty by the appeal to morality, conscience and conviction. In
international relations Vattel was a fervent supporter of the subordination of morality to political exigency, but within the confines of the nation-state he championed
freedom of philosophy, political tolerance, public candour and morality. The energy
expended on the pursuit of these objectives was indicative of the quality of a
government: 'La Nation connoitra en cela l'intention de ceux qui la gouvernent'.
Vattel adds a moral appeal to this assertion: 'Peuples, gardez-vous de ces corrup-
teurs; ils cherchent à acheter des Esclaves, pour dominer arbitrairement *sur eux*'
(Ibid., I, 9, para. 116). Furthermore, in the chapter on the civil war we learn that the
more just and real legitimacy of rule grows out of the wishes of a society based on
morality. 'Le plus sûr moyen d'appaiser bien des séditions, est en même temps le plus
just; c'est de donner satisfaction aux peuples' (Ibid., III, 18, para. 291). The ambivalence of Vattel, ostensibly a rational champion of Absolutist policies who kept them
free of the moral arguments with which he simultaneously undermined Absolutist
rule internally is typical of the bourgeois situation. The new world blossomed under
the aegis of an international order which, according to Raynal, it undermined from
within. (Cf. Rousseau, *Oeuvres complètes*, III, 13: ' . . . si la guerre des Rois est
modérée, c'est leur paix qui est terrible: il vaut mieux être leur ennemi que leur
sujet'.) In external relations Vattel supports the subordination of morality to politics,
while inside the nation he wants to moralise politics. Thus it should come as no
surprise that now and then we find that moral categories have crept into his external
policies. This explains how, on the one hand, he could use the category of 'ennemi du
genre humain' in international law to designate immoral rulers, yet at the same time
assert that a radical moralisation of foreign policy is a 'renversement total de la saine
politique' (Vattel, *Les Droits des Gens* II, 1, para. 3; III, 3, para. 34). On the
international level Vattel thought in terms of the State, on the national level in terms
of society. Bourgeois society developed within the State under the aegis of Absolutism. (Only after its victory — and after the occupation of the States and their
transformation into bourgeois legal and constitutional entities — could the bourgeois
elite also speak of the primacy of foreign policy, which was to play such an important
part in German history.)

still be uncertain, but when it occurs he will be in the right. The blamelessness of a pure conscience is transferred to the deed, while the deed — though itself no longer non-violent — is given legitimation.[44] In the event the roles of guilt and innocence are already assigned. And the potential emergency exists so long as the sovereign does not subordinate himself to morality.

The moral new beginning is so profoundly at odds with the Absolutist system that the political legitimation of the State, namely the subjugation of 'morality' to the power of the sovereign, becomes the legitimation of revolution. On the other hand, sovereign power, so long as it bases itself on the sovereign freedom of decision, in itself conjures up civil war. 'Sovereign power', wrote Holbach in 1773, 'is nothing more than the war of the individual against all when the monarch oversteps the limits imposed by the will of the people.'[45] From the vantage point of moral-social totality, Absolutist rule *per se* is civil war. Turgot's view differs from Holbach's radical formulation only in degree, not in principle. What Holbach says directly and openly — that the sovereign rule of an absolute monarch is tantamount to (civil) war — Turgot says indirectly by granting moral legitimacy to the revolt against such rule.[46] Turgot does not pursue a directly political objective in his indirect justification; he offers it not because he wishes to overthrow the Absolutist system. If he favoured a revolution at all it was in the form of a gradual change in the existing order, a revolution directed from above. Still, Turgot was following the trend of dualistic thought that lent moral legitimation to the revolution as a political upheaval — a revolution Turgot hoped to direct person-

44. *Oeuvres de Turgot*, I, 421 (1753). 'Si ses subjets [d'un tyran] sont en état de lui résister, leur révolte sera juste', Turgot declared, referring to 1688.
45. Holbach, *Politique naturelle ou discours sur les vrais principes du gouvernement*, II, 44. In his economic views Holbach sided with the physiocrats, but he did not share their political hopes for a legitimate despotism; rather he favoured a parliamentary constitution. Interestingly enough, Holbach, unlike Turgot, derived his ideas on morality from physical laws of motion. He entered the political arena as the spokesman of society, yet the political theoretical component of his 'morale universelle' held to the same interpretation of the existing government as Turgot.
46. Turgot's essay 'Fondation' (I, 584) for the *Encyclopédie* treats the continuous changes in ideas, manners, industry, work — in short all areas of life — and compares them to the existing institutions. The discrepancies discovered lead to the conclusion of 'un droit légitime de les changer'; Condorcet comments thus (*Oeuvres*, V, 23): 'M. Turgot ne développe pas les conséquences de ces principes que tous les bons esprits ne pouvaient manquer d'apercevoir et d'adopter: il pensait qu'il y avait des circonstances oú il fallait laisser au public le soin de l'application.' Turgot (*Oeuvres*, I, 290) himself said in 1751 in his *Discours sur l'histoire universelle:* 'Si le despotisme ne révoltait par ceux qui en sont les victimes, il ne serait jamais banni de la terre.'

ally, that is, to prevent as a political upheaval. It was inherent in the indirect political function of society's moral dualism within the Absolutist State that this very dualism exacerbated the crisis that manifested itself in the confrontation between morality and politics. Dualistic thought made possible the indirect legitimation of revolution beyond the radical critique and beyond the indirect occupation of the State associated with it. Yet Turgot, who was aware of the threatening civil war and legitimised it indirectly, is a typical example, bringing to light the hidden explosive force of enlightened thought as the omen of the coming decision.

CHAPTER 11

Crisis, Consciousness and Historical Construction (Rousseau, Diderot, Raynal, Paine)

'Crisis' as a central concept was not part of the century of criticism and moral progress. And this is altogether understandable, given that the inherent dialectic of antithetical thought served to hide the intended decision of this thought-process. Even when the critical polemic against the State turned into consciously voiced political demands, even when a political action on the part of the populace seemed inevitable, the realistic view of the existing tension remained bound up with dualism. In that situation, according to L.S. Mercier,[1] the voice of the philosophers lost its power; in other words, a situation had developed in which the bourgeoisie came to realise that the power of the spirit, the power of morality, had grown so greatly that it could now seek to assert itself in the political arena. This meant that the road into the future was not tantamount to unlimited progress, but that the future held the open question of a still unresolved political decision. How did the bourgeoisie react to this question; how, given the crisis situation, did they change and politicise moral dualism; that is, how were they able to view the crisis directly yet still look at it from the vantage point of moral dualism?

In the eyes of the intellectual spokesmen of the new society the reality of crisis is nothing more than the transfer of the battle of presumably polar forces into the political arena. Moral jurisdiction

1. L.S. Mercier, *L'an 2240*, London, 1772, 3.

determines the growing political awareness of that conflict and the crisis is further intensified by the increasing role played by the dialectic of the disintegrating dualism in the determination of political life. The political decision becomes the determinant of a moral process. This, too, intensified the crisis morally but shrouded its political aspect. Providing a veil for this concealment became the historical function of the bourgeois philosophy of history. History is now experienced in historico-philosophical terms. The unresolved decision in fact accords with a moral judgement, the 'governing practical sense', as Kant calls it,[2] it can supply the 'authentic' interpretation of history, of history as a process of moral laws — that is the historico-philosophical reinsurance by which the bourgeoisie anticipated the end of the crisis. Thus, the civil war was conjured up to the same extent as its outcome was already certain, that is, to the extent that the political nature of the crisis was concealed. To demonstrate this will be the last step in our investigation.

Rousseau, the first to direct his criticism with equal vehemence against the existing State and its social critics was also the first to sum up their interplay under the concept of crisis. 'Vous vous fiez à l'ordre actuel de la société', he wrote in 1762 in *Emile*, 'sans songer que cet ordre est sujet à des révolutions inévitables, et qu'il vous est impossible de prévoir ni de prévenir celle qui peut regarder vos enfants.'[3] Inevitably the social order was subject to changes that were neither predictable nor preventable, and, said Rousseau, 'it is impossible for the great monarchies of Europe to continue for long'.[4] The revolution Rousseau predicted, would overthrow the existing order; the States would not wither away non-politically, transformed progressively into a successful revolution which Voltaire regretted he would not live to see, but instead their overthrow would spell the beginning of the state of crisis. 'Nous approchons de l'état de crise et du siècle des révolutions.'[5]

Rousseau incorporated the crucial idea of crisis into his prediction of revolution. In doing so he differed from the Enlightenment, which was on familiar terms with the 'revolution' it had been predicting so confidently, but a revolution which, rooted in the

2. Kant, *Gesammelte Schriften*, VIII, 264.
3. Rousseau, *Oeuvres complètes*, III, 347f.
4. Ibid.
5. Ibid.

belief in progress, derived its political meaning from the moral antithesis to 'despotism', a revolution whose political core — that is, civil war — remained hidden.[6] In his recognition of the crisis

6. The eighteenth-century idea of revolution was a foreign-policy and supra-political concept, which means that like most other ideas of the Enlightenment it was indirectly political. However, even when applied to politics it supplanted the term *guerre civile*, which had become something of an abstraction. The application of internal moral progress to the external realm of history left no room for a *guerre civile*, but did allow for 'revolution'. That term runs throughout the publications and conversations of the new elite. The enormous change is felt everywhere; *le bouleversement, la révolution* — it affects ideas, manners, culture, the economy; in short, every aspect of life; it changes the face of the world. Bonnet, in one of his works, sees man's moral development as deriving from geological and biological revolutions (*La Palingénésie philosophique* . . ., Munster, 1770); Raynal opens each chapter of his *Histoire philosophique et politique* with the 'anciennes revolutions' which the countries he describes had undergone, particularly with regard to their economy; 'La constitution physique du monde littéraire entraîne, comme celle du monde matériel, des révolutions forcées, dont il serait aussi injuste de se plaindre que du changement des saisons', wrote d'Alembert in the *Encyclopédie*. 'Les révolutions sont nécessaires', Diderot asserted in the same work (*Oeuvres*, XIV, 427), voicing the general perception 'il y en a toujours eu et il y en aura toujours'. L.S. Mercier outdid him by proclaiming that 'Tout est révolution dans ce monde' (*L'An 2240*, p. 328). As evident as the revolution in morality and intellectual life is, one was living, according to Condorcet, in a 'milieu des révolutions des opinions' (*Oeuvres*, 5, 13 (1786)) — thus so self-evident are revolutions in their entirety. 'Revolution' in the eighteenth century is a commonly applied, historico-philosophically fixed category which as Rosenstock ('Revolution als politischer Begriff') points out, still contains the cosmological urgency of a planetary revolution. Revolutions can further the advance of reason, or they can mean a change in a natural circulatory process. In its historico-philosophical context the concept of revolution goes far beyond the political, just as — applied to the political sphere — it implies the a priori necessity of overthrow while at the same time making the concrete event appear harmless. The self-evidence of the moral revolution embodied by the new elite is transferred to the eagerly awaited political revolution, and with it the concrete extent of a 'revolution totale' in the political area becomes neutralised. 'Loin de craindre les révolutions on les désire, les uns hautement, les autres dans le fond du coeur', wrote de Mopinot in 1761. A revolution is not a civil war. This contention was supported by the Glorious Revolution; its significance, as Rosenstock has shown ('Revolution als politischer Begriff', 97), lay in the fact that it was a 'revolution without arbitrariness and violence'. 'Ce que devient une révolution en Angleterre n'est qu'une sédition dans les autres pays', Voltaire said admiringly in 1733 (*Lettres philosophiques*, VIII, *Oeuvres*, XXII, 104). He was considering the outcome of the English Civil War, its glorious end, the 'revolution', and comparing it to the continental civil wars. 'Les guerres civiles de France ont été plus longues, plus cruelles, plus fécondes en crimes que celles d'Angleterre . . .'. Even the English Civil War is surrounded with some of the reflected glory of the Revolution. Montesquieu used the same antithesis, if not the overall concept of revolution in the English sense, as Rosenstock. Civil wars, says Montesquieu, take place only in countries with intermediary powers; the rebels remain committed to the principle of the State and do not aim at its complete overthrow: ' . . . toutes nos histoires sont-elles pleines de guerres civiles sans révolutions; celles des Etats despotiques sont pleines des révolutions sans guerres civiles (*Esprit des lois*, V, 11). A revolution is more terrible than a civil war because its cause, a despotic regime, already contains the consequences within itself; if it takes place then, 'Tout est perdu' (Ibid., III, 9). With this comparison Montesquieu in effect did what Voltaire had done already, even if he did not share the latter's euphoric view of revolution: to the extent that the moral indictment of Absolutist

Rousseau, here as elsewhere, proved himself to be a political thinker.[7] Unlike others, he did not yearn in Utopianist fashion for revolution; not only did he foresee its arrival but with its coming he expected a general condition of insecurity and uncertainty once the existing order had collapsed: 'Qui peut vous répondre de ce que vous deviendrez alors?'[8] The crisis was recognised. The revolution which Rousseau foresaw was a revolution simultaneously of the State and of society; its coming would mean more than a 'grand changement',[9] more than a change that would bring victory to the social interests. The crucial factor that distinguished the revolution prophesied by Rousseau from a progressive uprising was crisis. The nineteenth century was to bring many revolutions, but one situation, that of crisis, persisted.

Because of its diagnostic and predictive meaning, the term 'crisis' became the indicator of a new awareness. Even if the heralds of progress had seen the situation as clearly as d'Argenson or Turgot, they could not have recognised the phenomenon of crisis as such. A crisis borne by belief in progress does not lend itself to planning, to rational direction. The term is found not in the work of the progressives but in the writings of philosophers committed to the cyclic view of history: in Rousseau, who saw 'despotism' as the

---

rule as despotic gained in intensity one could hope for revolution without thereby meaning a *guerre civile*. Voltaire's increasingly great expectations of the 'belle révolution' (*Oeuvres*, 43, 506, 519ff.; 44, 462; 45, 349, 531; 46, 274; 49, 380, 484) and the indirect invocations that underscored his expectations are eloquent testimony to this view. The question is no longer seen in terms of the political contrasting of State and civil war but as the moral antithesis of slavery and revolution. The general tenor of the Enlightenment is this: revolutions are necessary. If they do not take place the people are at fault, but if they do — and this is the other side of the moral dichotomy — then the prince is to blame. The State as a despotic entity is itself the incarnate principle of civil war; and if that State is overthrown then the situation is not one of civil war but of revolution. The concept of revolution — harnessed to the dualism of morality and politics — in fact invokes civil war morally and conceals it politically. Wieland in 1788 still used the concept of revolution — ambivalent in itself (cf. Condorcet, *Oeuvres*, 5, 13) — in its moral application to politics as the counterpart of civil war: ' . . . the present situation in Europe [seems to] approach a benevolent revolution; a revolution that will be brought about not through violent uprisings and civil wars . . . not through the destructive battle of might against might' but it will be the work of morality and enlightenment, 'without flooding Europe with blood and putting it to the torch . . .' (Ibid., II, 15, 223).

7. Cf. B. Groethuysen, *J.J. Rousseau*, 4th edn, Paris, 1949, 206ff. Groethuysen offers a compilation of the warnings sounded by Rousseau, because the evils of a revolution were greater than the evils it wished to eradicate.

8. Rousseau, *Oeuvres complètes*.

9. Voltaire, *Oeuvres complètes*, 45, 349 (1767); 49, 483f. (1776). Voltaire liked to used this term for the onset of the 'beau temps'.

closing of the circle that would lead to a new state of nature,[10] and in Rousseau's amicable opponent Diderot, who described man as waging a lifelong civil war within himself.[11] The concept of the circularity of history made it easier to conceive of a turning-point, a *peripeteia* for which planned progress makes no allowance. However, this initially formal assumption cannot in itself explain Rousseau's concept of crisis. Before we can do so we must first define the historical role that Rousseau inherited.

The Genevan Rousseau, a foreigner in the French State, a petty-bourgeois outsider among the *grande bourgeoisie*, pre-eminent among democrats, was predestined to see the volatile relationship of State and society in a new light. 'Ceux qui voudront traiter séparément la politique et la morale n'entendront jamais rien à aucune de deux.'[12] Rousseau, who feared the revolution he was destined to witness, was also the first to see the fiction of secular dualism. And yet, in trying to amalgamate enlightened morality and the State, Rousseau, more than any other thinker, paved the way for revolution. He, too, remained caught up in the dialectic of the Enlightenment, which shrouded its political content in direct proportion to the uncovering of it. Despite his unquestionable political acumen, Rousseau was the captive of the Utopian fiction pursued by the Enlightenment in its hypocritical stage.

Rousseau raised the question of the political system 'through which each man is united with all yet still obeys only himself, and moreover remains as free as before'.[13] That is to say, he conceived of a condition in which the new society exercises power yet still remains what it was. His *Contrat social* offers the solution to this paradox which can be understood from the historical genesis. As a member of Bayle's Republic of Letters, Rousseau could imagine the neutralisation of the bruising contradiction of subject and man in no other way than through the subjugation of all to one and one to all.

---

10. Rousseau, *Contrat social* III, 10; *Discours sur l'origine et les fondements de l'inégalité parmi les hommes*: ' . . . la plus aveugle obéissance est la seule vertu qui reste aux esclaves. C'est ici le dernier terme l'inégalité, et le point extrême qui ferme le cercle et touche au point d'où nous sommes partis . . .'.
11. Diderot, *Oeuvres*, II, 240.
12. Rousseau, *Emile*, IV.
13. Idem., *Contrat sociale*, I, 6. 'Trouver une forme d'association . . . par laquelle chacun s'unissant à tous n'obéisse pourtant qu'à lui-même et reste aussi libre qu'auparavant.' The real problem that had to be resolved, according to Rousseau in his essay 'Economie' in the *Encyclopédie*, 'est d'assurer à la fois la liberté publique et l'autorité du gouvernement'.

What the early Enlightenment shied away from, Rousseau in his naivety took seriously. The *République des lettres*, in which each is sovereign over the other, controls the State.[14] Since then society, in pursuit of an unattainable norm, has begun to process itself. In the 'miraculous state' in which no one rules yet everyone obeys and is at the same time free,[15] the revolution is sovereign. All representative bodies are eliminated, and in their place society, as the nation, wins the right to abrogate its constitution and its laws whenever, however, and wherever it wishes.[16] Bayle's perceptions had been forgotten, but his Republic was about to be victorious, to be realised in an unexpected way — that of permanent revolution.

In his quest for the true state Rousseau unwittingly unleashed the permanent revolution. He was looking for the unity of morality and politics, and what he found was the total state, that is to say, the permanent revolution in the guise of legality. Rousseau's crucial step was to apply the concept of sovereign will, which the Enlightenment had excluded from its purview, specifically to the moral autonomy of society. He claimed the sole, unconditional will, the accepted basis of the sovereign decision of the absolute ruler, for society. The result was the *volonté générale*, the absolute general will as a law unto itself. The ostensible ruler, the bearer of power condemned to corruption, is dethroned, but the sovereign will as the political principle of decision is retained and transferred to a society which as society has no jurisdiction over that will. The sum total of voluntative individuals does not develop a total will, nor does the sum total of individual interests add up to the general interest.[17] Rather, the *volonté générale* is the emanation of a totality, the expression of the nation that became a national entity through that will. Hobbes's logical paradox, that the State rests on a contract but then continues to exist as an autonomous entity, was politically realisable because through it the sovereign will of the ruler rep-

14. 'Économie', section I. This takeover of the State by the *philosophes* appears in L.S. Mercier (*L'An 2240*, 57): ' . . . et lorsque l'intérêt de la patrie l'exige, chaque homme dans son genre est auteur, sans prétendre exclusivement à ce titre . . . tout le monde est auteur . . . tout un peuple auteur'.
15. Rousseau, *Contrat social*, I, 6.
16. Ibid., II, 12. ' . . . en tout état de cause, un peuple est toujours le maître de changer ses loix, même les meilleurs; car s'il lui plaît de se faire mal à lui-même, qui est-ce qui a droit de l'en empêcher'. For the sovereign nation every basic law was a contradiction in itself (ibid., I, 7).
17. Ibid., I, 7. 'En effet chaque individu peut comme homme avoir une volonté contraire ou dissemblable à la volonté générale qu'il a comme citoyen.'

resenting the State was set free. Rousseau's paradox, on the other hand, that the national entity possesses a common will that makes it into a national entity, is not readily politically realisable: it sets free a will which at the outset has no executor. Neither delegated nor representable,[18] the will as sovereign becomes invisible. The identity of State and society, of sovereign decision-making bodies and the totality of citizens, is from the very outset destined to remain a mystery.

The will striving for fulfilment is the true sovereign. This anticipates the metaphysic of the permanent revolution. The end product is the total State. It depends on the fictive identity of bourgeois morality and sovereign decision. Every expression of the general will becomes a general law because its own totality is its sole objective.[19] The *volonté générale*, the absolute general will that recognises no exception, supersedes the nation. This sovereignty, simply by its existence, is always what it is supposed to be — and totally so.[20] The absolute general will that recognises no exception is alone the exception.

So Rousseau's sovereignty turns out to be nothing other than permanent dictatorship. It shares its origins with the permanent revolution into which his State has turned. The functions of the dictatorship are carried out by the one who executes the hypostatised general will. The presumption of the *volonté générale* as the new political principle radically alters the executor of that principle, namely society. It becomes nationalised into the collective.[21] The collective grows out of the sum of individuals absorbed by the very state that first brought them into being as political individuals. The nation, the collective that governs itself, presupposes the general will, just as that will is based on a collective created by it. Rousseau, by explaining one factor by another, is able to make the postulated unity of both appear as the ultimate reality. However, this rational totality has a crack through which that reality becomes apparent. The citizen gains his freedom only when he participates in the general will, but as an individual this same citizen cannot know when and how his inner self is absorbed by the general will.

18. Ibid., II, 1, 2.
19. Ibid., II, 6
20. 'Le Souverain, par cela seul qu'il est, est toujours tut ce qu'il doit être' (ibid., I, 6).
21. Ibid., I, 6. 'A l'instant, au lieu de la personne particulière de chaque contractant, cet acte d'association produit un corps moral et collectif . . .'.

Individuals might err, but the *volonté générale* never does.[22] The rational totality of the collective and of its *volonté générale* thus compels a constant correction of reality, namely of those individuals who have not yet become part of the collective.[23] This correction of reality is the task of the dictatorship. The difference between dictatorship and the Absolutist State is exemplified by the effort of the former to bring the private inner space which Hobbes had excluded from the reach of the State under its sway. The Absolutist State was destroyed by the unresolved problems of religious civil war which resurfaced in the altered situation, of the Revolution. The people, even when in the majority, cannot know their true will;[24] they need guides, leaders. The leader rules not by virtue of his own decision but because he is better informed about the hypostatised general will than the sum total of individuals. It is up to him to create the fictive identity of morality and politics. The people always want the good without knowing that they do. To lead them towards the good requires — quite in keeping with the lodges — more than Absolutist rule, which encompasses only the external. 'L'autorité la plus absolue est celle qui pénètre jusqu'a l'intérieur de l'homme.'[25] Not only actions, but above all ideas, must be co-ordinated. Once the rule of the princely will is replaced by the rule of the general will, then logically the unity of interior and exterior must be forced. 'C'est sur les volontés encore plus que sur les actions, qu'il [le véritable homme d'état] étend son respectable empire.'[26] The realisation of the initial postulate of the collective — and it is precisely this that proves its fictive nature — depends on the co-ordination of the individuals. Its route is terror, its method, ideology. If the 'Machiavellianism' of the Absolutist rulers, which was based on the separation of morality and politics, was still an emanation of the thereby liberated sovereign conduct — the princes could also dispose differently — then the head of the Rousseauesque democracy was under constant pressure to create ideology, to bring about the

22. Ibid., II, 3, which highlights the difference between the general will and the collective will.
23. 'Voulez-vous que la volonté générale soit accomplie, faites que toutes les volontés particulières s'y rapportent; et comme la vertu n'est que cette conformité de la volonté particulière à la générale, pour dire la même chose en un mot, faites régner la vertu (Rousseau, 'Économie', II).
24. 'Il faudra d'autant moins l'assembler [le peuple], qu'il n'est pas sûr que sa décision fût l'expression de la volonté générale' (ibid.).
25. Ibid., I.
26. Ibid., and Rousseau, *Contrat social*, II, 12.

fictive unity of ideas and action. The leader must forever instruct the people, who do not know their true will, by showing them things as they really are — or how they are supposed to appear.[27] The longed-for rule of ideas, of public opinion, is realised only by determining in each specific situation which of the ideas are valid. Since the Enlightenment had eradicated all distinctions between internal and external, unmasked all arcana, the public became the ideology. Ideology rules by the mere fact of its having been brought into existence. In Rousseau, moral censorship is national-ised; the public censor becomes the chief ideologue.[28]

Rousseau makes obvious that the secret of the Enlightenment, the concealment of its power, has become the principle of politics. The power of the Enlightenment, which grew invisibly and secretly, became the victim of its own disguise. Having obtained power, and especially then, the public shields the sovereign. The crucial task of the new law-maker (on which all else depends) consists in replacing authority by the power of the public. It is a task which the leader undertakes only in secret.[29] And his greatest achievement lies in his ability to hide his power from the people and direct it so peacefully that the State appears to be in no need of leadership. 'Il est certain, du moins, que le plus grand talent des chefs est de déguiser leur pouvoir pour le rendre moins odieux, et de conduire l'état si paisiblement qu'il semble n'avoir pas besoin de conducteurs.'[30] The Enlightenment as such rules only by veiling its rule. The postulated identity of moral freedom and political compulsion, by which Rousseau hoped to root out the evils of the Absolutist system, turns out to be the ideological dictatorship of virtue, which hides its dominance behind the mask of the general will. The presumed unity of man and citizen stands revealed as the process of a forced identification. The sovereign is always what he is supposed to be. Everyone believes he knows who he is, but for that very reason no one does. The subject becomes a citizen, but Rousseau was as unsuccessful in eliminating the difference between man and citizen

27. Rousseau, *Contrat social*, II, 6. 'La volonté générale est toujours droite, mais le jugement qui la guide n'est pas toujours éclairé. Il faut lui faire voir les objets tels qu'ils sont, quelquefois tels qu'ils doivent lui paraître, lui montrer le bon chemin qu'elle cherche ... Le public veut le bien qu'il ne voit pas. Tous ont également besoin de guides.'
28. Ibid., IV, 7.
29. Ibid., II, 12.
30. Rousseau, 'Économie', I.

as conversely every man lives with the bad conscience of his separate identity as a citizen. The *volonté générale* is always right, and as such it continues to look over the shoulder of the sovereign citizen into his private life. Man as citizen apparently controls the general will; in fact, however, it is the leaders who do and who know how to hide their real power through the pressure for conformity. The balance between the morality of the citizens and the politics of the State is a fragile one, since the ideological cover of their identity is in constant danger of tearing apart. To make the appearance into reality requires the perpetuation of the means of identification — terror and ideology — the perpetuation of the dictatorship, the state of emergency. The sovereign is always what he is supposed to be.

Rousseau logically developed all the elements of the permanent revolution which in differing degree, yet increasingly, marked the crisis after 1789, by taking the past verdicts more seriously than the moral judges themselves. He perpetuated their steady flow of opinions as prejudices. The acceptance of, the possibility and desirability of the indisputable general will brought on terror and ideology, the weapons of dictatorship, as a means of correcting an intrusive reality. This elevated the method of progressive criticism, of taking the rational demand for the true reality (before which the presence disappears) to a political principle. Loans without collateral are constantly being drawn on the future. In pursuit of the fiction of a rationally planned reality the revolution will continue on its course, just as it will continue to give birth to dictatorship in order to redeem unsecured bills.

In this respect Rousseau was the first executor of the Enlightenment, ruling over the young generation on the eve of the Revolution. He turned the polemical fiction into political reality and his failure to see this deception attests to the power of a Utopia that develops precisely when it sees itself as political.

This is further borne out by the concept of crisis as Rousseau understood it. His vision of the perfect State did not allow for crisis; he recognised its existence only as the critical judge of the status quo. Given the prevailing view of the State as a body, it was not far-fetched to apply the medical term 'crisis' to the political arena. But Rousseau was the first to apply the term to the body politic, the 'corps politique'.[31] The collapse of the existing order would not

---

31. Rousseau, *Oeuvres complètes*, V, 315. The transfer of the concept of crisis

only mean the end of that order, 'le grand devient petit, le riche devient pauvre, le Monarque devient sujet',[32] but the collapse of the State itself. Crisis meant, the condition of lawlessness, of anarchy.[33] The 'état de crise' held a political meaning for Rousseau; it implied 'la crise de l'état'.

To that extent the concept of crisis encompasses a spectrum of events, with no room for dualistic dichotomies that do not touch on areas outside the State. However, crisis in the Rousseauesque sense of political anarchy, crisis as the end of order, the collapse of all property relations, convulsion and unpredictable unrest; crisis as the political crisis of the State as a whole, was not the central meaning which bourgeois crisis-consciousness attached to it. Rather, pre-revolutionary crisis-consciousness fed on the type of political criticism practised by the bourgeoisie within the Absolutist State. This also becomes apparent if one traces the course by which Rousseau

---

from medicine into politics took place in England back in the seventeenth century. In his celebrated controversy with Swift, Steele, towards the end of the Spanish War of Succession, published his pamphlet *The Crisis*. Consequently, after the change of government in 1713, he was expelled from Parliament (A.C. Baugh, *A Literary History of England*, London, 1950, 880). However, the concept had not yet become firmly fixed in the political sense, as Johnson's *A Dictionary of the English Language* (London, 1755) makes clear. Here the third definition of 'state' still reads 'stationary point, crisis, height'. But the aspect of danger and looming catastrophe is clearly indicated in Junius, who, in a letter of 1769, wrote that he wanted 'to escape a crisis so full of terror and despair'. During the American War of Independence the term 'crisis' begins to crop up in pamphlets, debates and letters. In French, Diderot uses the term in its changed meaning: 'Ces bruits ont été et seront partout des avant-coureurs des grandes révolutions. Lorsqu'un peuple les désire, l'imagination agitée par le malheur, et s'attachant à tout ce qui semble lui en promettre la fin, invente et lie des événements qui n'ont aucun rapport entre eux. C'est l'effet d'un malaise semblable à celui qui précède la crise dans les maladies: il s'élève un mouvement de fermentation secrète au dedans de la cité; la terreur réalise ce qu'elle craint . . .'. A thousand prophets would appear and anticipate the coming end, the catastrophe that could not happen in a well-governed country. These passages, which Diderot ostensibly wrote about first-century Rome but which applied indirectly to the French situation of 1778 — a parallel which, according to Grimm 'ne rend l'ouvrage ni moins piquant ni moins original' — are among the clearest symptoms of crisis and testify to an awareness of crisis on the part of French society (Diderot, *Oeuvres*, III, 169, 'Essay sur les Règnes de Claude et de Néron'). Strangely enough, I have been unable to find any specific verbal juxtaposition of criticism and crisis. Like morality and politics, the two concepts appear to be mutually exclusive in polemical usage.
32. Rousseau, *Oeuvres complètes*, III, 348.
33. See *Considérations sur le Gouvernement de Pologne* (1772), chap. 9: 'Causes particuliers de l'Anarchie'. 'Par-tout où la liberté régne, elle est incessamment attaquée et très souvent en péril. Tout État libre où les grandes crises n'ont pas été prévues, est à chaque orage en danger de périr' (Rousseau, *Oeuvres complètes*, V, 318). Rousseau discusses the unrest connected with crisis — in the statist and political sense — in *Jugement sur la Polysynodie* (1760): 'Qui pourra retenir l'ébranlement donné, ou prévoir tous les effets qu'il peut produire?' So long as society does not change itself it is pointless to change the existing order.

arrived at his crisis prognosis, that is, his understanding and formulation of the concept of political crisis.

Before he prophesied the return of the States to their original natural condition — to use Hobbes's terminology — Rousseau specifically mentioned the fear of death which, as in Hobbes, is uppermost in man. Nature tells man to use every means at his disposal in order to avoid death.[34] But this natural urge to thwart death does not lead to the same conclusion as Hobbes, namely to seek salvation in the State. On the contrary, Rousseau sees the State itself as a fatal threat.

Rousseau carries the revaluation of the natural condition under the aegis of the State to the extreme.[35] He no longer sees the natural state as civil war but as the realm of virtue and innocence with which he polemically confronts both the existing State and society. 'S'il est quelque misérable État au monde, où chacun ne puisse pas vivre sans mal faire, et où les citoyens soient fripons par nécessité, ce n'est pas le malfaiteur qu'il faut pendre, c'est celui qui le force à le devenir'.[36] Via the realm of nature through which he had led Émile, Rousseau dialectically arrived at the notion of the inhumanity of the existing State. Viewed from the vantage-point of moral innocence, the existing State is the factor that prevents man from exercising his innate virtue, from 'living', and, in polemical terms, compels him to resort to all available means to save his life and to overthrow an immoral rule.

This meant a change from a purely moral dualism to a political dualism. The opposition to the state is detached from its indirect relationship. Enlightened society thought of the government as immoral, but of itself as just. Rousseau went one step further: not only was the ruling State immoral, but it also compelled society, man, to be immoral. The existing State corrupts man. This situation left Rousseau with no choice but to call openly for the overthrow of the State. And he did just that, although he himself was reluctant to do so. As the executor of the Enlightenment he became the victim of its hypocrisy.

34. On Hobbes cf. p. 25 above. Based on this, Rousseau, *Oeuvres Complètes*, III, 346: 'Il faut que tout homme vive,' and everyone recognises this, depending on the depth of his humanity; 'puisque de toutes les aversions que nous donne la nature, la plus forte est celle de mourir, il s'ensuit que tout est permis par elle à quiconque n'a nul autre moyen possible pour vivre'.
35. Cf. G. Chinard, *L'Amérique et le rêve exotique dans la littérature française au XVIIᵉ et au XVIIIᵉ siècle*, Paris, 1913.
36. Rousseau, *Oeuvres Complètes*.

Rousseau conjures up the image of original, natural and moral man alongside whom existing society and the ruling State blend into one another. This Utopian vision of the *homme isolé* obsessed with the innate innocence of his origin outside the State is the fictive guideline for Rousseau's prognosis. Regardless of whether or not his concept of crisis was framed in purely political terms, the tenor and course of his prophesy had the overtones of a moral judgement. Master and servant are equal; in the midst of crisis man reverts to his origins; man is tested internally and externally and only the true, the virtuous man, the man who works, will survive.[37]

His vision of the innocent 'état d'homme' led Rousseau to turn the political crisis of the State, which had been a frequent subject of his topical writings, into a moral crisis. And in doing so he gave voice to what his contemporaries both understood and ultimately wanted to hear.

This challenging manifestation of crisis surfaced in fact only when the verdict of the Enlightenment, based on the underlying political postulates, had to be carried out. The unpolitical or indirect political attitude of the new elite toward the State, the dialectical product of the monopolisation of power by the Absolute sovereign in 1770 in France, reached the stage of autonomous political consciousness.[38] More and more, the will to link political rule — via the *parlements* or in the form of a constitution — to the eternally valid laws discovered and proclaimed by society, joins the theoretical link of the supreme State power to the interests of society. Armed with its postulates, the new elite entered the arena of political dispute with the existing State. In doing so it did not relinquish the moral position that gave support to its inner superiority and innocence. On the contrary, it broadened it. The critical disjunction between the realm of natural goodness and a polity which this division had turned into a realm of sheer power became intensified. It now served to insure the innocence of the attack. Up to this time, according to a pamphlet published in 1780,[39] there existed a power equilibrium in France — the bourgeoisie already considered itself an

37. Ibid., III, 348ff.
38. 'Les Français ne se bornaient plus à désirer que leurs affaires fussent mieux faites; ils commençaient à vouloir les faire eux-mêmes, et il était visible que la grande Révolution que tout préparait allait avoir lieu, non-seulement avec l'assentiment du peuple mais par ses mains' (De Tocqueville, *L'Ancien Régime*, 215, on the situation of 1771, when Louis XV dissolved the *Parlement*).
39. Raynal, *Histoire philosophique*, IV, 513.

independent political factor — the 'action de la force et la réaction des volontés' formed a 'balancement des puissances'. The new society confronted the *ancien régime* in full awareness of its political equality, but in doing so the popular will continued to hide its aggressiveness behind the necessity and innocence of being merely reactive. The bourgeoisie's view of itself as simply a 'reaction' created the revolutionary ferment of its ideology. For innocence obligates, it makes for revolution. And here Rousseau's influence, his support of the progressive Enlightenment and his injecting the powers of the heart and emotions (and the *volonté générale*) into the political dispute, was telling. The threat of civil war lay not in dissatisfaction and Enlightenment; it appeared in the shape of the virtuous man. No longer is his moral judgement confined to the realm of political non-commitment; rather it compels him to execute it. 'Car la vertu s'aigrit et s'indigne jusqu'à l'atrocité. Caton et Brutus étoient vertueux; ils n'eurent à choisir qu'entre deux grands attentats, le suicide ou la mort de César.'[40]

Society, to save itself, not only appoints itself moral judge, but feels compelled to ensure its existence, to carry out its verdict. Suicide or the death of the ruler — that is the choice, and with that choice moral dualism becomes crucial. The polar categories are transferred to the political condition, and through their influence on it they create a hopeless either/or situation. Moral dualism becomes the determinant of the crisis. The validity of this was borne out by the bourgeoisie's prognoses of an uncertain future.

These prognoses both attested to the reality of the crisis and determined its nature, and crucially so. 'Heads became hot', wrote Diderot[41] to Princess Dashkova in St Petersburg, when in 1771 Louis XV drove the *Parlement* from Paris and thereby seemed to eliminate the last vestige of legal protection against arbitrary rule. But the flames spread, and the principles of freedom and independence which up to then had lain hidden in the hearts of thinking men, now established themselves openly and frankly. Reviewing the past, Diderot argued that the spirit of the century was one of freedom and that it would now be impossible to halt its advance.

40. Ibid., 538.
41. Diderot, *Ouevres*, XX, 26ff. In his letter of 3 April 1771, Diderot implores the addressee, the President of the Petersburg Academy, not to let the letter fall into other hands. The 'crisis' is still treated as a secret.

Une fois que les hommes ont osé d'une manière quelconque donner l'aussaut à la barrière de la religion, cette barrière la plus formidable qui existe comme la plus respectée, il est impossible de s'arrêter. Dès qu'ils ont tourné des regards menaçants contre la majesté du ciel, ils ne manqueront pas le moment d'après de les diriger contre la souveraineté de la terre.[42]

The earlier course of the Enlightenment, that is, the criticism of Church and State that furnished the dualistic counterpart for the development of the bourgeois sense of self[43] openly and plainly threatened the existing State. Furthermore, the threat to princely sovereignty made the political crisis obvious. 'Telle est notre position présente, et qui peut dire où cela nous conduira?' Certainty gave way to insecurity and the critical situation conjured up the question of the future. Diderot had a ready answer. It was unambiguous and dualistic, indeed the unambiguity lies in the duality: 'Nous touchons à une crise qui aboutira à l'esclavage ou à la liberté.'[44] Once the State becomes involved in the critical process, its 'pour et contre' turns into the either/or of a crisis that inevitably forces the political decision.

For Diderot the crisis represents not only a time of lawlessness, of anarchy, but the political crisis itself makes a dualistic prognosis[45]

42. Ibid.
43. 'Le câble qui tient et comprime l'humanité est formé de deux cordes; l'une ne peut céder sans que l'autre vienne à rompre', says Diderot, thus describing not only the internal connection between religious and political criticism, but also the growing polemical character of man and society, which develops in the antithesis to the prevailing religion and the inhumane policy.
44. Diderot leaves open the actual outcome of the crisis. If the Jesuits were still in power there would be no doubt about a relapse into radical despotism and absolute barbarism. However, as things now stood, and without putting too severe a strain on his prophetic gift, he wished to point out that it was much easier for an enlightened people to relapse into barbarism than to take even one step toward civilisation. Good, like evil, had its maturation point. 'Quand le bien atteint son point de perfection, il commence à tourner au mal; quand le mal est complet, il s'élève vers le bien.' The philosophy of circularity leaves all options open, while at the same time offering the possibility of a reversal and complete change of power relationships without basking in progressive self-confidence.
45. An observation of Calonne's in 1790 throws light on the influence of such dualistic choice prognoses on the contemporary consciousness: 'Chacun gémit de l'état présent, chacun aspire à un meilleur avenir', and there existed only two views. The one relied on the operations of the Assemblée, 'et se persuadent que leur dernier résultat fera succéder une prosperité durable à une crise momentanée', while the other saw the same measures as nothing but anarchy; the first saw revolution as a necessary process of crystallisation, while the other did not think that evil would disappear with the passage of time, nor that this would happen through the dissolution of the 'corps politique'. '. . . Pour se décider entre ceux deux opinions, et juger sainement ce qu'on doit prévoir . . .', one would have to examine the present state of the Assemblée (Calonne, *De l'État de la France, présent et à venir*, London, 1790, 8).

which anticipates its possible outcome. The crisis will result either in freedom or slavery; that is to say, the end of the crisis is in accord with the sense of self that gave rise to the prognosis. The view of the crisis as anarchy, as a condition of uncertainty, as civil war, is certainly part of the prognosis, but the nature of that crisis is determined by its outcome. It is in fact merely the end of the critical process launched by a society that stood outside the State and against that State. The crisis turned into a moral tribunal whose laws were engraved in the hearts of the bourgeois critics.[46] The beginning of the crisis not only brought political uncertainty, the end of which — as in Rousseau — was unpredictable, but the political crisis was a transitory moment whose outcome had already been determined by the categories of bourgeois criticism. The critical separation between moral innocence and a power that innocence called immoral shaped the political decision. Diderot seems to leave the outcome of that decision open, but when it is made — and it is certain to be made — only two possibilities are entertained: despotism or freedom. The same politically indirect, moral sense of self of the new elite that had marked the criticism also marks the end of the crisis once the elite decides to confront the State directly. Dualistic choices and related pleas to opt radically either for freedom or slavery abound; the political fact of crisis associated with this, the crisis as civil war, is rarely mentioned. (This question is enlarged upon in the Excursus, pp. 186–8 below.)

Contained in this ambivalence — whether to confront the ruling State directly or indirectly, to stir up an internal political debate yet to continue to look on this political process as a moral tribunal whose verdict, whatever it may be, anticipates the political outcome — it is the crisis-awareness of the enlightened bourgeoisie, the outgrowth of the political criticism.

Since such a rigorous criticism had made the existing order a crime, it followed that in the eyes of the citizens the overthrow of this regime, the *crise*, was simply a judgement. Up to the present, according to Abbé Raynal among others, the balance of power had prevented revolution and violence, 'a prévenu ces éclats, ces vi-

46. The Johannine experience of the Last Judgement is the theological counterpart of the idea that the certitude of critical judgement contained within itself the end of the crisis. Even if the judgement itself is still outstanding the decision has already been made by the Incarnation of Christ and the Crucifixion. This, in its ostensibly self-evident fashion, makes clear the transformation of Christian eschatology into Utopia.

olences, d'où résulte ou la tyrannie, ou la liberté populaire'.[47] But now, he wrote in 1780, the despots can no longer count on permanent immunity; society and the laws would avenge themselves: 'Ainsi, quand la société et les loix se vengent des crimes des particuliers, l'homme de bien espère que le châtiment des coupables peut prévenir de nouveaux crimes'.[48] The dualistic choice prognosis, which reflected the uncertainty of the threatening civil war, ultimately turned out to anticipate the execution of the moral verdict against the old world. The crisis ends with the chastisement of the criminals. This means that the civil war is conjured up in the present, as its course is seen as the execution of a moral judgement.

The dualistic interpretation which the 'philosophers' bestowed on the crisis, the choice predictions that tended towards either/or were nothing but an application of the forensic categories of the enlightened conscience, the rigorous verdicts of a moral judiciary against history. This eliminated the dubiousness of the critical situation; the crisis was concealed yet the concealment served to intensify it. The political guise of the crisis constituted its intensification, just as its intensification served to conceal it. The crisis of the eighteenth century was so contained in the dualistic categories that seemingly eliminate the political factor that it may be said to be the product of the dialectic of morality and politics, at the same time as being the dialectic itself. In other words, the crisis was a crisis only because its political nature was essentially covered over.

Concealing this concealment was the historical function of the Utopian philosophy of history. It was responsible for the further intensification of the crisis because it made evident that the decision yet to come would take the form of a moral judgement. It proved the cogency of a history with which the bourgeoisie identified so as to carry out its moral judgement along the lines of the historico-philosophical approach to history. The philosophy of history gave the bourgeoisie the vitality and certainty needed to bring about the crisis as a moral judgement.

To clarify this let us listen to what Abbé Raynal,[49] a man who exerted considerable influence in the two decades preceding the

---

47. Raynal, *Histoire Philosophique*, IV, 153.
48. Ibid., 455; the issue under discussion is the 'leçons pour des despots' in the wake of the American War of Independence.
49. On Raynal, cf. A. Feugère, *Un précurseur de la Révolution: L'abbé Raynal*, Angoulême, 1922; and G. Esquer, 'L'anticolonialisme au XVIIIe siècle' in *Colonies et Empires*, Paris, 1951, II, 8. Concerning the various co-authors of his work, above all

Revolution, had to say on this subject. Raynal was a true prophet of the crisis, both in its sense as the threat of civil war and as a moral judgement invoked in the historico-philosophical certainty that it will follow his prognosis: 'J'ai cru m'entretenir avec la Providence', said Frederick the Great about Raynal after a conversation with him, the irony of which completely eluded that refugee from the French police.[50] Raynal was a typical *philosophe de l'histoire* who had hardly a single original idea, but as a popular figure of the Paris salons he was a zealous collector of the wisdom of others.[51] He was the leading spokesman of the *République des Lettres*, and his work was the yardstick for the dominant philosophy of history. In his personal demands and hopes Raynal was progressive and moderate; he supported the prudent, gradual change of things as they existed — the goal being a *constitution tempéré*.[52] In his political theory however, he supported Rousseau, coming out in favour of undivided popular sovereignty[53] and, though a cleric, championing the natural religion of the heart. A man of virtue, this 'inquisitif' (the sobriquet bestowed on him by his friends) passed moral judgement, dividing the world into two parts and subordinating them to that judgement. 'Il s'agit avant tout d'être vrais, et de ne pas trahir cette conscience pure et droite qui préside à écrits et nous dicte tous nos judgements.'[54] Raynal exemplifies the leap from moral jurisdiction to historico-philosophical reinsurance. In him, the sure judgement about despotism delivered from a position of morality takes on the aura of the Last Judgement.[55]

In 1770 Raynal anonymously published his *Histoire philosophique et politique des établissements et du commerce des Européens dans les deux Indes*, a historico-philosophical view of political crisis.

Diderot, which Dieckmann's findings were able to clarify, cf. Hans Wolpe, *Raynal et sa machine de guerre*, Paris, 1956.

50. Frederick the Great's letter to d'Alembert, dated 18 May 1782, quoted in Fuegère, *Un précurseur*, 82.

51. Cf. Esquer, *L'anticolonialisme*, 3ff., 27.

52. Raynal, *Histoire Philosophique* (1780 edn), IV, 473 *passim*.

53. Ibid., chap. 'Gouvernement', and I, 85. Raynal or, respectively, his co-author Delayre adopted the concept of a state religion from Rousseau: 'L'État n'est pas fait pour la religion, mais la religion pour l'État' (IV, 533).

54. Ibid. (1780 edn), IV, 456.

55. In terms of the history of ideas, this of course is one of the modes of secularisation of Christian eschatology. Man, having supplanted God as moral judge, assumes control of history and, via the medium of his philosophy of history, believes the course of history to be certain according to his jurisdiction: the Last Judgement is incorporated into the progressive course of history as an ongoing process — with, in Raynal, completely eschatological structures.

The critical situation furnished the impulse for this work, which begins with these words: 'Tout est changé et doit changer encore. Mais les révolutions passées et celles qui doivent suivre, ont-elles été, peuvent-elles être utiles à la nature humaine?'[56] Here is a question posed by the Paris salons, the question of crisis. What, it is asked, is the 'benefit' of revolution? — and history supplies the answer. But history is understood by the categories of moral criticism.

Raynal wrote the history of two worlds, the Old and the New. In it the natural and innocent realm of the transoceanic wilderness, up to then the vast reservoir of the indirect criticism of despotism,[57] takes over the historical role of the new society. Raynal does not

56. Raynal, *Histoire Philosophique* (1770 edn), I, 4.
57. Cf. Chinard, *L'Amerique et le rêve exotique*, 390ff. Chinard exemplifies the increasing reassessment of the *bon sauvage*, first used by the Jesuits to exhort society towards religious contemplation, or at least to guide it in the direction of moral improvement by revealing a higher nature in America; however, the concept was subsequently taken over by society as a vehicle of political criticism of the State.
See also Fay, *L'esprit révolutionnaire*, chap. 1, 'A la recherche d'un monde nouveau'. The moral and historico-philosophical significance of the trans-oceanic world was not fully understood in the eighteenth century. The indirect political contribution of the 'outside world' to the shaping of the new society which shattered the Absolutist States has not, as far as I can see, received the scholarly attention it deserves. In its historical sense the 'outside world' of the modern subject is the world beyond Europe. In his 'provisional moral treatise', Descartes, interestingly enough, compares the outside objects inaccessible to man with China and Mexico (*Discours de la Méthode*, III). The expanding discovery, conquest, and control of this outside world is the historical expression of the modern philosophy of history. The belief in progress receives historical substantiation through overseas conquests. This is yet another crucial presupposition of the modern philosophy of history. 'Lacking familiarity with modern discoveries, says Leibniz in the *Theodizee*, 'St Augustine was greatly embarrassed when it was a matter of excusing the predominance of evil. The Ancients thought that only our earth was inhabited, and even here they shied away from the antipodes.' Expansion overseas made for the multitude of Utopias that marked temporal progress, and at the same time society discovered the realm of nature in which all men are equal, in which the 'morale universelle' was a reality, the ideal world which furnished the yardstick for the indirect political criticism of the Absolutist States. The consciousness of global unity, the corresponding philosophies of history and the indirect political criticism of the Absolutist regimes are all part of the same movement. 'Chacun s'étend, pour ainsi dire, sur la terre entière, et devient sensible sur toute cette grande surface', declares Rousseau in *Emile* (III, 104) describing modern man, the product of Absolutism. The difference between Europe and America is far more trenchant in terms of the modern consciousness than, for example, the difference with 'exemplary China'. The superiority of the civilised, progressive Europeans became manifest only on the other side of the Atlantic. There they educated the 'savages' who, on the other hand, personified the ideal of the theories of nature and circularity, an ideal that conjured up a turn for the better for ('decadent') Europe, a further sign of progress, so to speak. Raynal was a philosopher both of progress and circularity. The American colonies were the historical site at which the internal contradiction lost its meaning: the most progressive constitution in the world was to be found in this realm of most primitive nature. After America won its independence, the intellectual contrast (in the political meaning which Voltaire and Rosseau symbolised in France) became insignificant: progressives and philosophers of circularity agreed on the necessity and exemplariness of the Ameri-

speak directly of the French State and its 'natural' enemy, patterned on the ideal example of the *bon sauvage*; instead, he describes the history of two continents in making the *état actuel de l'Europe* his indirect target.[58] In the course of his economic and colonial history of Europe overseas, world history is transformed into Judgement Day. Transatlantic natural innocence and European tyranny confront one another as two Manichean realms, 'séparés par une mer immense'.[59]

The discovery of the New World set in motion a vast process between America and Europe. The historical course of this process followed the same pattern as that of the indirect criticism. The polemical contrast of moral innocence and immoral despotism is transposed geographically and projected into the past so as to arrive at a final judgement via an historical and simultaneously moral necessity. Oppressed and exploited, the New World — the arena of virtue and of natural laws — managed to free itself of the despotic rule of its colonial tyrants. The rise of the New World and the decline of the old world of despotism are a single, connected, reciprocal movement. The two continents, America and Europe, are like the two pans of a scale: when one goes up the other goes down. The turning-point, the change, has been reached. The work ends with the description of the smouldering independence movement of the American colonists and a prediction of ultimate victory.[60] More than twenty-five thousand copies of Raynal's book were distributed in the American colonies.[61] The indomitable resistance of the ingenuous yet enlightened settlers was certain to throw off the yoke of the overseas despots. 'Réduit à opter entre esclavage et la guerre',[62] they would take up arms, and American innocence would surely be victorious. The imminent political independence of the virtuous settlers would end an historically determined, factually moral process between the Old and the New World. Via the geographically

can Revolution. The two intellectual currents merged, and by 1789 had coalesced into a single flood tide.

58. An insertion at the end of the last volume of the first edition (IV, 426) specifically points out that the previously announced description of the existing situation in Europe was missing from the manuscript. The reader familiar with the 'manière indirecte' undoubtedly noticed the description of Europe, and of France in particular.

59. Ibid., 1770 edn, VI, 42.
60. Ibid., 426.
61. Wolpe, *Raynal et sa Machine de guerre*, 9.
62. Raynal, *Histoire philosophique*, 1770 edn, VI, 421.

obvious detour of the separation of Europe and America, the
separation of morality and politics ultimately leads to the triumph
of the new society.

The historico-philosophical ferment permeating this work gave
meaning and internal cohesion to the historical and geographic
facts. Raynal's method, to expose and understand the French situation, which he believed to be on the verge of resolution, remained
indirect. His was a double detour, one via geography, the other via
history. It is the detour taken by the philosophy of history to
understand the existing crisis — and to conjure it up.[63]

The entire last chapter of Raynal's work, written in 1770, is an
indirect description of the French situation and at the same time a
summons to emulate the acclaimed American movement. Each
sentence takes the reader back and forth between the overseas
colonies and the ideal new society in France; he describes the
American relationship with London, but really he is talking about
the French court.

The brutal tax laws of the English Parliament (read the French
court) were responsible for the exemplary 'résistance indirecte et
passive'[64] of the innocent settlers in the New World. They are
penalised without having committed a crime, so long as they do not
tax themselves — the goal of the French bourgeoisie.[65] The difference between the *ancien régime* and the new society is extracted
from the social context and given a geographic guise. The moral
dualism that had guided the criticism was expanded into an Atlantic
contrast between the Old and the New World. That contrast
becomes a universal signal of the crisis that compelled a conclusive
change. The codification of a global construct of history conjures up
the decline of the Old World. The victory of the new society over
despotism is as morally certain as the unbridgeability of the gulf
separating America and Europe.

Hélas! . . . les crimes des rois et les malheurs des peuples rendront même

---

63. On this, cf. a voice from the German territory: 'All of our literature is stamped
by our slavish century, the newspapers in the lead. Under these circumstances what
better course than to slip away from our decadent hemisphere and see what is going
on in the other half! There we find that there are still men who believe that they are
not destined to live as slaves . . . '. The Americans would show what man is capable
of. They would rise up like giants and win the battle (Schubart, *Teutsche Chronik*,
III, no. 41, 321, 20 May 1776).
64. Raynal, *Histoire philosophique*, 1770 edn, VI, 409.
65. Cf. pp. 63–4 above.

universelle cette fatale catastrophe qui doit détacher un monde de l'autre. La mine est préparée sous les fondements de nos empires chancelants; les matériaux de leur ruine s'amassent et s'entassent du débris de nos loix, du choc et de la fermentation de nos opinions, du renversement de nos droits qui faisoient notre courage . . . de la haine à jamais irréconciliable entre des hommes lâches qui possèdent toutes les richesses et des hommes robustes, vertueux même qui n'ont plus rien à perdre que leur vie.[66]

Two worlds are breaking apart. To the extent that moral dualism can also be found in the geographic polarity the social world is also unbridgeable. In complete contradiction to the actual situation both in France and America, there are only two classes: rich and poor, haves and have-nots, 'c'est à dire les maîtres et les esclaves'.[67] According to the dualistic world-view of the propertied but politically powerless bourgeoisie, the social classes become involved in the crisis, which makes it possible for the group that is virtuous but does not govern to triumph, like the Americans. The contrasts are as unbridgeable as the Atlantic that separates virtue from vice. 'En vain . . . d'établir un traité de paix entrè ces deux conditions.'[68] It is delusory to believe that the tension can be eased or relaxed; only a radical decision can do so.

In the concrete situation — and Raynal leaves no doubt on this score — civil war is the moral tribunal conjured up via a global philosophy of history.

Gardons nous en effet de confondre la résistance que les colonies Angloises devroient opposer à leur métropole, avec la fureur d'un peuple soulevé contre son souverain par l'excès d'une longue oppression. Dès qu'une fois l'esclave du despotisme auroit brisé sa chaîne, auroit commis son sort à la décision du glaive, il seroit forcé de massacrer son tyran, d'en exterminer la race et la postérité, de changer la forme du gouvernement dont il auroit été la victime depuis des siècles. S'il osoit moins, il seroit tôt ou tard puni de n'avoir eu qu'un demi courage . . .[69]

66. Raynal, *Histoire philosophique*, VI, 425f.
67. Ibid., 398.
68. Ibid.
69. Ibid., 422. That same year brought a prognosis of revolution akin to that of Frederick the Great who arrived at his forecast by drawing the political consequences from Holbach's *Système de la Nature*: 'If the high-flown ideas of our philosophers are to be fulfilled, then the forms of government of all the states of Europe would have to be reshaped.' . . . 'il faudrait encore que la râce détrônée fût totalement extirpée, ou se seraient des aliments de guerres civiles, et des chefs de partis toujours prêts à se mettre à la tête des factions pour trouble l'Etat'; in any event, in the wake of the new form of government a flood of new men lay claim to rule; revolts and revolutions are never-ending and the government faces threats a thousand times more

Raynal, being an optimistic progressive, legitimises the civil war he hopes to avert by his moral reduction of the existing situation to two radical contrasts. 'Les partis extrêmes et les moyens violents' — in themselves not justified — are made just by the immorality of authority.[70] Once virtue enters the arena of political action, then the moral dualism that, within the framework of the existing State, had guided the indirect assumption of power and made possible an overweening criticism, automatically justifies civil war. Civil war is an innocuous occurence. Although it does lead to violence and murder, it is none the less shaped by political criticism. The moral indictment of the State, its identification with naked power inherent in the dualistic approach to reality, its characterisation as slave-master, turns a revolt against such rule into a moral tribunal. Civil war means a crisis for the State, but for the 'citizen' the crisis represents a judgement. The political innocence of a philosophy of history that invokes this crisis not as civil war, but civil war as a moral tribunal, carries within it the assurance that the political crisis will be resolved favourably amidst the threatening uncertainty.

Events in America soon bore out Raynal's prophesy of revolution. Thomas Paine's commentaries on the developments from 1776 to 1783 radically and aggressively defended the position of freedom. He chose the title *The Crisis* for his periodical. With the instinctive certainty of the propagandistic populariser (which in his way Raynal was also)[71] Paine's use of this term compromised the dual sense of a civil war that was also the execution of a moral verdict which would lead to the victory of innocence and freedom as surely as two continents were breaking apart. The War of Independence ushered in an era in which the lines were drawn between virtue and vice, for the hearts of men were being put to the test. 'These are the times that try men's souls.'[72] For Paine, the civil war between the colon-

---

dangerous than foreign wars (Frederick the Great, *Oeuvres*, IX, 166). Frederick the Great's prognosis is remarkable for its concrete presentation of political developments following the overthrow of the government, whereas Raynal partly fails to see them and partly conceals them with the moral pathos with which he invokes the victory of the victims of centuries of oppression.

70. Raynal, *Histoire philosophique*, 1770 edn, VI, 421.

71. Cf. Fay, *L'esprit revolutionaire*, 12. Raynal admits that compared to the elegant personages of the Enlightenment, his was a crude and bold approach: 'Mais combien les gens de goût délicat me trouveront encore éloigné du ton réservé aux Écrivains de génie!' (Raynal, *Histoire philosophique*, 1780 edn, I).

72. Thomas Paine, *The Crisis*, I (23 December 1776), in *The Writings*, New York, 1894, I, 170.

ists and the British troops was a moral crisis, and by the end of the war, in 1783, a verdict had been reached in favour of morality: Tyranny — like hell, not easily vanquished[73] — had been overthrown, 'and the greatest and completest revolution the world ever knew, gloriously and happily accomplished'.[74]

The American War of Independence turned the moral certainty that the key to the end of the crisis lay in the critical separation of morality and immorality into an historical fact and political truth. Even where violence was used, the victory was credited to innocence — 'the harder the conflict the more glorious the triumph'.[75] The end of the military conflict lay in fact in the moral starting-point, and thus its morally certain outcome justified the civil war.[76] This was the lesson of the American example.

The American civil war lent concrete historical and geographical support to the universal exaggeration of the polemical antithesis posited by Raynal through his historical and global expansion of moral dualism. He incorporated entire sections of Paine's comments, and the most revolutionary at that, in his own work, whose fifty-four editions claimed an avid readership in France.[77] The Manichaean categories of the Old and the New World, and the related push towards a final resolution akin to that in America, welled up with growing force. The secret that had been hidden for so long now came to light. 'Leur cause est celle du genre humain

---

73. Ibid.
74. Ibid., 370.
75. Ibid., 170.
76. 'You, or your king, may call this "delusion", "rebellion", or what name you please. To us it is perfectly indifferent. The issue will determine the character, and time will give it a name as lasting as his own' (ibid., 86, 21 November 1778). The American War of Independence had proved that a bloody civil war — in contrast to the Glorious Revolution of 1688 — could be a 'revolution' that wins political freedom. Raynal, for example, no longer adheres to Montesquieu's differentiation of *guerre civile* and revolution. 'Les guerres civiles qui mènent les peuples libres à l'esclavage, et les peuples esclavages à la liberté, n'ont fait en France qu'abaisser les grands sans relever le peuple' (Raynal, *Histoire philosophique*, 1780 edn, IV, 512). The idea of freedom is no longer linked solely to 'revolution' but also to *guerre civile*. This linkage is a yardstick for the growing aggressiveness of the bourgeois thinkers, above all of those who are influenced by Rousseau, and Raynal.
77. Raynal borrowed entire sections of *Common Sense* in his book explaining the American events and tried to keep up to date by bringing out revised editions. Cf. the edition of 1780, IV, 391ff. 'C'est à l'une (la société) à commander: c'est à l'autre (le gouvernement) à la servir.' 'Mais dites vous ce sont de rébelles! . . . Des rébelles! Et pourquoi? parce qu'ils ne veulent pas être vos esclaves.' England wanted slaves, America freedom. 'Chacun a trahi son secret. Dès ce moment plus de traité . . . Le Roi? Il est votre ennemi . . . ' (IV, 413).

tout entier: elle devient le nôtre . . .'[78] And in view of the American experience there was reason to believe that the threatening crisis would in fact take the form of a moral process. The glorification of the American revolt gave the imminent civil war in France, clearly foreseen by Raynal, the aura of a transcendent, well-nigh trans-oceanic necessity. An armed clash between the *ancien régime* and the new society, if it was to come about, remained securely en-sconced in the global philosophy of history that culminated in the inevitable crisis of two worlds.

Thus Raynal answered the initial critical question about the usefulness of revolutions by way of the philosophy of history. The indirect political crisis which from the very outset was relegated to a Utopian future found spurious fulfilment in a philosophy of history that assured the execution of its verdicts. Progressive certainty of victory and eschatological visions of Doomsday did not cancel each other out, since both were based on the unpolitical self-confidence of bourgeois verdicts. They were projected into the future, and for enlightened man they also determined the course, nature and end of the crisis. The future had already arrived. The critical separation of laws and the ruling authority had indicted the existing State, so that the decision the crisis was bound to bring about was in effect an execution of the moral verdict of the bourgeoisie. It was, said Raynal, the spirit of justice, 'l'esprit de justice, qui se plaît à compenser les malheurs passés par un bonheur à venir'.[79] Further-more, the application (with naturalistic vigour) of the antithesis of morality and politics to America and Europe further substantiated

78. Raynal, *Histoire philosophique*, 1780 edn, IV, 456. On the influence of the American independence movement on France and the pre-Revolutionary mood which was systematically stirred up by the Masons under Franklin's guidance, cf. Fay, *L'esprit revolutionaire*, 90ff. Thus Turgot, writing in 1778: 'Ce peuple nouveau, situé si avantageusement pour donner au monde l'exemple d'une constitution où l'homme jouisse de tous ses droits, exerce librement toutes ses facultés, et ne soit gouverné que par la nature, la raison et la justice . . .'. This nation was the hope of mankind, 'il peut en devenir le modèle'. The wealth of literature with analogous views is listed in Fay, *L'esprit revolutionaire*.

79. Raynal, *Histoire philosophique*, 1780 edn, IV, 455. 'La liberté naîtra du sein de l'oppression . . . et le jour du réveil n'est pas loin' (IV, 552). Moral certainty persuaded the majority of the people that the political crisis was merely a transitory moment and would necessarily lead to something better. Dupont's reports to Minister Edelsheim of Baden concerning events after 1787 are typical of this belief. The concept of crisis now crops up more frequently, but always embedded in the progressive revolution. At the close of the Assembly of Notables, Dupont wrote: 'La France sera sortie d'un moment de crise plus puissante, mieux constituée et plus heureuse qu'elle ne l'avait encore été' (25 May, 1787; K. F. von Baden, *Politische*

Utopian certainty. For Raynal, overseas and the future were the fictive area of exculpation that indirectly guaranteed the triumph of morality. The crisis was mastered historico-philosophically. However, this very mastery contained its intensification. Raynal's colonial history which foresaw the threatening civil war was at the same time a historico-philosophically disguised invocation of revolution. Crisis and historical philosophy thus proved to be a complementary, internally linked phenomenon. That internal connection was rooted in the bourgeoisie's critical indictment of the State. The criticism gave rise to the philosophy of history while the criticism was precursor of the crisis. The uniqueness of the crisis, recognised and yet not recognised by the bourgeoisie, of being both desired and not desired, was connected with the ambivalence of the Enlightenment, wherein the process of unmasking simultaneously caused political blindness. The uncertainty of crisis was identical with the certainty of Utopian historical planning. The one challenged the other and, conversely, both perpetuated the process unwittingly set in motion by the educated bourgeoisie against the Absolutist State.

The bourgeois Utopia was the 'natural child' of Absolutist sovereignty. With it the State became the victim of its own restrictions. The State as the answer to the self-disintegrating Christian catholicity was a formal, orderly structure which consciously had to exclude man as man if it wanted to preserve its form. The subject was privatised as man. To assure its sovereignty the Absolutist State had to create a realm of indifference, beyond religion and politics, to protect man against the horror of civil war and enable him to tend to his affairs in peace. Disintegrated man as subject — initially at the highest levels of the educated class — joined together to form bourgeois society and tried to find refuge in the realm outside politics and religion. He found that refuge in morality, the product of privatised religion in the perfectly structured State. Its field of operation was the one, infinite, world. The Absolutist political system was vanquished by the indirect assault of a society which referred to a universal morality the State had to exclude, and

---

Correspondenz, I, 268). 'Out of every crisis mankind rises with some share of greater knowledge, higher decency, purer purpose', said Franklin Delano Roosevelt in the twentieth century, thereby testifying to the uninterrupted effectiveness of the Utopia of progress which invokes the crisis to the same extent to which it obscures its experience.

through which — without apparently touching on the Absolutist system politically — destroyed that very system from within. The concentration of power in the hands of the Absolute sovereign afforded political protection to a nascent society that Absolutism as a political system was no longer able to integrate. The State, as the temporally conditioned product of the religious wars whose formality had mediated the religious conflicts, had become the victim of its historic certainty.

The disintegration of Absolutism was part of an impetuous process into which history had been drawn by bourgeois criticism. The verdicts of the moral inner space saw the existing situation simply as an immoral being that provoked its indictment so long as, and to the extent which the moral judges themselves were powerless to execute their verdicts. However, the new elite was to the same extent strengthened in its belief that it personified the true, the moral, the essential being. History was stripped of its factualness in order to give bourgeois morality legitimacy. The apolitical bourgeoisie, alienated from historicity, maintained that the rescision of the view of history as nature's fall from grace was to be expected. Henceforth, history could only be seen in historico-philosophical terms, as a process of innocence that had to become fact. The sovereignty of society seems to spring apparently unchecked from sovereign criticism. As author the bourgeois man of letters believes himself to be the creator of authority. For the bourgeoisie the threatening civil war, whose outcome was unpredictable, had already been morally decided. The certainty of victory lay in the extra- and supra-political consciousness which — initially as the answer to Absolutism — intensified into Utopian self-assurance. Bourgeois man, condemned to a non-political role, sought refuge in Utopia. It gave him security and power. It was the indirect political power *par excellence* in whose name the Absolutist State was overthrown.

In the *bellum omnium contra omnes* of the Republic of Letters, morality continued to invent new reasons for pre-empting sovereign action which was essentially groundless. It fed on the constant change in the argumentation because access to power had been denied to it. Ultimately it had to decapitate the monarch. In despair over its inability to recognise the nature of power, it took refuge in naked force. It usurped power with the bad conscience of a moralist who claims that it is the intention of history to make power superfluous.

Thus, Utopia as the answer to Absolutism ushered in the modern age which had long since outdistanced its starting-point. Yet the heritage of the Enlightenment was still omnipresent.

The transformation of history into a forensic process conjured up the crisis to the extent that the new man believed himself able surreptitiously to transfer his moral self-insurance to history and politics, that his, in his guise as philosopher of history. Civil war, whose laws continue to govern us to this day, was recognised but made to appear harmless by a philosophy of history for which the intended political resolution only represented the predictable and inevitable end of a moral process beyond politics. This guise of harmlessness, however, served to intensify the crisis. According to the postulate of the bourgeois disputants based on a dualistic world-view, the moralisation of politics meant the unleashing of civil war, whereas the 'revolution' was not seen as civil war but rather as the fulfilment of moral postulates. The concealment and intensification of the crisis are part and parcel of the same process. Inherent in the covering up was the intensification, and vice versa.

Criticism had set this process in motion, and in so far as the critical judges maintained an indirect relationship to the dualistically excluded politics, they blinded themselves to the challenge and risk of all political actions and decisions; yet these are the expression of all historical movements.

The fact that they failed to realise this was one of the tricks played on them by the existing situation. The Enlightenment, compelled to camouflage itself politically, was the victim of its own mystique. The new elite lived with the certainty of a moral law whose political significance lay in its antithesis to Absolutist politics — the dichotomy of morality and politics guided the pre-eminent criticism and legitimised the indirect taking of power whose actual political significance, however, remained hidden to the protagonists precisely because of their dualistic self-understanding. To obscure this cover as cover was the historic function of the philosophy of history. It is the hypocrisy of hypocrisy to which criticism had degenerated. With this, a qualitative leap was made which prevented all participants from gaining insight into their own delusion. The political anonymity of the Enlightenment found fulfilment in the rule of Utopia. The dubiousness and openness of all decisions still historically outstanding seem thereby to have been eliminated, or the decisions are manifested in the bad conscience of those who are subject to them. For the indirect relationship to politics — Utopia, which, after society's secret closing of ranks against the absolute sovereign surfaced dialectically — changed in the hands of modern man into a politically unsecured loan. The French Revolution was the first instance of that loan being called in.

Excursus

Even where reference to civil war is made the choice is never between civil war and slavery, but inevitably between revolution and slavery. 'Regardez toujours la guerre civile comme une injustice . . . c'est la doctrine la plus contraire aux bonnes moeurs et au bien public. . . . Choisissez entre une révolution et l'esclavage', proclaimed Mably (quoted in D. Mornet, *Les Origines intellectuelles de la Revolution française*, Paris, 1933, p. 233). Revolution spells freedom and marks both the end of political crisis and civil war.

In the eighteenth century civil war as an existential and political phenomenon which, as for Hobbes, was the historical antithesis of the State, was no longer part, in the perception of the bourgeoisie, of a legitimate State (see pp. 49–50, n. 26 above). Pierre Bayle was familiar with the dialectic of civil wars. 'Il aimoit trop la paix pour s'embarquer dans cette guerre de Religion', he wrote about a scholar living in the era of the religious civil wars (essay on Eppendorf, 1090 b).

> Mais ce fut en vain qu'il espéra de se tenir sur le rivage, spectateur tranquille des émotions de cette mer. Il se trouve plus exposé à l'orage que s'il eût été sur l'une des flotes. C'est là le destin inévitable de ceux qui veulent garder la neutralité pendant les guerres civiles soit d'Etat soit de Religion. Ils sont exposés à l'insulte des deux partis tout à la fois; ils se font des ennemis sans se faire des amis, au lieu qu'en épousant avec chaleur l'une des deux causes, ils auroient eu des amis, et des ennemis. Sort déplorable de l'homme, vanité manifeste de la raison philosophique . . .

The spirit and verve of the innovator were undoubtedly needed, 'car sans eux pourroit-on faire des progrès considérables?' (essay on Aureolus, I, 399 b). 'Il n'est pas jusques aux guerres civiles dont on n'ait pu quelquefois assurer cela.' Civil wars, it was said, were a cleansing, a curry-comb of mankind, but he would like to be spared such benefits. The price was too great: 'Il vaut mieux demeurer malade, que de guérir par un remède d'une charité si terrible'. As far as Bayle is concerned, the road to progress came

187

to a stop at the line he drew between the *Règne de la Critique* and the State. To the extent that criticism was extended to the State, i.e., to the extent that the progressive movement of the moderns within the Republic of Letters was applied to all of history and also encompassed the State, the citizens ceased to know about civil wars and the original function of the State that emerged from the religious civil wars by ending and suppressing them.

The *Encyclopédie* contained eight articles treating different aspects of war under the heading 'guerre': 'guerre civile' is nowhere to be found. The term is rarely heard in the eighteenth century, as though it had been suppressed, and when it does appear it is incorporated into the progress of history and made harmless. 'Guerres civiles utiles aux talents et aux lettres par le mouvement qu'elles donnent aux esprits . . .', noted Turgot in 1750 (II, 670). Civil war aids progress; it is just if it does away with tyranny, the obstacle to progress, concludes Vattel (III, XVIII), and, moreover, is preferable to tyranny: 'il vaut mieux s'exposer à une guerre civile', than be the subject of a despot (I, 3, § 51). Holbach offers the same argument in his 'Essay sur les préjugés' (1770) (quoted in Mornet, *Les Origines intellectuelles*, p. 103): 'Quand même la vérité ferait dans l'esprit des peuples un progres assez rapide pour produire des factions et même des révolutions . . . les troubles passagers sont plus avantageux qu'une languer éternelle sous une tyrannie continuée . . . que la citoyen n'obeisse qu'a la loi', thereby radicalising an oft-quoted statement of Montesquieu to the effect that unrest within a country is preferable to the calm of despotism (*Grandeurs des Romains . . .*, chap. 9).

Beyond being just, civil war becomes a necessity, and in eras of progress will lead to freedom. 'A certains états', Mercier tells us, 'il est une époque qui devient nécessaire; époque terrible, sanglante mais le signal de la liberté. C'est la guerre civile dont je parle.' But even this civil war of Mercier's is basically a revolution: 'la plus heureuse de toutes a eu son point de maturité, et nous en recueillons les fruits . . . c'est là que s'élèvent et paraissent dignes de commander à des hommes' (*L'an deux mille quatre cent quarante*, p. 329). Mercier did not see civil war as an event that creates conflicting parties and feeds on their differences, as he later discovered to his horror (see Mornet, *Les Origines intellectuelles*, p. 239), but as the breakthrough of the hitherto unseen new man into political power. Linear progress seems assured. Civil war is invoked because its result — revolution — has become a certainty. 'Revolution', not civil war nor crisis is the slogan of the new elite. Only after 1789 will Bayle's existential experiential outlook be reached again. 'So this is the comfortable and secure position of a merely neutral spectator. Happy is he who *can* and *may* be neutral. However the longer one *wishes* to be neutral, the more onerous and dangerous does a war become in the moral as well as the political world.' The intellectual distinction between morality and politics became a split into warring civil factions which were political and also appealed to morality. 'Both parties proclaim with equally strong voices: He who is not with me is against me, and their conduct matches their words. . . . We live in an era of extremes' (F.C. von Moser, *Politische Wahrheiten* [Zurich, 1796], XII).

Bibliography

Primary Sources
arranged chronologically by date of birth

Luther, Martin (1483–1546), *Werke, Krit. Ges.-Ausg.*, Weimar, 1883 *et seq.*

D'Aubigné, Agrippe (1552–1630), *Œuvres complètes*, ed. Réaume and Caussade, Paris, 1877

Hooker, Richard (1554–1600), *Of the Laws of Ecclesiastical Polity*, ed. C. Morris, 2 vols., London, 1954

Shakespeare, William (1564–1616), *The Complete Works*, Oxford, 1954

James VI [I] (1566–1625), *The Basilikon Doron*, 2 vols., Edinburgh and London, 1944

Barclay, John (1582–1621), *Argenis, Editio V*, Frankfurt, 1626

Richelieu, Cardinal de (1585–1642), *Testament politique*, ed., Louis André, Paris, 1947

Hobbes, Thomas (1588–1679), *Thomae Hobbes Malmesburiensis Opera philosophica quae latine scripsit omnia, in unum corpus nunc primum collecta studio et labore Gulielmi Molesworth*, London, 1839–45

——, *The english Works of Thomas Hobbes of Malmesbury, now first collected and edited by Sir William Molesworth*, 11 vols., London, 1835–45

——, *Behemoth or The Long Parliament*, ed. Tönnies, London, 1889

——, *Leviathan*, ed. Lindsay, London, 1949

Descartes, René (1596–1650), *Œuvres*, Paris, 1887

Hyde, Edward, Earl of Clarendon (1608–74), *The History of the Rebellion and Civil Wars in England*, 6 vols., Oxford, 1888

Spinoza, Benedictus de (1632–77), *Opera*, ed. Gebhardt, Heidelberg, n.d.

Locke, John (1632–1704), *An Essay Concerning Human Understanding*, ed. C. Fraser, Oxford, 1894

Simon, Richard (1638–1712), *Histoire critique du Texte du Nouveau Testament*, Rotterdam, 1689

——, *Histoire Critique du Vieux Testament*, Paris, 1680

Leibniz, G.W. (1646–1716), *Die philosophischen Schriften*, ed. C.H. Gerhardt, 7 vols., Berlin, 1875

Bayle, Pierre (1647–1706), *Dictionnaire Historique et Critique*, 3rd edn, Rotterdam, 1720

Fénelon de la Mothe, François (1651–1715), *Œuvres Complètes*, Paris, 1850

Vico, Giambattista (1668–1744), *Opere*, ed. F. Nicolini, Milan and Naples, 1953

——, *De Nostri Temporis Studiorem Ratione* (Latin/German; *Vom Wesen und Weg der geistigen Bildung*), Godesberg, 1947

St Simon, Duc de (1675–1755), *Mémoires compl. et auth.*, 20 vols., ed. St Beuve, Paris, 1857

Desaguliers, J.T. (1683–1744), *The Newtonian System of the World, the best Model of Government: Allegorical Poem*, Westminster, 1728

Anderson, James (1679–1739), *The Constitutions of Freemasons 1723; Reproduced in Facsimile from the original Edition: with an Introduction by Lionel Vibert I.C.S.*, London, 1923

Anderson, Jacob (1679–1739), *Des verbesserten Konstitutionenbuches der alten ehrwürdigen Brüderschaft der Freymaurer erster Theil. Geschichte des Ordens auf Befehl der großen Loge aus ihren Urkunden, Traditionen und Logenbüchern zum Gebrauch der Logen verfaßt von Jacob Anderson, D.D., aus dem Engl. übersetzt*, 4th enl. edn, Frankfurt, 1783

——, *Des verbesserten Konstitutionenbuches... zweiter Theil. Verordnungen, Gesetze, Pflichten, Satzungen und Gebräuche nebst historischer Nachricht von dem Ursprung des Ordens aus den Hellmundschen Urkunden gesammelt von dem Bruder Kleinschmidt f. d. A.C.Z.F.*, Frankfurt, 1784

Pope, Alexander (1688–1744), *Collected Poems*, London, 1951

Montesquieu, Charles de (1689–1755), *Esprit des lois* [1748], Paris, 1845

d'Argenson, René-Louis (1694–1757), *Mémoires publ. p. R. d'Argenson*, Paris, 1825

——, *La France au milieu du XVIIIᵉ siècle d'après le Journal du M. d'Argenson*, ed. Brette, Paris, 1898

Voltaire, F.M. (1694–1778), *Œuvres complètes*, 52 vols., Paris, 1877–85

——, *Dictionnaire Philosophique*, ed. Benda, Paris, 1954

Home, Henry [Lord Kames] (1696–1782), *Versuche über die Geschichte der Menschen*, 2 parts, Leipzig, 1774–5 (German transl. of *Sketches of the History of Man*)

Johnson, Samuel (1709–84), *A Dictionary of the English Language*, 2 vols., London, 1755

Frederick the Great (1712–86), *Œuvres*, Berlin, 1846 *et seq.*

——, *Die politischen Testamente*, ed. Volz, Berlin, 1922

Rousseau, J.J. (1712–78), *Œuvres complètes*, Paris, 1823 *et seq.*

——, *Du contrat social*, ed. Halbwachs (Aubier), n.p., 1943

Diderot, Denis (1713–84), *Œuvres Complètes*, ed. Assézat and Tourneux, Paris, 1875–9

——, *Œuvres Philosophiques*, ed. Vernière, Paris, 1956

D'Alembert, Jean (1717–83) and Denis Diderot, *Encyclopédie ou dictionnaire raisonné des sciences, des arts et des métiers, par une société de gens de lettres;... Edition exactement conforme à celle de Pellet*, 72 vols.,

Berne and Lausanne, 1778

[Raynal] (1713–96), *Historie Philosophique et Politique des établissements et du commerce des Européens dans les deux Indes*, 6 vols., Amsterdam, 1770

Raynal, ibid., 8 vols., The Hague, 1774

——, ibid., 4 vols., Geneva, 1780

——, *Philosophische und politische Geschichte der Besitzungen und des Handels der Europäer in beiden Indien*, 7 vols., Hanover, 1774/9, transl. by J. Mauvillon

Uriot, Joseph (1713–88), *Le secret des Francs-Maçons mis en Evidence*, Frankfurt and The Hague, 1744

Vattel, E. de (1714–67), *Les Droits des Gens ou Principes de la Loi Naturelle*, London, 1758; Washington, 1926

Vauvenargues, Marquis de (1715–47), *Œuvres*, ed. P. Varillon, 3 vols., Paris, 1929

Helvetius, C.A. (1715–71), *De l'Esprit*, Paris, 1758

d'Alembert, Jean le Rond (1717–83), *Discours Préliminaire de l'Encyclopédie, publié intégralement d'après l'édition de 1763*, Paris, 1919

Bonnet, Charles (1720–96), *La Palingénésie philosophique*, Munster (Perrenon), 1770

Holbach, P.H. von (1723–89), *Système sociale*, 1773; German transl., Umminger, *Soziales System oder Natürliche Prinzipien der Moral und der Politik mit einer Untersuchung über den Einfluß der Regierung auf die Sitten*, Leipzig, 1898

Moser, F.C., Frhr. von (1723–98), *Politische Wahrheiten*, Zürich, 1796

Kant, Immanuel (1724–1804), *Ges. Schriften*, ed. Preuß. Akademie d. Wissenschaften, Berlin, 1902 *et seq.*

Turgot, A.R.J. (1727–81), *Œuvres et Documents*, ed. Schelle, 5 vols., Paris, 1913–23

[Stattler, Benedict] (1728–97), *Das Geheimnis der Bosheit des Stifters des Illuminatismus, zur Warnung der Unvorsichtigen hell aufgedeckt von einem seiner alten Kenner und Freunde*, Munich and Augsburg, 1787

Karl Friedrich, Großherzog von Baden (1728–1811), *Politische Correspondenz*, eds. Erdmannsdörffer and Abser, 6 vols., Heildelberg, 1888 *et seq.*

Lessing, G.E. (1729–81), *Sämtliche Schriften*, eds. Lachmann and Muncker, 22 vols., Leipzig, 1886

[Bode, J.J. Chr.?] (1730–93), *Gedanken über die Verfolgung der Illuminaten*, Frankfurt/M., 1786

Adelung, J. Chr. (1732–1806), *Versuch eines vollständigen, grammatischen kritischen Wörterbuchs der Hochdt. Mundart . . .*, 4 vols., Leipzig, 1774 *et seq.*

Wieland, Chr. M. (1733–1813), *Gesammelte Schriften*, ed. Preuß. Akademie d. Wissenschaften, Berlin, 1909 *et seq.*

[Weissenbach, J.A.] (1734–1801), *Der letzte Vorbothe des Neuen Heidenthums Horus! oder das Endurtheil, das man dies Jahr übers Evangelium abgesprochen und zum Handbuch der Freymaurer gemacht hat*, Basel, 1784

[——], *Kritisches Verzeichnis der besten Schriften, welche in verschiedenen*

Sprachen zum Beweise der Religion herausgekommen, Basel, 1784

Calonne, Ch. Alex. de (1734–1802), *De l'Etat de la France, présent et à venir*, London, 1790

Schlözer, A.L. von (1735–1809), *Briefwechsel meist histor. und polit. Inhalts*, 8 vols., Göttingen, 1777–80

Paine, Thomas (1737–1809), *The Writings*, coll. and ed. by M.D. Conway, 4 vols., New York and London, 1894

Schubart, Chr. F.D. (1739–91), *Teutsche Chronik*, Augsburg, 1774 *et seq.*

Mercier, L.S. (1740–1814), *Tableau de Paris*, Amsterdam, 1782/3

——, *L'an deux mille quatre cent quarante*, London, 1772

Göchhausen, E.A.A., Frhr. v. (1740–1824), *Die Enthüllung des Systems der Weltbürgerrepublik*, Rom (Leipzig), 1786

Grolmann, L.A. Chr. v. (1741–1809), *Die neuesten Arbeiten des Spartakus* [Weishaupt] *und Philo* [Knigge], 2nd edn, 1794

Condorcet, Ant. Nic. M. de (1743–93), *Correspondence inédite de Condorcet et Turgot*, ed. C. Henry, Paris, 1882

——, *Œuvres*, ed. A. Condorcet, O'Connor and Arago, 12 vols., Paris, 1847

Hamberger, G. Chr., and J.G. Meusel (1743–1820), *Das Gelehrte Teutschland oder Lexicon der jetztlebenden teutschen Schriftsteller*, 4th edn, vols. 1–4 and 9, addenda in 11, Lemgo, 1783–1806

Desèze, Romain (1748–1828), *Défense de Louis XVI*, Leipzig, 1900

[Weishaupt, Adam] (1748–1830), *Schilderung der Illuminaten, Gegenstück zu Nr. 15 des grauen Ungeheuers* [Nürnberg], 1786

[——], *Schreiben an den Herrn Hofkammerrath Ut[z]schneider in München*, 1786

[——], *Anzeige eines aus dem Orden der Frei-Maurer getretenen Mitglieds (Cosandey) m. Anmerkungen (von Weishaupt)*, Sparta [Ravensberg], 1786

[——], *Kurze Rechtfertigung meiner Absichten*, Frankfurt/M. and Leipzig, 1787

de Maistre, Joseph (1753–1821), *La franc-Maçonnerie, mémoire au Duc de Brunswick*, ed. E. Dermenghem, Paris, 1925

Rivarol, Antoine de (1753–1801), *Mémoires*, ed. Berville, Paris, 1824

Babo, Joseph M. (1756–1822), *Über Freymaurer, erste Warnung*, 1784

——, *Politische Numern, enthaltend eine kurze Übersicht der gegenwärtigen Angelegenheiten Europas*, II, Frankfurt/M., 1786

Schiller, F. (1759–1805), *Sämtliche Werke*, Säkularausgabe (= Centenary Edition), Stuttgart and Berlin, 1904 *et seq.*

——, *Sämtl. Schriften, Hist. Krit. Ausg.*, ed. Goedecke, Stuttgart, 1867 *et seq.*

Meggenhoffen, Ferd. v. (1761–90), *Meine Geschichte und Apologie*, 1786

Buhle, J.G. (1763–1821), *Grundzüge einer allgemeinen Encyklopädie der Wissenschaften*, Lemgo, 1790

Cosandey, Renner, and Utzschneider (1763–1840), *Drey merkwürdige Aussagen die innere Einrichtung des Illuminatenordens in Baiern betreffend* [Munich], 1786

Saint-Just, Louis de (1767–94), *Œuvres*, ed. Jean Gratien, Paris, 1946

[Anon.], *Die entdeckte Heimlichkeit der Freymäurer* [1779]

[Anon.], *Kurze historische Nachricht von dem Ursprung der Freymaurer-Gesellschaft und deren Gehemnissen mit unpartheiischer Feder in Sendschreiben vorgestellt* [Frankfurt], 1742

[Anon.], *Nachricht, welche Herr Generalvicarius von Monalto im Jahre 1752 aus Neapel über die dort einreissende und von dem Könige verbothene Freymäurerei erhalten hat. Aus dem welschen Manuskript ins Deutsche übersetzt*, 1785

[Anon.], *Nachtrag von weiteren Originalschriften, welche die Illuminatensekte überhaupt, sondernbar aber den Stifter derselben Adam Weisshaupt betreffen*, Munich, 1787, 2 parts

Einige Originalschriften des Illuminatenordens, welche bey dem geheimen Regierungsrath Zwack *durch vorgenommene Hausvisitation zu Landshut den 11. und 12. Oktober vorgefunden wurden*, Munich, 1787

Secondary Sources

Details of sources not listed here, especially of the most common works of reference, may be found in the notes

Albertini, Rud. v., *Das politische Denken in Frankreich zur Zeit Richelieus*, Marburg, 1951 (vol. 1 of *Arch. f. Kult.-gesch.*)

Arendt, Hannah, *Elemente und Ursprünge totaler Herrschaft*, Frankfurt/M., 1955

Bahner, Werner, 'Der Friedensgedanke in der Literatur der französischen Aufklärung, in *Grundpositionen der Französischen Aufklärung*, Berlin, 1955

Bäumler, Alfred, *Kants Kritik der Urteilskraft, ihre Geschichte und Systematik*, Halle, 1923

Becker, C.L., *Der Gottesstaat der Philosophen des 18. Jahrhunderts*, Würzburg, 1946 (transl. from the English by A. Hämel)

Bénichou, Paul, *Morales du Grand Siècle*, Paris, 1948

Berger, *Schiller*, 6th edn, 2 vols., Munich, 1910

Böhn, Max v., *Rokoko. Frankreich im achtzehnten Jahrhundert*, Berlin, 1921

Bousset, W., *Der Antichrist*, Göttingen, 1895

Bowle, John, *Hobbes and his Critics*, London, 1951

Brinton, Crane, *Europa im Zeitalter der Französischen Revolution*, Vienna, 1938 (German transl. of *A Decade of Revolution*)

Brockdorff, Baron Cay von, *Die englische Aufklärungsphilosophie*, Munich, 1924

Buddeberg, K. Th., 'Descartes und der politische Absolutismus', in *Archiv für Rechtsgeschichte und Sozial-Philosophie*, XXX, Berlin, 1936/7

——, 'Gott und Souverän', in *Archiv. d. öffentl. Rechts*, NF, vol. 23, 1937

Burckhardt, C.J., *Richelieu, Der Aufstieg zur Macht*, Munich, 1935

Cassirer, Ernst, *Die Philosophie der Aufklärung*, Tübingen, 1932

Chinard, Gilbert, *L'Amérique et la rêve exotique dans la littérature française au XVIIᵉ et au XVIIIᵉ siècle*, Paris, 1913

Cochin, Augustin, *Les sociétés de Pensée et la Révolution en Bretagne*, 2 vols., Paris, 1925

Dakin, Douglas, *Turgot and the Ancien Régime in France*, London, 1939

Dermenghem, E., *Joseph de Maistre Mystique*, Paris, 1946

Dilthey, Wilhelm, *Gesammelte Schriften*, 9 vols., Leipzig and Berlin, 1921 *et seq.*

Dörries, E., 'Gottesgehorsam und Menschengehorsam bei Luther', in *Arch. f. Ref.-Gesch.*, 39, 1942

Engel, Leopold, *Geschichte des Illuminaten-Ordens, ein Beitrag zur Geschichte Bayerns*, Berlin, 1906

Esquer, G., 'L'Anticolonialisme au XVIIIe siècle', in *Colonies et empires*, II, 8, Paris, 1951

Fay, Bernard, *La Franc-Maçonnerie et la Révolution intellectuelle du XVIIIe siècle*, Paris, 1935

——, *Benjamin Franklin*, Paris, 1929

——, *L'esprit révolutionnaire en France et aux Etat-Unis à la fin du XVIIIe siècle*, Paris, 1925

Feugère, A., *Un précurseur de la Révolution. L'abbé Raynal*, Angoulême, 1922

Findel, J.G., *Geschichte der Freimaurerei*, 3rd edn, Leipzig, 1870

Le Forestier, *Les Illuminés de Bavière et la Franc-Maçonnerie allemande*, Paris, 1914

Freyer, Hans, *Weltgeschichte Europas*, 2nd edn, Stuttgart, 1954

Garnier, A., *Agrippe d'Aubigné et le Parti protestant*, 3 vols., Paris, 1928

Giercke, Otto, *Johannes Althusius und die Entwicklung der naturrechtlichen Staatstheorien*, 3rd edn, Breslau [Wrocław], 1913

Glagau, Hans, *Reformversuche und Sturz des Absolutismus in Frankreich (1774–1788)*, Munich and Berlin, 1908

Göhring, Martin, *Geschichte der Großen Revolution*, 2 vols., Tübingen, 1950

——, *Weg und Sieg der modernen Staatsidee in Frankreich*, Tübingen, 1946

Groethuysen, Bernhard, *Die Entstehung der bürgerlichen Welt- und Lebensanschauung in Frankreich*, 2 vols., Halle, 1930

——, *Jean-Jacques Rousseau*, 4th edn, Paris, 1942

Hanotaux, Gabriel, *Histoire du Cardinal de Richelieu*, 5 vols., Paris, 1893

Hartung, Fritz and Roland Mousnier, 'Quelques problèmes concernant la monarchie absolue', in *Storia Moderna, Relazioni del X. Congresso Internazionale di Scienze Storiche*, vol. IV, Florence, 1955

Haüsser, Ludwig, *Geschichte der Rheinischen Pfalz*, 2 vols., Heidelberg, 1856

Hazard, Paul, *Die Krise des europäischen Geistes*, Hamburg, 1939 (German transl. of *La Crise de la Conscience Européenne*)

——, *Die Herrschaft der Vernunft. Das europäische Denken im 18. Jahrhundert*, Hamburg, 1949 (German transl. of *La Pensée Européenne au XVIIIe siècle de Montesquieu à Lessing*)

Hettner, Hermann, *Geschichte der deutschen Literatur im achtzehnten Jahrhundert*, 4 vols., 7th edn, Brunswick, 1925

——, *Geschichte der französischen Literatur im achtzehnten Jahrhundert*, Brunswick, 1894

Bibliography

197

Hinterhäuser, Hans, *Utopia und Wirklichkeit bei Diderot*, Heidelberger
Forschungen, Heft 5, 1956
Hönigwald, R., *Hobbes und die Staatphilosophie*, Munich, 1924
Horkheimer, *Die Entstehung der bürgerlichen Geschichtsphilosophie*, Stutt-
gart, 1930
—— and T.W. Adorno, *Dialektik der Aufklärung*, Amsterdam, 1946
Janet, Paul, *Histoire de la Science politique dans ses rapports avec la morale*,
2 vols., 3rd edn, Paris, 1887
Jodl, Friedrich, *Geschichte der Ethik als philosophischer Wissenschaft*, 2
vols., Stuttgart and Berlin, 1906
Kluxen, Kurt, *Das Problem der politischen Opposition. Entwicklung und
Wesen der englischen Zweiparteienpolitik im 18. Jahrhundert*, Munich
and Freiburg, 1956
Knoop, D., and G.P. Jones, *The Genesis of Freemasonry*, Manchester, 1947
Kohut, A., *Die Hohenzollern und die Freimaurerei*, Berlin, 1909
Koser, Reinhold, 'Die Epochen der absoluten Monarchie in der neueren
Geschichte', in *HZ*, 61, 1889
Kühn, Johannes, *Toleranz und Offenbarung*, Leipzig, 1923
Labrousse, C.E., *La crise de l'économie française à la fin de l'ancien régime
et au début de la Révolution*, Paris, 1944
Lantoine, Albert, *Histoire de la Franc-Maçonnerie Française*, Paris, 1925
Lecky, W.E.H., *A History of England in the Eighteenth Century*, 3 vols.,
London, 1892
Lennhoff, Eugen, *Politische Geheimbünde*, Zürich, Leipzig and Vienna,
1930
—— and O. Posner, *Internationales Freimaurerlexikon*, Zurich, Leipzig
and Vienna, 1932
Lipowsky, F., *Karl Theodor, Churfürst von Pfalz-Baiern*, Sulzbach, 1828
Löwenstein, K., 'Zur Soziologie der parlamentarischen Repräsentation in
England vor der ersten Reformbill', in *Erinnerungsbuch für Max Weber*,
II.B., Munich, 1923
Löwith, Karl, *Weltgeschichte und Heilsgeschehen*, Stuttgart, 1953
Lubienski, Z., *Die Grundlagen des ethisch-politischen Systems von Hobbes*,
Munich, 1932
Meinecke, F., *Die Idee der Staatsräson*, 3rd edn, Munich and Berlin, 1928
Mornet, Daniel, *Les Origines intellectuelles de la Révolution française 1715
à 1787*, Paris, 1933
Näf, Werner, 'Frühformen des modernen Staates im Spätmittelalter', in
HZ, 171, 1951
——, Die Epochen der neueren Geschichte, Staat und Staatsgemeinschaft
vom Ausgang des Mittelalters bis zur Gegenwart, 2 vols., Aarau, 1945
Peters, Richard, *Hobbes*, Harmondsworth, 1956
Peuckert, W.E., *Geheimbünde*, Heidelberg, 1951
Plechanow, G.W., *Beiträge zur Geschichte des Materialismus*, Berlin, 1946
Polin, Raymond, *Politique et philosophie chez Thomas Hobbes*, Paris, 1953
Priouret, Roger M., *La Franc-Maçonnerie sous les lys*, Paris, 1953
Ranke, Leopold, v., *Sämtliche Werke*, 3rd edn, Leipzig, 1867
Rall, Hans, *Kurbayern in der letzten Epoche der alten Reichsverfassung*,

1745–1801, Schriftenreihe zur bayerischen Landesgeschichte, vol. 45, Munich, 1952

Rein, Adolf, 'Über die Bedeutung der überseeischen Ausdehnung für das europäische Staatensystem', in *HZ*, 137, 1927

——, *Die europäische Ausbreitung über die Erde*, Potsdam, 1931

Riegelmann, H., *Die europäischen Dynastien in ihrem Verhältnis zur Freimaurerei*, Berlin, 1942

Ritter, Gerhard, 'Der Freiherr vom Stein und die politischen Reform programme des ancien régime in Frankreich', in *HZ*, 137, 1927

Rocquain, Félix, *L'Esprit révolutionnaire avant la Révolution 1715–1789*, Paris, 1878

Rommen, Heinrich, *Die Staatslehre des Franz Suarez SJ.*, Mönchen-Gladbach, 1926

Rosenkranz, K., *Diderots Leben und Werke*, 2 vols., Leipzig, 1866

Rosenstock, Eugen, 'Revolution als politischer Begriff der Neuzeit', in *Abh. der schles. Ges. für vaterl. Lit., Geisteswiss. Reihe, H. 5, Festgabe für Paul Heilborn*, Breslau [Wrocław], 1931

Roßberg, A., *Freimaurerei und Politik im Zeitalter der Französischen Revolution*, Berlin, 1942

Runkel, F., *Die Geschichte der Freimaurerei in Deutschland*, 3 vols., Berlin, 1931

Sagnac, Philippe, *La Formation de la société Française moderne*, 2 vols., Paris, 1945–6

Sauter, *Die philosophischen Grundlagen des Naturrechts*, Vienna, 1932

Say, L., *Turgot*, 2nd edn, Paris, 1891

Schelsky, H., 'Die Totalität des Staates bei Hobbes', in *Arch. f. Rechts- und Sozialphil.*, XXXI, 1937/8

Schilling, Kurt, 'Naturrecht, Staat und Christentum bei Hobbes', in *Ztschr. f. Phil. Forschung II*, 2/3, Reutlingen, 1948

Schmitt, Carl, *Politische Theologie, Vier Kapital zur Lehre von der Souveränität*, Munich and Leipzig, 1922

——, *Der Nomos der Erde im Völkerrecht des Ius Publicum Europaeum*, Cologne, 1950

——, *Die Diktatur*, 2nd edn, Munich, 1928

——, *Der Leviathan in der Staatslehre des Thomas Hobbes*, Hamburg, 1938

Schneider, J.F., *Die Freimaurerei und ihr Einfluß auf die geistige Kultur in Deutschland am Ende des 18. Jahrhunderts*, Prague, 1909

Schnur, Roman, 'Die französischen Juristen im konfessionellen Bürgerkrieg des 16. Jahrhunderts, ein Beitrag zur Entstehungsgeschichte des modernen Staates', in *Festgabe für Carl Schmitt*, Berlin, 1959

Schott, T., 'Das Toleranzedikt Ludwigs XVI.', in *HZ*, 61, 1889

Schreihage, H., 'Thomas Hobbes' Sozialtheorie', in *Abh. des Instituts für Politik, ausländisches öffentl. Recht und Völkerrecht an der Universität Leipzig*, Heft 33, 1933

Sée, Henri, *L'évolution de la pensée politique en France au XVIIIᵉ siècle*, Paris, 1925

Sieburg, Fr., *Robespierre*, Frankfurt/M., 1935

Söderberg, Hans, *La Réligion des Cathares. Etude sur le gnosticisme de la basse antiquité et du moyen age*, Uppsala, 1949

Sorel, G., *Les illusions du progrès*, Paris, 1908

Strauß, Leo, *The Political Philosophy of Hobbes, its Basis and its Genesis*, Oxford, 1936

Taine, H., *Die Enstehung des modernen Frankreich*, 3 vols. (in 6), Leipzig, 1891–3 (German transl. of *Les origines de la France contemporaire*)

Taubes, J., *Abendländische Eschatologie*, Berne, 1947

Texte, J., *Jean-Jacques Rousseau et les origines du cosmopolitisme littéraire*, Paris, 1895

Tocqueville, A. de, *Œuvres complètes*, ed. I.P. Mayer, Paris, 1952

Tönnies, Ferdinand, *Thomas Hobbes, Leben und Lehre*, 3rd edn, Stuttgart, 1925

Troeltsch, Ernst, *Ges. Schr.*, 4 vols., Tübingen, 1912

Valjavec, Fritz, *Die Entstehung der politischen Strömungen in Deutschland 1770–1815*, Munich, 1951

Villat, Louis, *La Révolution et l'Empire*, I, Clio, Paris, 1947

Wahl, Adalbert, *Vorgeschichte der Französischen Revolution*, 2 vols., Tübingen, 1905

Weiß Eberhard, *Geschichtsschreibung und Staatsauffassung in der Französischen Enzyklopädie*, Wiesbaden, 1956 (vol. 14 of *Veröffentlichungen d. Instit. für europ. Geschichte, Mainz*)

Weiß, M., *Histoire des réfugés protestants de France*, 2 vols., Paris, 1853

Wenck, Waldemar, *Deutschland vor hundert Jahren*, Leipzig, 1887

Wolf, Erik, *Grotius, Pufendorf, Thomasius*, Tübingen, 1927

Wolfram, L., *Die Illuminaten in Bayern und ihre Verfolgung, Erlangen 1899 und 1900* (2 Programmhefte des Gymnasiums zu Erlangen)

Wolfstieg, A., *Bibliographie der freimaurerischen Literatur*, 3 vols., Burg b. M., 1913

Wolpe, Hans, *Raynal et sa machine de guerre*, Paris, 1956

Wright, Qincy, *A Study of War*, 2 vols., 4th edn, Chicago, 1944

Wundt, Max, *Kant als Metaphysiker. Ein Beitrag zur Geschichte der deutschen Philosophie im 18. Jahrhundert*, Stuttgart, 1924

Indexes

Name Index

Subject Index